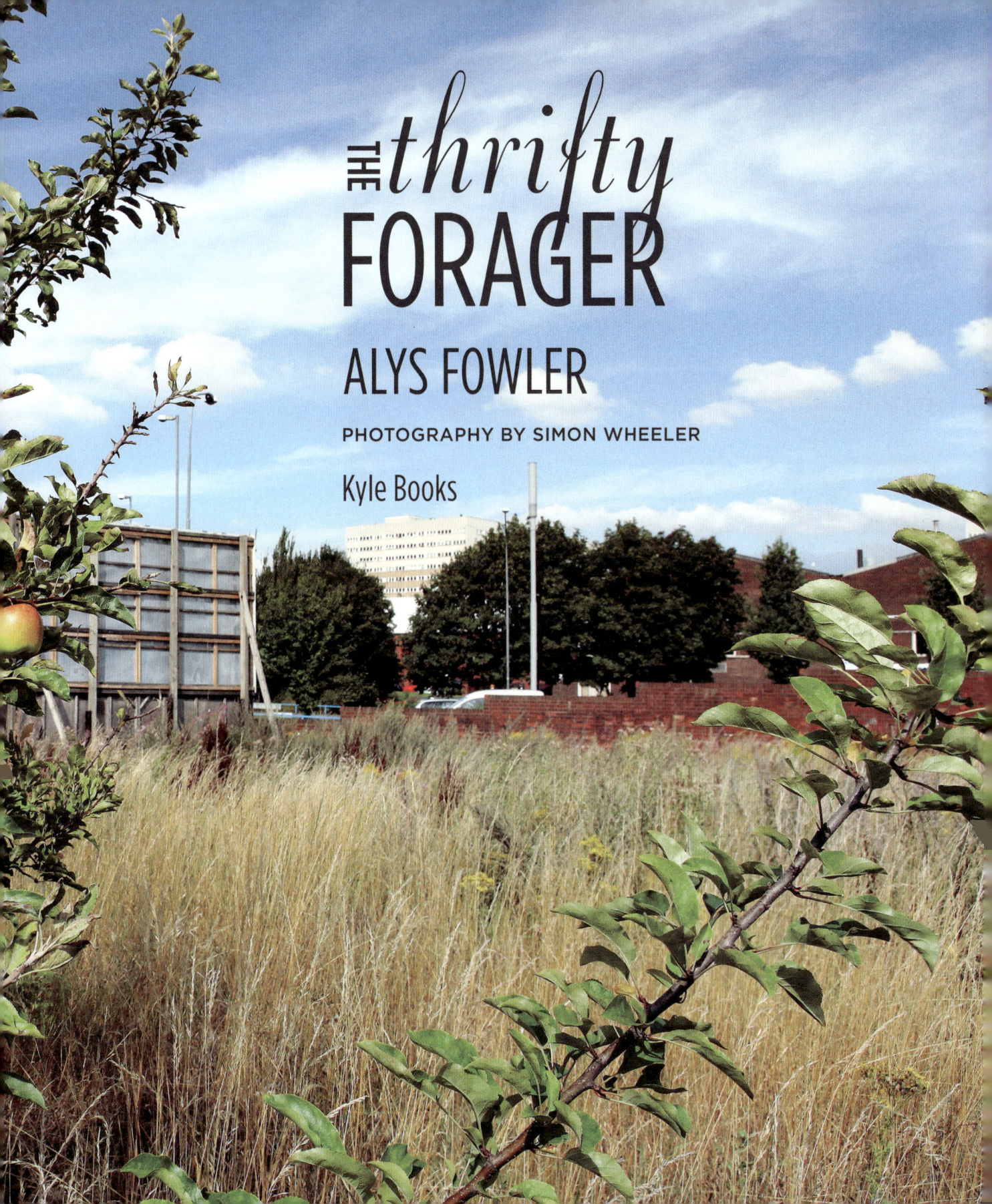

'YOU CANNOT BUY
THAT PLEASURE
WHICH IT YIELDS
TO HIM WHO TRULY
PLUCKS IT'

HENRY DAVID THOREAU,
WILD FRUITIST

For my mother
Thank-you for teaching me
to eat my weeds

This edition published in Great Britain in 2015 by Kyle Books, an imprint of Kyle Cathie Ltd.
192–198 Vauxhall Bridge Road
Lonond, SW1V 1DX
general.enquiries@kylebooks.com
www.kylebooks.com

First published in Great Britain in 2011 by Kyle Cathie Ltd.

ISBN: 978 0 85783 314 3

10 9 8 7 6 5 4 3 2 1

A CIP catalogue record for this title is available from the British Library

Alys Fowler is hereby identified as the author of this work in accordance with section 77 of Copyright, Designs and Patents Act 1988.

All rights reserved. No reproduction, copy or transmission of this publication may be made without written permission. No paragraph of this publication may be reproduced, copied or transmitted, save with written permission or in accordance with the provision of the Copyright Act 1956 (as amended). Any person who does any unauthorised act in relation to this publication may be liable to criminal prosecution and civil damages.

Text copyright © 2011 by Alys Fowler
Photographs copyright © 2011 by Simon Wheeler
Illustrations copyright © 2011 by Marcus Oakley
Design copyright © 2011 by Kyle Books

Design: Lawrence Morton
Photography: Simon Wheeler
Project editor: Sophie Allen
Copy editor: Charlie Ryrie
Production: Sheila Smith and Nic Jones

Colour reproduction by Scanhouse

Printed and bound in China by Toppan Leefung Printing Ltd.

# CONTENTS

**INTRODUCTION** 6
**SO IS IT SAFE?** 10
**WHY FORAGED FOODS ARE GOOD FOR US** 12

## HOW TO FORAGE 14

**HOW TO WORK OUT WHAT TO EAT** 16
**WHO SHOULD EAT WHAT** 16
**SO WHERE SHOULD YOU GO** 18
**LAND USE** 21
**THE LAW** 21
**A GOOD RULE** 22
**SPIT OUT YOUR SEEDS** 25

**NORWAY CASE STUDY:** A Modern Monk 26
**USA CASE STUDY:** City Fruits 42
**UK CASE STUDY:** Incredible Edible Todmorden 50

**HOW TO SET UP A COMMUNITY ORCHARD** 56

## THE PLANT DIRECTORY 62

**WHAT TO PICK WHEN** 64
**LEAF DESCRIPTIONS** 66
**HOW TO PRESERVE FRUITS** 76
**BIRGIT'S KITCHEN** 82
**WILTED GREENS** 84
**A–V PLANT DIRECTORY** 86

**RESOURCES** 186
**INDEX** 188
**ACKNOWLEDGEMENTS** 192

Darling,

I have something to admit.

I've been lying to you.

Every time I've served you up spinach, be it in soup, pies or risotto, I've actually been feeding you wild things. You've had stinging nettles, dead nettles, purslanes and oraches; I've fed you fat hen, good King Henry and goosegrass. You've had dandelions and thistles. They've come from the side of the train tracks, along the river, in the parks and, sometimes, my garden.

You've gone back for seconds and had it the following day so I guess you've liked some of it? Actually I think, by now, you must know that spinach is a pretty loose term in our kitchen. I hope you don't mind, but I don't intend to start growing it anytime soon.

Lots of love
A

**IT'S TRUE** that I've been less than truthful to my husband for the last couple of years about where our dinners have come from. I can see his point, it is a little weird to go out and forage when there's a supermarket at the bottom of our road. But I gain so much pleasure from foraging: every leaf, seed and berry that I pick somehow seems to connect me both to my past and my future. I think about what my mother has taught me about the outdoors. I think of the many women over millennia that have done this. How our roles have been constructed out of the idea that we're destined to forage and gather. And I am good at gathering; I can pick fast, note exactly when a bush is ripe with berries, I can climb high into the tree to pick those fat mulberries, and where others see weeds or see nothing at all, I can see our supper.

More importantly I'm not alone. Last year I offered to take some people around my park to show where and how to forage sustainably. I thought at best 10 or 20 hardy souls would turn up, I never expected 60 to come and take notes so eagerly. This makes my heart sing. There were old people, hipsters, youngsters, mums and dads and dog walkers all interested in looking and participating in their park in a different way. Foraging is exciting because it offers a sort of freedom with food that many of us have never experienced before. Foraging or wild-food walks are popping up all over the country – all you need to do is surf the web to find like-minded folk who want to get to grips with identifying edible plants and using them.

Which brings me to this book. I guess I should lay my wares bare. This is no ordinary foraging book. It is not full of folklore, not because I don't think that history is not important but because there are many brilliant foraging books that explore this (they're all hanging out in the resource section on page 186 if you want a little light reading). Foraging stories are important because they are there to help you remember a certain plant and I have included my own stories about how I came to certain plants in the hope that you might create some of your own. Teach your children your stories, tell them how you learnt to recognise a certain plant or what recipe brings out the best

Introduction | 7

flavour. When I asked my neighbour about bilberry picking in Birmingham she told me that everyone of a certain generation knew where to go because the bilberry hill was also one of the best places to take a date. She said half of Birmingham probably lost their virginity or were conceived amongst those berries. And, personally, I like that story (though I might censor it for the very young).

You do not have to go to the countryside to find these foods, though of course you can, but in some cases you may do better in a car park than a field. The plants in this book are just as likely to have come originally from faraway shores as from home, so this is not a book about native foraged foods. This is also not a book about eating weird things. I have been ruthless about taste. There are many things you can eat in this world. As Simon (the photographer) pointed out, if it doesn't make you sick it's edible, but whether you want to eat it is another thing. I have stuck to plants that taste good enough to want to go back for more, that don't have difficult or laborious processing to get to the good bits and, most importantly, that are readily available in most places. There is nothing rare in this book and there's good reason for that.

Some of these foods can be grown at home, whether this is making use of the weeds already in your garden or introducing attractive ornamentals with an edible bent. I have also included people (and their plants) who have consciously decided to create edible landscapes for foraging, including community orchards and edible trails around towns. I hope this book will inspire you to look a little differently at your landscape and to add something a little wilder to your supper.

As Henry David Thoreau wrote in his last unfinished manuscript *Wild Fruits*, 'the value of these fruits is not in the mere possession or eating of them, but in the sight and enjoyment of them'. He goes on to write that the word fruit comes from the Latin, *fructus*, meaning 'that which is used or enjoyed' and suggests that 'if it were not so, then going a-berrying and going to market would be nearly synonymous experiences'. I have spent many wonderful afternoons gathering wild foods with friends, and then cooking them down in jams and pies. These are good memories and each year I find myself anticipating the ripening of damsons or the next batch of brambles. I cannot say the same of any visit to the supermarket.

Let's face it, the supermarket is never going to be that much fun because someone else has made all the choices for you. Knowing about what your local area has to offer makes you and your community independent, resilient even to certain sorts of global change (who cares about the prices of cherries in the US if your local trees provide fruit for free). But mostly it's fun, there is nothing like the free find. I put foraging for supper up there with finding a designer piece in a charity shop. It's an independent choice and that feels great.

Foraging, the act of looking for food, helps us to map the world around us, to give it meaning. If you know that in the park on a certain corner breakfast beckons in the form of damson jam then you start to care about that place in a very different way. I believe wholly that an awareness of our landscape is important. It is our best conservation tool, it builds community and defines where we live, and perhaps it could be the starting point for deciding how the place we live in will work in the future.

This book has taken me around the world to meet women and men who are creating a new form of foraging. This new foraging is more likely to be done in towns and cities than in the wilderness. It's not about survival but about celebrating our spaces. In this form of foraging, domesticated and wild plants are equals, the abandoned orchard is as important as the native berry. What defines these forays is the picking as much as what is picked.

# bilberry picking in Birmingham

# SO IS IT SAFE?

**THE THING** I hear most about foraging is that surely it's unclean and polluted, particularly if you're foraging in the city (which is pretty much where all my foraged food comes from). I'm going to hit this one on the head so we can move swiftly on to the more joyous elements. Supermarket food is no cleaner than things that you forage for. It could possibly be more polluted, it is definitely more unknown. Vegetables and fruit that you buy at the supermarket may say where they have come from, what they are, even who grew them. There will be best-before dates and washing instructions – but that doesn't mean much. It's just labelling.

Our current global farming system is in a bit of mess, it relies on all sorts of less than desirable practices and is less than transparent about what the end product is. If you want to really know about how something is grown, the husbandry practice, about which way the prevailing wind blows (and with it the pollution), you need to ask the growers and see where it is grown. Farmers' markets and CSAs (Community Supported Agriculture) are great for this, stuff you grew yourself even better. Or you can go and forage. As a competent forager I know about the land management practice of where I can pick (mostly parks), I make choices about what and when I pick, I observe the landscape, I watch for changes. I can make informed choices about what I eat and I believe that often what I pick from around me is far more beneficial to me and my surroundings than anything I buy out of a packet.

Fruit, particularly tree fruit such as apples and pears, is perhaps the safest urban food. Fruit trees tend to sequest minerals and toxins into their heartwood or bark, not into the fruit. This makes sense as the fruit makes the trees of the future. Berries, such as blackberries and raspberries, are shallow-rooted and this means they can take up more pollutants. In 2000 the government body MAFF (Ministry of Agriculture, Fisheries and Food) undertook a study into heavy metal pollution in wild blackberries. This found that blackberries picked at urban sites or on busy roads do have higher levels of certain heavy metals compared to those picked in rural areas, but none of the blackberries picked had significant levels that might pose a risk to human health. The sensible route is to pick your blackberries away from roads (or at least on the far side of the hedge), to wash them before eating them, and not to eat blackberries for breakfast, lunch and tea every day of the month.

Leafy greens, such as fat hen, nettles and brassica family greens, are likely to accumulate the most toxins so you want to pick these from the cleanest sites and stay away from roadsides or old industrial sites.

rocket and mallow leaves

# WHY FORAGED FOODS ARE GOOD FOR US

**WE'VE BEEN** on this earth for roughly 200,000 years. Agriculture appeared about 10,000 years ago, before that we were strictly dependent on nature for our food. As hunters and gatherers, we ate a wide variety of foods, particularly plants, far greater than anything we eat now. Basically our genetic constitution, the way we digest food, was formed at a time when the environment was hugely different from today. Our environment may have changed, but our constitution has evolved very little in the last 10,000 years.

It's important not to glorify those ancient diets – life expectancy was short and hunger always prevalent. Our ancestors lived off a boom and bust diet, but it is important to understand that our history informs the way we have evolved, and until the last century or so we ate very differently. For instance, we eat a lot less greens today and the greens that we do eat are all highly cultivated, which is not altogether good.

All plants are a source of alpha-linolenic acid, the parent Omega-3 fatty acid that is an important essential fatty acid for the healthy development of our brain, eyes and nerves. There is also evidence to suggest that this fat helps prevent cardiovascular diseases. Omega-3s are mainly found in fish oil and plants, but unfortunately many fish are now also full of lots of less than desirable things, such as heavy metals and oceanic pollutants.

Alpha-linolenic acid is an incredibly important fat in plants, it's found in the membrane that surrounds the chloroplast, which is basically the centre of energy production, where photosynthesis occurs. The problem with alpha-linolenic acid is that it affects the shelf life of vegetables. Over the centuries we've been unwittingly selecting and breeding vegetables that will store well, but contain less essential fatty acid – alpha-linolenic acid.

In the 1980s Greek scientist Artemis Simopoulos found that purslane growing wild in Crete had an Omega-3 content four times higher than cultivated spinach. These same wild greens from Crete were also found to have more flavonoids that an equal quantity of red wine. They also had a higher content of antioxidants than cultivated vegetables. Could it be that wild greens from Crete are actually the superfood that we've been searching for? Or is it just that wild plants are a little better adapted to survive than cultivated ones? Anyone who has dabbled in gardening can tell you that weeds are pretty tough, less likely to wither from drought, able to grow well in poor soils and often able to stand high levels of pest attack.

Antioxidants are present in plants because of high levels of phenolic compounds which are essential for plant growth and produced as a response for defending injured plants against pathogens. It makes sense that weeds have high levels of these and thus more antioxidants. Weeds are self-reliant because no-one looks after them.

When you eat your weeds or gather wild berries you're not just re-enacting a part of your ancestral behaviour, you are also eating food that is more appropriate to the food your bodies evolved to digest, definitely a lot more appropriate than eating a chocolate bar.

# HOW TO FORAGE

Sometimes I gather with nothing more than my pockets to take home my bounty, but when I am on a foraging mission I go equipped with a sturdy pair of boots, plastic bags, containers, a pair of rubber gloves, scissors, a knife, a bit of string, and often the dog too. A lot of city foraging is opportunistic, my handbag has had its fair share of fruit stuffed into it, and during peak foraging times I always have some plastic bags for greens (which don't fare well at the bottom of a purse). I find that scissors or a small penknife are very useful for cutting greens off at the base so you carry around the minimum amount of dirt. For something like stinging nettles, a pair of rubber gloves is essential. I have come to think of Isabel, my dog, as a key foraging tool as all dogs spend much of their time marking territory. Where she goes I steer clear of. But the only thing you really need is knowledge.

# HOW TO WORK OUT WHAT TO EAT

**PLANTS ARE** much like people, once you know someone you can recognise them even if they change their hat or put on a different coat. When you get an eye for a certain favourite food you'll be able to recognise it from afar (or at least its territory). However, plants do adapt and change. Leafy plants growing in poor soils may have smaller leaves, change their leaf colour (often showing more reds and purples due to signs of stress) or have more leathery, tougher leaves. Put that same plant in lush conditions with good soil and plenty of water and it may grow considerably larger and look a lively bright green – just like people, if plants feel neglected, they tend to look it too.

Plants often change their appearance considerably as the year progresses and they live out their cycle – a sorrel leaf in spring is just a mass of spear-shaped green leaves, but come late summer the plant is a tall stalk covered with pink seeds and very few leaves.

The best way to learn how to recognise a plant is to go out and find a plant you already know, such as a stinging nettle or bramble. Take a long, good look at it and then go home and read about it (it might be a good idea to take a sample of the plant home with you). Botanical descriptions can be a little overwhelming at the beginning. They are full of odd, archaic words, like ovate and lanceolate that are there to clarify things, but it doesn't always seem that way initially. The photos of leaf shapes, margins and arrangements *(on pages 66–75)* will help you get your eye in. It is a bit of an odd language, but it doesn't take long to figure out and, once you've got it, we will all be on the same page, so to speak.

Initially, start off with plants with easy-to-read descriptions, try out some with the plants you know, and then move on to the unknown. If, after reading the description, you are still unsure, don't pick but do more research. Google the plant, ask another forager, look in a plant encyclopedia, join your local botanical society if there is one and pester them to help you, or if you're lucky enough to have a local botanical garden, ask for help. If you're still not clear, just don't eat it. Not until you're sure. It's fun foraging, but not worth getting sick over.

# WHO SHOULD EAT WHAT

**WILD FOOD** is good for you but, like all foods, some people should steer clear of certain food groups. It goes without saying that pregnant women should be extra careful with what they eat. There is nothing in this book that would cause harm, but unknown pollutants and traces of animal urine or faeces can be harmful, so perhaps stay away from foraging for nine months or so. If you have kidney stones (or similar ailments) then you should not eat borage, and you may wish to stay away from fat hen, oraches, nettles and sorrels that all contain notable levels of oxalic acid.

Wild foods can have a pretty powerful effect on your body, not because they are bad, but because they are so raw, for want of a better word, compared to a lot of our processed foods. If you go mad on, say, fat hen or blackberries and decide to eat them every day at every meal for a month, you might well end up with diarrhoea. I'm just trying to say be sensible, eat wild things a few times a week perhaps. Most foraging isn't about finding food for survival, it's just about adding some truly diverse and delicious things to your meals.

The Thrifty Forager

## SO WHERE SHOULD YOU GO?

**WILDER PARKS,** canal and riverside pathways, those funny bits of urban wasteland that actually look more like the countryside than city, allotments, churchyards – they'll all throw up something edible.

Dense woodlands aren't very productive as there is little light at ground level for plants to grow. As many of the berries and green plants that you want to eat are most often at or near ground level, head to the margins. Hedgerows are ideal, as are the banks of streams and open areas.

Clearly try and choose the places which are least polluted, the furthest corner from the road and so on. If you are after fruit and are in any way unsure about ground pollution, only pick from trees. I'd stay clear of picking greens in car parks, or along busy roads, and head into parks for them or choose plants protected from heavy pollution by, say, a fence or a dense hedge.

# SOME POSSIBLE FORAGING PLACES

**PARKS**
- **Hawthorn** Crataegus spp
- **Mulberry** Morus nigra
- **Walnut** Juglans regia
- **Hazelnut** Corylus avellana
- **Raspberry** Rubus idaeus
- **Juneberry** Amelanchier lamarckii
- **Ornamental quince** Chaenomeles spp
- **Rowan** Sorbus aucuparia
- **Cherry plum** Prunus cerasifera
- **Cherry** Prunus avium
- **Crab apple** Malus sylvestris
- **Daylily** Hemerocallis spp
- **Apple** Malus domestica
- **Rose and rosehip** Rosa spp
- **Fig** Ficus carica
- **Stinging nettle** Urtica dioica
- **Garlic mustard** Alliaria petiolata
- **Goosegrass** Galium aparine
- **Sheep's sorrel** Rumex acetosella
- **Dandelion** Taraxacum officinale

**PATHWAYS**
- **Mallow** Malva sylvestris, Malva neglecta
- **Chicory** Cichorium intybus
- **Dandelion** Taraxacum officinale
- **Chickweed** Stellaria media, Cerastium vulgare
- **Garlic mustard** Alliaria petiolata
- **Stinging nettle** Urtica dioica

**CAR PARKS**
- **Ornamental quince** Chaenomeles spp
- **Ornamental pear** Pyrus spp
- **Crab apple** Malus sylvestris
- **Blackberry** Rubus fruticosus
- **Chinese bramble** Rubus tricolor
- **Oregon hollygrape** Mahonia aquifolium
- **Oregon grape** Mahonia nervosa
- **Darwin's barberry** Berberis darwinii
- **Walnut** Juglans regia
- **Hazelnut and cobnut** Corylus avellana

**GARDENS AND ALLOTMENTS**
- **Thistle** Cirsium vulgare
- **Sowthistle** Sonchus oleraceus
- **Chickweed** Stellaria media
- **Broad-leaved willowherb** Epilobium montanum
- **Garlic mustard** Alliaria petiolata
- **Dandelion** Taraxacum officinale
- **Stinging nettle** Urtica dioica
- **Ground elder** Aegopodium podagraria
- **Herb Bennet** Geum urbanum
- **Bittercress** Cardamine spp
- **Sorrel** Rumex acetosa
- **Oregon grape** Mahonia nervosa
- **Barberry** Berberis spp
- **Apple** Malus domestica
- **Pear** Pyrus spp
- **Ornamental quince** Chaenomeles spp
- **Lime tree** Tilia cordata
- **Hazelnut** Corylus avellana
- **Mallow** Malva sylvestris, Malva neglecta
- **Chamomile** Chamaemelum nobile, Matricaria recutita
- **Field poppy** Papaver rhoeas

**ABANDONED GROUND**
- **Blackberry** Rubus fruticosus
- **Apple** Malus domestica
- **Crab apple** Malus sylvestris
- **Fig** Ficus carica
- **And if the land and soil is not polluted (say it's a back garden)**
- **Mallow** Malva sylvestris, Malva neglecta
- **Chickweed** Stellaria media, Cerastium vulgare
- **Dandelion** Taraxacum officinale
- **Chamomile** Chamaemelum nobile
- **German chamomile** Matricaria recutita

# crab apples

## LAND USE

**EVERY CITY** is just layers upon layers of habitation, the soil is often not much more than building rubble and layers of detritus built up over the years. A place's past life is not always obvious, it can literally be deeply buried. Parks can once have been industrial sites, playing fields are built on top of old gas works, petrol stations come and go. Toxic chemicals can build up in the soils and plants will accumulate these toxins from the soil. In some ways plants are part of the clean-up process, but you don't want to eat part of that. Local knowledge is probably one of the best ways to find out about former land uses, though it is possible to get a quick preliminary check through the Homecheck website (www.homecheck.co.uk). This runs what's known as an environmental search to look at risks such as flooding, local landfill, radon and coal mining. It also looks at local historical use, though it is quite vague. Your local library may have detailed historic maps that will help you out.

## THE LAW

**HERE'S THE** tricky bit: plants, even weeds are owned, or at least the land they sit upon is. Although in the UK we have the 'right to roam', thanks to the Countryside Rights of Way Act 2000 and foraging is a traditional use of the countryside, there is no law saying that you have the right to do it.

If you want to eat free, wild food you are supposed to ask permission from the landowner first. And it is completely against the law to dig up any plants without permission. It is also illegal to collect plants from national Nature Reserves or Sites of Special Scientific Interest without permission from Natural England and the landowner. There are a number of plants that are protected because they are so rare and it is illegal to collect these without a licence. Those licences don't cover collecting the plant to eat. None of these plants are in this book, but for a list you can look up The Botanical Society of Great Britain's website.

If there is no history of permissive foraging, which means known foraging on the site in the past, then the landowner has the right to deny any future foraging. Proving that someone has previously foraged, or just finding the right person from whom to ask permission, can often be tricky.

In some cases, having to ask would be ridiculous. Can you imagine phoning up your council to ask if you could take a dandelion leaf from a pavement or pick lime flowers off a street tree? But asking permission from your local park does make sense. All parks will prohibit picking of plants for obvious reasons – they want their roses to stay in their gardens – but they're unlikely to have a problem with you picking nettles or helping them weed, as long as you ask.

# A GOOD RULE

**'NON-COMMERCIAL** gathering of berries, nuts and mushrooms for the table is a traditional use of the countryside and probably does no harm to the plant, providing it is carried out in moderation and the plant is common.' This comes from the code of conduct for the conservation and enjoyment of wild plants written by The Botanical Society of Great Britain.

Apart from the fact that it seems to state that all foraging should happen in the countryside, it is a good rule. It is grounded in common sense – don't profit, don't harm and don't take too much. However, there's a big but, because this general rule only stands 'so long as no conservation legislation and byelaws apply'.

The byelaws and conservation legislation are complicated. Every bit of land is owned by somebody and everyone has their own rules, from the National Trust to Wildlife Trusts and Local Authorities. For instance, National Trust byelaws state that 'No unauthorised person shall dig up or remove, cut, fell, pluck or injure any flowers, plants, fungi, moss, ferns, shrubs, trees or other vegetation growing on Trust property or remove any seeds thereof or injure any grass or climb any tree.'

These sorts of prescriptive rules potentially have implications for foragers as more land increasingly comes under the care of local authorities and quasi-governmental organisations with their associated byelaws. They could gradually limit the land that is available for casual foraging. But it's rarely entirely black and white and, in fact, organisations like the National Trust have allowed commonsense foraging for years.

At the end of the day it is all about communication – good foraging practices rely on good relationships. If what you are seen to be doing shows no threat to the wildlife and is courteous to the people (and the plants), then you may not be within the letter of the law, but it's unlikely you are going to fall foul of anyone and get prosecuted. But if you can find someone to ask permission from, do so, and if you decide to take the law into your own hands, do it respectfully – take a little, take responsibly and take with the future in mind.

sloes and haws

MY PERSONAL RULES

Ask permission. If you can't ask an authority, then get permission from the earth, and be thankful. What comes around goes around, if you don't respect the plants your pickings might be slim the next time round.

Be clever. Eat only what you know.

Don't be greedy. Think of the wildlife that need this food, do not take more than your fair share.

Be respectful. If you can harvest from the plant and keep it growing, then do so. Make sure you leave plenty of seed behind to self-sow.

Teach others. Don't be secretive, if people ask what you are doing, explain. Knowledge is only useful if it's shared. Stewardship will only work if everyone is on board.

Go forth and propagate. Do something useful with your pips and seeds by sowing them.

# SPIT OUT YOUR SEEDS

**MANY OF THE FRUITS** that you forage will have considerably bigger pips than those from tamer fruit. One of the first things plant breeders do is to breed out the breeding possibilities – think of the banana or the seedless grape – to make a fruit more edible. The Darwin's barberry has bitter, slightly chewy almond-flavoured seeds that require you to lightly roll the berry round in your mouth to release the sweet flesh and then spit out the many seeds. The plant created something so sweet and delectable for you to snack upon so that you would eat it and disperse the seeds. Spit as far away from the parent plant as possible, into the best place you can find for a seed to start its new life (spitting onto concrete is neither pleasant nor useful).

If you want to take it a step further, collect some of your pips, stones and seeds and start a seedbed. You'll be starting your own very local gene bank. Some of your seeds will have all the good characteristics of the parent plant, others will differ wildly, but maybe somewhere in there will be a future foragers' dream – a perfect plum, a beautiful apple, a lovely haw.

Many tree species will take up to two years to germinate, so you'll need to make your seedbed somewhere out of the way, protected from wind. Good compost mixed with leaf mould is ideal in a large deep box or individual deep pots (trees often have long taproots) if you don't have soil to plant into. Your seedbed needs to be free of weeds and well-drained, 10-20cm deep and up to 1 metre wide.

Sow your seeds roughly 10-15cm apart, at a depth of at least twice their diameter. If possible, cover your soil with a 2cm-deep layer of grit to help to keep weed growth down. Leave the seedlings to grow on for up to a year before transplanting on to a new home. Expect your success rate to be very low and sow as many seeds as you have space for.

NORWAY CASE STUDY

# A MODERN MONK

There's a moment in any new hobby when you realise you need to find someone else to share your passion and that person has to get it. You need someone who knows exactly what you mean when you say you've found something. So I went out looking for another forager, someone who wouldn't see the boundaries and wasn't all about just native plants. Basically, I wanted to find someone as geeky about the subject as me. I found someone one step further – Stephen Barstow.

Stephen is English, but lives in Norway. He has many attributes to his name (he is a leading voice in wave technology, a brilliant academic, a cross-country skier, a cook, a Frank Zappa fan, an owner of an impressive beard), but the one that truly won me over was his salad. Stephen Barstow has put together the world's largest salad. It had 536 ingredients and took him three days to make.

There are over 15,000 or so edibles in the world and Stephen is, in his own words, 'eating his way through them'. His garden houses as many of these as he can cram in, but when Simon the photographer and I arrived it was late and, although it wasn't exactly dark (it is the land of 24-hour daylight in summer), we were exhausted and headed straight in to eat. The garden had to wait till morning.

Gardeners' interiors are often something else. It is hard to care too much about what the inside of your house looks like when your heart lies outside. Stephen's house was full of extraordinary house plants – a coffee plant with ripening beans (we ate the fleshy beans for dessert, spitting out the seeds to be roasted for coffee some other time), various tropical edibles, seeds drying on plants, others starting to germinate, and books, articles and reference material everywhere. I wondered secretly whether I was mad to bring along Simon. I consider him a good friend, but I realised I might be seriously testing that friendship with this rather indulgent adventure. Then we opened a bottle of wine.

The next morning I awoke to a view that stole my breath away. A view that leaves you incapable of doing anything else but staring. It is mesmerising, all encompassing, the sky and sea barely split by the distant mountains. With a view like that it is hard to imagine how Stephen can spend any spare time squirreling yet more plants into less than easy gardening terrain. The slope is steep, the sort that means one too many glasses of wine and you could topple to the water below. The soil is thin, a mere couple of feet before you hit hard rock. And the seasons, I suppose, are best described as very long and very short. In the winter, there are two months with no sun and, when I saw the garden, there was no night.

Breakfast was suitably Norwegian, flat breads, pickled fish, old cheese (it's a Norwegian thing, truly odd, old mouldy stuff) and Stephen's dried berries and fruit with muesli. I tried to work out what the berries were. And then we went out into the garden for a tour.

Stephen's garden doesn't have much space, partly due to the difficult terrain, partly a collector's habit. Paths are merely thin tracks on very steep slopes and everywhere, every second, there is something incredibly exciting. There are plants so ancient we've almost forgotten how to eat them, others so pretty you could barely bring yourself to do so (Martagon lily bulbs for tea, for example).

Stephen calls his work edimental – ornamental edibles. He has meticulously researched what other communities forage to eat and then found the garden-worthy version. He says he has no eye for design, just plants those that like each others' company beside each other, but I disagree. The garden is wonderful, like some psychedelic wildflower meadow. It has an air of slightly dishevelled grace and what's most amazing is the way it offers a huge variety of year-round food, grown in a simple sustainable way.

He doesn't feed his plants much, just a yearly mulch with rotted-down seaweed from the shore. His weeding is done with thick carpets of newspaper to suppress weeds and, after a year, once the newspaper rots, he's created a new bed. Many of his plants are not winter-hardy so these spend the winter with him in various parts of the house. He doesn't own any machines, and scythes the grass of his steep hill.

Someone once called Stephen a modern monk and this makes sense. It's nothing to do with design – monastery gardens are all parterres and cloisters – but something about his strange compelling collection, the wonderful view, the clean air, his simple, structured life and the immense hard work that he puts into his garden. That great beard helps too. There really is something very special about the space, I only spent three days there but it felt far longer. We talked lots, ate plenty of lovely things and spent a long, long time contemplating the view, before eating a little more of it.

And if you want to know why he made such as large salad, I think it's just because he can.

# SOME NEW FAVOURITES FROM STEPHEN'S GARDEN

## LEAFY GREENS

### Hostas

I used to hate hostas. They were one of those plants that meant a battle to grow anything good. But now I know I can beat the slugs to eating them, I am quite quickly falling in love.

In Japan, hostas are known as *Sansai*, or wild mountain plants, as they were traditionally harvested from the wild and sold at market. Their immense popularity now means they are grown as a crop, sold as *urui*. You eat the young tender stems and shoots and can start to pick them the minute they appear in spring, but it's best to wait till there is 10cm or more of shoot and just the beginning of an unfurled leaf. At this point, the stem is sweet and tender. It will become bitter with age, probably to defend itself against the slugs who'll race you to get a good harvest. Eat the very young shoots raw, but as they age you'll first need to lightly boil them and then run them under cold water, then you can use them much as you would spinach. Stephen makes something called 'Hostakopita', a hosta-filled version of the Greek spinach pie, spanikopita.

You can also marinate the young stems in sugar, soy and salt or a basic *su* – equal parts sugar and white vinegar, dissolved over a little heat with salt to taste.

There are thousands of hostas; Stephen grows those known to be edible, including the popular garden form *Hosta sieboldiana*, *H.* 'Sagae' (a variety from the city of Sagae where hostas were grown as crops) and the native Japanese *H. montana*. If you have other species growing in your garden and want to try them, I recommend caution, try a little bit and see how it goes. I would be very wary of eating a hosta straight from the garden centre. Few growers are growing hostas for food and they may use chemicals not suitable for human consumption.

**How to grow** Hostas thrive in damp, shady conditions (along with slugs). They need to grow in soil rich in organic matter, so dig some homemade or shop-bought compost into the planting hole first. If you have leaf mould (rotted-down leaves), add this too. Many people find growing hostas in pots helps combat the slug problem – fill these with good quality compost and water regularly. Used coffee grounds are particularly good at keeping slugs away from young leaves.

Hostas are perennial and can be long-lived, but not if you eat all the leaves every year. You should divide them every five years or so. I think the best way to harvest from hostas is to thin out the growth, leaving a good amount to grow into summer. This way you can maintain a decent patch for eating and enjoying for years to come (and there's great satisfaction in beating the slugs to dinner).

hostas

30 | The Thrifty Forager

## AGASTACHE FOENICULUM
### Anise hyssop

This plant is a joy to grow, simple, tasty and pretty. It is a North American herb used widely by the native community, mostly as tea for colds and to aid with chest pains from coughs. The young leaves have a delicious aniseed flavour and are good mixed in salads or made into a tea. Unopened florets and leaves can be used as an aniseed substitute in recipes. Try using a few florets when baking biscuits or teacakes. It tastes a bit like sweet cicely *(see page 148).*

**How to grow** Although usually thought of as a sun-loving herb, agastache actually does fairly well in shade. It is tall, 90-150cm (a bit shorter if growing in shade), so best towards the back of a border. Dense spikes of blue flowers with violet bracts appear from mid summer to late autumn, growing above lance-shaped downy leaves that are whitish green beneath. Grow in organic-rich, but well-drained soil and, if your plant gets too big, divide it in spring. Powdery mildew may affect the leaves in dry summers and will be worse in shady conditions. Do not eat mildewy leaves. Sow seeds in early spring when frost has passed, or in the cold frame.

## MONARDA DIDYMA
### Bee balm, bergamot, Oswego tea

I'm a sucker for a cup of tea. If my day was represented by a piece of paper, tea would perforate it into a doily. Give me a plant to turn into tea and I'm suitably smitten. Bee balm is loved by bees and gardeners for its highly decorative flowers, which are also lovely in salads. These appear in late summer and positively hum with bees. It has a long history as a medicinal tea plant used by many Native American communities.

The tea tastes highly aromatic, a sort of Earl Grey of the herbal tea world. It also has useful medicinal properties as it's a source of thymol (also found in several thyme and oreganum plants), a naturally occurring antiseptic used in modern mouthwashes. Native Americans used the tea for mouth and throat infections.

If you get addicted to the taste, dry the leaves for winter use by cutting the whole plant down before it flowers. If you do this fairly early in the season it will re-grow, slightly shorter, and you should still get flowers. Hang the plant upside down, away from sunlight somewhere warm and dry and, in several days, the leaves will be crisp enough to store in an airtight container.

Young leaves can be added to salads in spring or steamed lightly, but once the leaves mature the taste is too aromatic for most.

**How to grow** This is a North American native that likes moderately fertile moist soil in full sun. It's best not to overcrowd monarda as poor air circulation leads to powdery mildew and no-one wants to drink mouldy-looking leaves. If the plant does get mildew, cut it back hard. Make sure bee balm doesn't dry out in summer or sit in too much wet over winter.

Mildew-resistant cultivars tend to be bred from a cross between *M. didyma* and *M. fistulosa* (both edible). 'Squaw' is a bright red variety, 'Cherokee' pink, 'Scorpion' a deep purple and 'Balance' a reddish pink. It's a good idea to label them as they are often the last to show any signs of growth in spring and it's easy to dig them up by mistake. The young foliage is susceptible to slugs in spring, so rather than mulching around the plants, which may encourage slugs, I like to feed them with chicken manure pellets.

caucasian spinach

HABLITZIA TAMNOIDES
## Caucasian spinach

Just being able to physically touch something I'd only read about, to finger the pretty leaves and nibble a little at the young vines made the long trip to Norway more than worthwhile. This plant is a rare find. I dream of one day owning it.

Stephen is one of a handful of seed guardians to this amazing plant. It comes from the Caucasus region and is naturally found growing clambering around in damp shady places, such as the edges of woodlands and riverside thickets. The ones I saw in Stephen's garden have scrambled up into trees and around porches.

This plant has a curious history and Stephen is now very much part of that, or at least the part about its reintroduction into our gardens. It was brought to Scandinavia in the 1820s as an ornamental plant to climb pergolas and porches. By the end of the century it was quite in vogue with the rich – if you had a large garden you probably had it covering a pergola somewhere. What's interesting is that someone somewhere cottoned on to how good it tastes, so they weren't just covering structures with the stuff, they were serving it up for dinner.

It dies back in the winter, but in mid summer I was looking at plants a good 5m in length, which shows just how rapidly it puts on growth. Stephen treats his as early spring greens that can be cut and will come again for three cuts before he lets it scramble up for the summer. It's a curiously attractive thing with heart-shaped leaves and tiny green flowers. Stephen describes the taste like spinach, if not better.

Around the Northern hemisphere all sort of gardeners are getting excited about this edible. Stephen is slowly distributing his seed around the world. It's not something you're going to find at your local garden centre any time soon, but keep your eyes open. Fully hardy (Stephen says his starts sprouting out of the snow), shade-loving (it withers away in sun) perennials are hard to come by, particularly ones that taste good. I predict quite a renaissance for this long-forgotten plant.

MALVA VERTICILLATA 'CRISPA'
## Curled mallow

This is perhaps the prettiest salad leaf I've ever eaten. It seems astonishing that something quite so charming has fallen by the wayside. Closely related to the marsh mallow, *Malva moschata*, it has a mild flavour so it's great to bulk up salads, or you can eat it lightly steamed, dressed with oil and lemon.

Curled mallow is an ancient, cultivated vegetable domesticated in East Asia thousands of years ago and appearing in old Chinese herbals, apparently as a remedy for constipation. It was superseded by brassicas in the Chinese diet, though it is still cultivated on a small scale. At some point it escaped and became naturalised in parts of Europe, particularly in France, where it became a foraged food. Growing to 45cm, *M. verticillata* 'Crispa' has rounded, bright green triangular-lobed leaves with a frilly edge, the can-can skirt of the salad world. It's an annual, not frost-hardy, and needs to be sown in good, free-draining soil and planted in full sun or partial shade. Sow in spring and plant out once all threat of frost has passed.

The Modern Monk

ALLIUM SPECIES
## Onions
*We ate plenty of onions whilst staying with Stephen; they appeared raw for lunch and cooked for tea. They came in all shapes and sizes, we ate all the parts. They were sweet, strong and delicious and made our own chives and bulb onions look rather dull. Bees, hoverflies, butterflies and other flying pollinators go wild for onion flowers that offer plenty of nectar and pollen all in one place. Even if you only eat a few leaves a year, it's worth putting perennial onions into your garden as the flowers are beautiful and distinctive and can be woven into pretty much any garden style.*

---

ALLIUM VICTORIALIS
## The victory onion or alpine leek

This is so handsome and fine-tasting that it is amazing that we've got stuck with standard yellow onions all this time. It's a perennial found growing in damp alpine forests and sub-alpine meadows in mountainous regions of Russia, China and Japan where it's considered a wild delicacy. It's a traditional food crop of the indigenous Ainu people of Hokkaido in Japan. Stephen even found reference to it in the Viking sagas – apparently they grew gardens full of the stuff. Once used against scurvy, more recent research suggests that this onion has powerful medicinal properties and contains high levels of ascorbic acid. It has traditionally been both eaten fresh and preserved by salting.

The raw leaves have a strong onion flavour, the small bulbs, only about 10mm in diameter, taste more of garlic. The flower stem grows between 30-85cm tall with a classic allium spherical flower head, made up of dense whiteish green star-shaped flowers appearing from late spring to mid summer. It usually has two or three large straplike leaves and could be misidentified before flowering with other plants including the poisonous lily of the valley, *Convallaria majalis*, that doesn't have a bulb but rhizomes. The easiest way to tell any allium is that the leaves smell strongly of onions or garlic when crushed. Fully hardy and not bothered by pests, the victory onion likes to grow in full sun or partial shade in well-drained but moisture-retentive soil, so enrich your soil with lots of leaf mould or compost. It doesn't like to be crowded out by other plants and would work well in a pot. Stephen suggests making a pesto out of the leaves in spring and freezing it in small batches suitable for portion sizes.

ALLIUM CERNUUM
## Nodding onion

This dainty little onion from North America is sometimes known as lady's leek. The bulbs taste strongly of onions and can be used like spring, bunching or Welsh onions, but this is far prettier that the other three. Long grass-like leaves are slightly pink at the base, and edible flowers in mid to late summer are like dainty chandeliers of a dozen or so clear pink or white, nodding flowers. Sweet and oniony, these are lovely in salads.

It's fairly easy to obtain plants from specialist bulb catalogues, but ask about how they've been grown before sampling them, as they won't have been grown for eating. Hardy nodding onions like sandier soils in full sun and will seed around in the right conditions.

the victory onion or alpine leek

The Thrifty Forager

nodding onion

*walking onion*

ALLIUM CEPA PROLIFERUM GROUP
## Egyptian walking onion

Egyptian walking onions are happy wanderers that like to move home with the seasons. Once they flower, they produce small bulbs on the flower head called bulbils. Their weight makes the flower stalk bend over to touch the soil where the bulbils root. Stephen, who has the sort of brain for this thing, has worked out that they walk at the pace of $3 \times 10^8$mm per second, or roughly one metre in the course of year, a fact I treasure and trot out whenever I can.

You can eat the leaves like spring onions or Japanese bunching onions. If they are re-homing themselves rather too freely, then you can eat the bulbils but they are slightly fiddly to peel. You can also dry mature bulbils to store.

Egyptian walking onions grow between 50–100cm and generally fit themselves in where they can. They are happy enough in any reasonably well-drained soil and prefer sun to shade. Slugs love them, especially when the base of the plant is in shade, but otherwise they are maintenance free. If you want to propagate them, just remove the bulbils and replant in a pot with the tips peeping through the soil – they will quickly resprout.

ALLIUM MOLY
## Yellow onion, lily leek

I'd forgotten how sweet Moly is (both in flavour and looks). I once bought a great batch of discount store bulbs and filled the beds of my rented house with this dainty yellow-flowering allium. Stephen has her growing on a terrace bed overlooking the fjord, a little dwarfed by the Egyptian walking onions, but still a pretty little blonde and worthy, I think, of any edible garden.

The yellow onion is a wild foraged food in its native habitat in Spain. Flowers, leaves and small bulbs are all edible and plants are happy in sun or partial shade, growing between 12-35cm high. The bulbs are about 2.5cm wide and produce many offsets so that the plant forms a dense cluster of bulbils. It has many nodding flowers, yellow on the outside, green-yellow on the inside. 'Jeannine' is a pretty cultivated form with larger bright yellow flowers. Plant bulbs in autumn or sow seed to overwinter in a cold frame in pots with good free-draining compost. If you have no cold frame, stratify the seeds for four weeks in the fridge before sowing.

CARUM CARVI
## Caraway

It's easy to see why caraway has become so established a flavour in north European food as Norway is awash with it, along the shoreline and right up into the grassy alpine meadows. Stephen is experimenting with wild collected seed to find strains with larger roots and those that will overwinter without losing their leaves. The poorer the soil, the stronger the flavour of the seed. Strong plants were growing in the thin sandy stuff that barely covered the rocks around the shore. Fresh seed is distinctly soapy tasting, but this tempers with drying, and young foliage and the roots can also be eaten. The foliage tastes a bit perfumed, but it's good in soups, stews and dotted through salads. Caraway is a biennial plant and its roots should be harvested around the autumn of the first year or spring of the second year before it flowers – they are small, but with a superior parsnip flavour.

There are some accounts of naturalised caraway in Britain, but I've never found any. Plants grow well in a sunny position in well-drained soil and the fat seeds are best harvested by picking the whole plant when it has turned a golden-brown colour. Hang upside down with the heads in a paper bag and, after a week or two and a lot of shaking, the seed will come off. Seed should be sown fresh for more supplies.

RUBUS ARCTICUS
## Arctic raspberry

Stephen had this fine-looking little raspberry growing in a big barrel, which was a lovely way to show it off. Only reaching about 30cm tall, it has bright, neon-pink flowers that appear from late spring onwards and, after them, red blackberry-like fruits which have a wonderful tart sweetness. I think you probably can pick a few all summer long, rather than any great number at once. It prefers slightly acidic conditions and is, as its name suggests, very hardy, naturally found growing in Canada and the Pacific Northwest, Russia, Norway, Sweden and Finland.

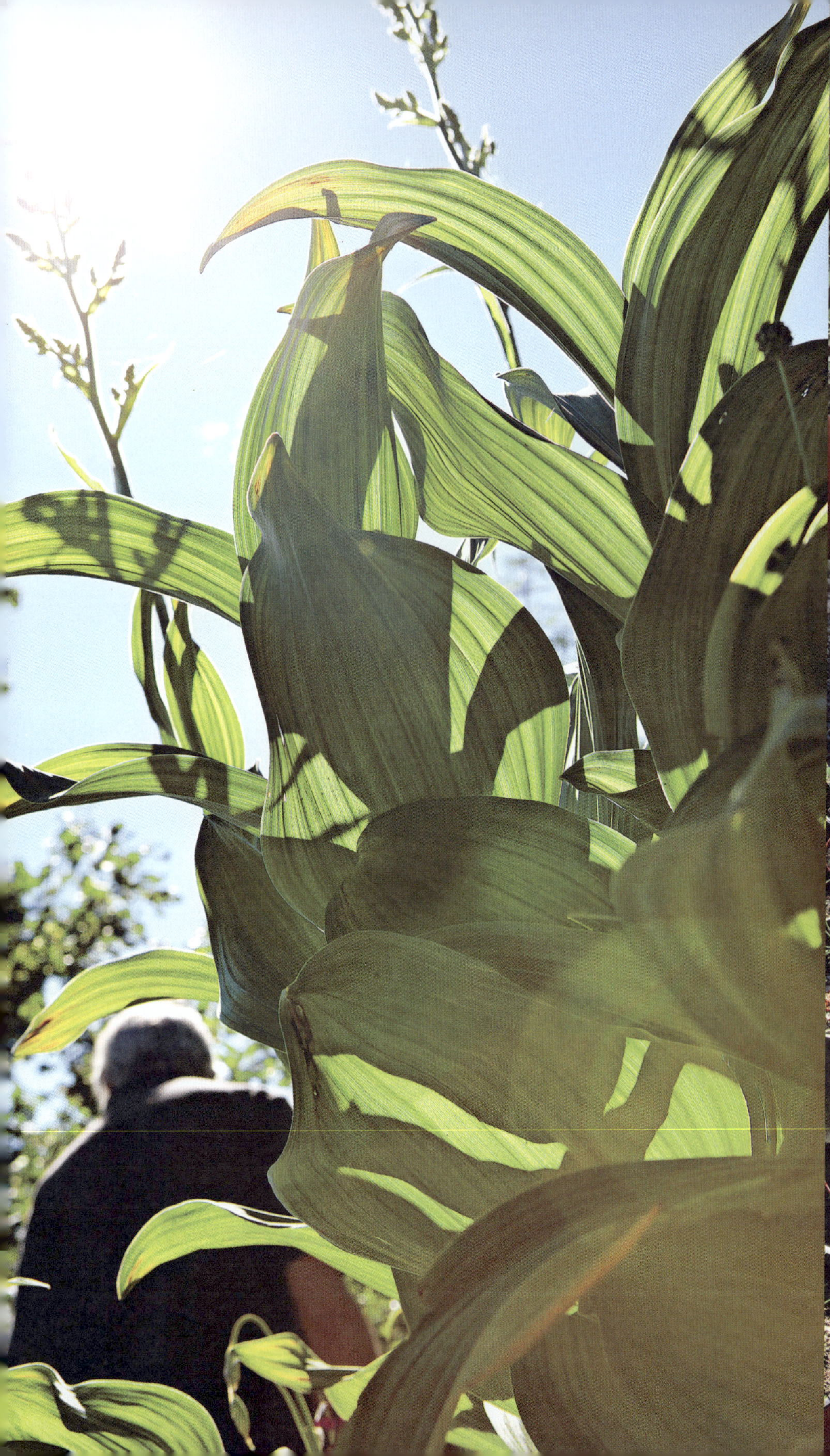
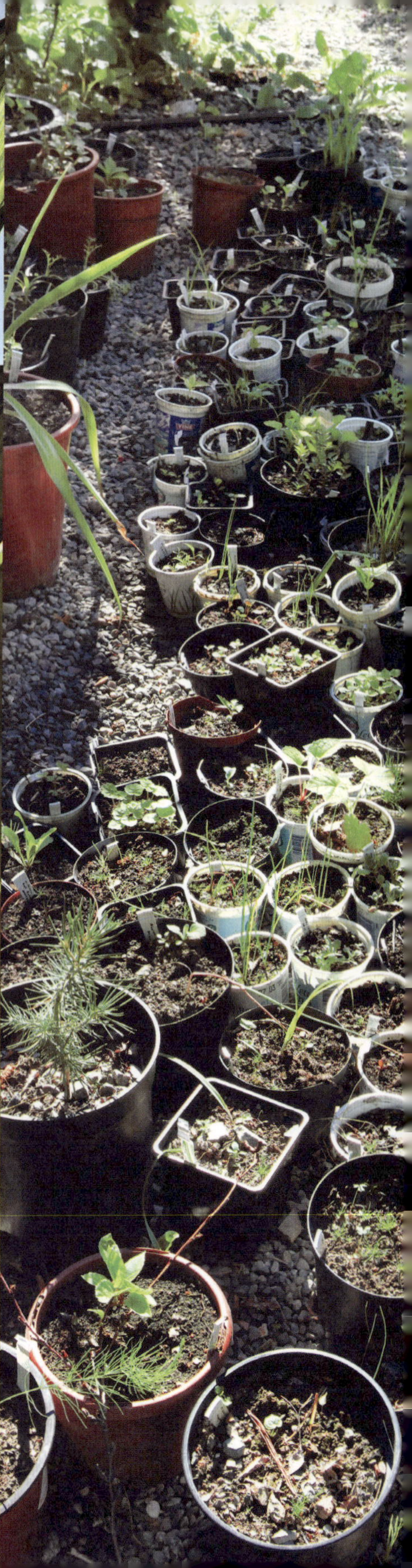

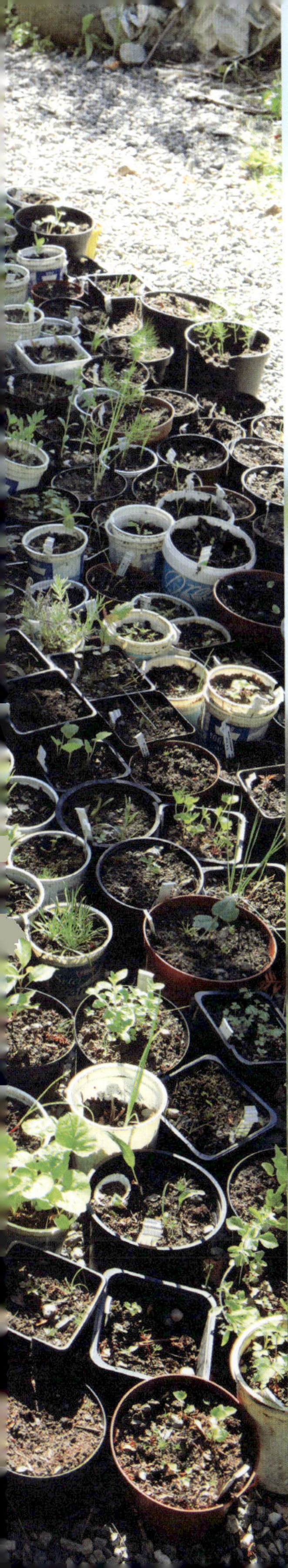

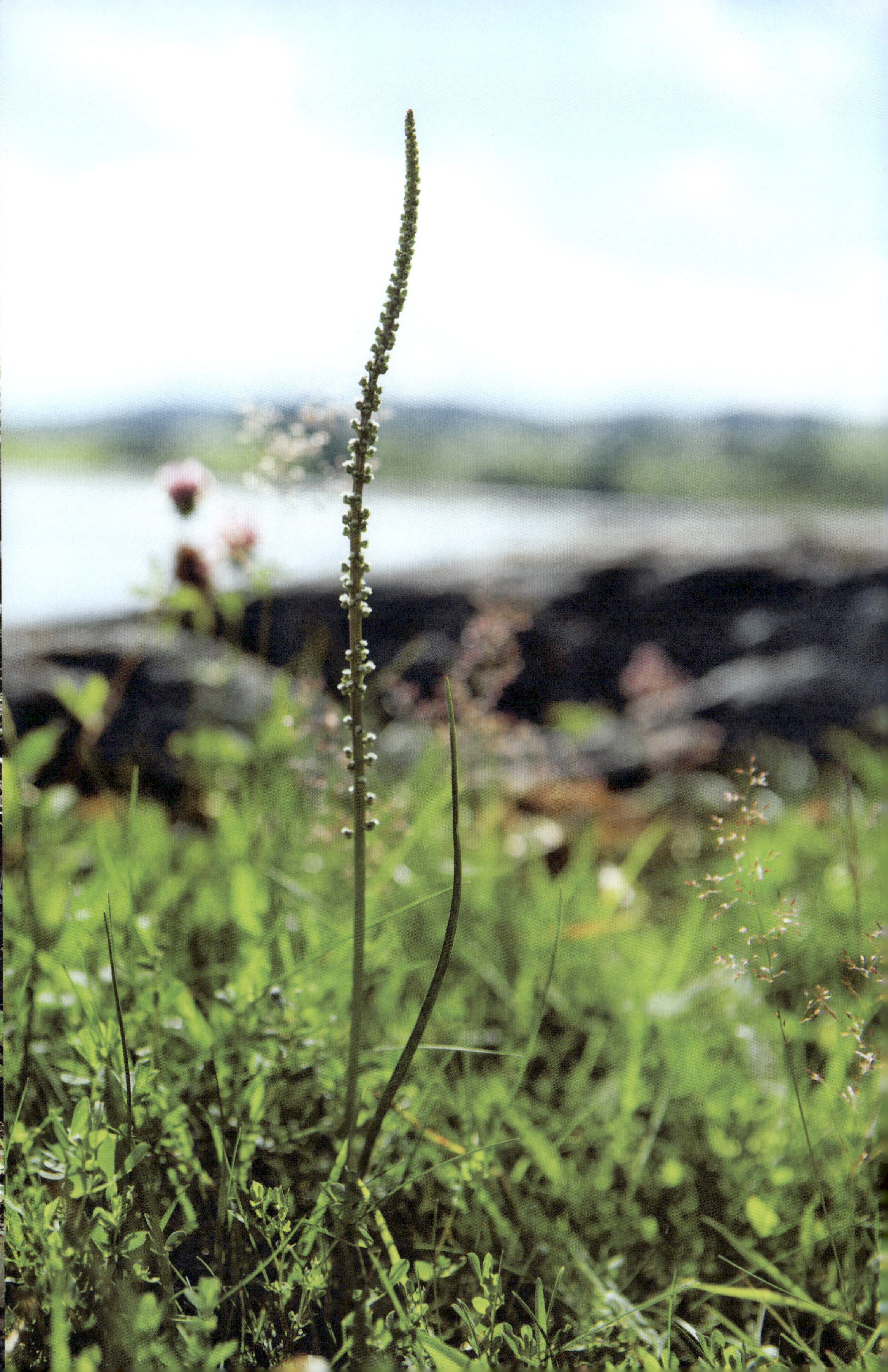

42 | The Thrifty Forager

USA CASE STUDY
# CITY FRUITS

Foraging is traditionally a countryside pursuit. That's certainly where I learnt its ways, but you don't have to go out of town to forage. You can stay in the city. It might even be important that you do so. The idea that nature can only be found outside of cities is damaging and incorrect. Nature is wherever you are. As you walk to the bus, you're pretty sure to pass edible weeds (though you might not actually want to eat them from the bus stop), and even a busy shopping centre often has something wild for you to eat, thanks to the unwitting edibles in most municipal plantings. There are edible plants literally all over the city, the only thing you need to do is to get your eye in – but that's not always so easy.

We are taught to see the countryside as an edible view, the fields will be processed into cereals, the cows will be milked and the hedgerows will provide wild fruits, but recognising the edible landscape in the city takes a whole new way of thinking. Thankfully, there are those prepared to take on this challenge. A growing number of groups in different countries are gradually mapping, collecting and distributing our neglected urban fruits.

Fallen Fruit is a Los Angeles based artist collective, a collaboration between artists David Burns, Mattias Viegener and Austin Young. They were all living in Silver Lake, a suburb of LA, and they noticed there was masses of fruit rotting all over the city. So they began by mapping out public fruit in LA, recording those trees and bushes that grow on or over public property in the city. It all started as a kind of treasure hunt, finding wonderful fruit for free.

Instead of just picking up the fruit for themselves, they set about mapping their neighbourhood so others could enjoy it. Their first map found over 100 fruit trees within the neighbourhood, providing year-round fruit. This came as a huge shock to most people. LA is a car culture, people drive everywhere, so there is often a sense of being disconnected from the street and even the neighbourhood. Despite the fact that LA is dripping in fruit, very few people ever notice it. And if they do see it, it's in rather an abstract way, almost like the original forbidden fruit – this land is abundant, but do not eat its fruits.

Fallen Fruit found that people were afraid to pick the fruit, they didn't know whether they were allowed to, or whether it was safe. So the original mapping project led to nocturnal public fruit forages. They led foragers on night-time public fruit walks, choosing the night because 'it makes it a little strange and that leads to more exchanges'. These, in turn, led to public jam-making sessions, and before they knew it, Fallen Fruit had become the poster boys of collective urban foraging.

Their work now takes them around the world creating maps, making short films about people's perception of fruit, creating public fruit orchards and generally charting the way private and public land use defines the way we live.

They consider public fruit as much a part of any place as its people. 'Fruit trees are like the older residents of the neighbourhood. The trees define the places, they tell us stories about those neighbourhoods'. They found that in more wealthy neighbourhoods there was little or no fruit out front. And, if there were fruit trees, they were usually ornamental varieties not known for eating (though one street was lined with bitter oranges perfect for marmalade making).

44 | The Thrifty Forager

45

In poorer immigrant neighbourhoods the fruit was more likely to be out front.

Although they got shouted at, they picked the bitter oranges from the rich neighbourhood and turned them into marmalade. Mattias explained that 'Fallen Fruit is really about letting as many people into the act and giving away as much as possible for free. It all comes back to public and private ways that we present ourselves to the world.'

Their take on urban foraging is extremely witty. When they take people on their nocturnal fruit forages, they dress up in clear plastic coveralls to highlight that this fruit, unlike supermarket fruit, is not wrapped in plastic: 'We wear plastic rather than wrap our fruit in it'. But at Fallen Fruit's roots lies a profound message. 'Fruit is not a natural object, it is deliberately created or selected, it's more of a cultural object than a natural one.'

## Public Fruit Jams

Fallen Fruit's jam-making sessions are like none other. They can make 1,400 jars in a couple of hours, but this isn't making jam like grandmother did. 'We want our jam-making to be playful, collaborative and experimental'. The public are asked to bring any spare fruit, and then encouraged to sit with strangers and pair up their wares, making their own recipes. So if you come with figs (LA is almost overrun with fig trees) you might be paired with lemons and perhaps someone who brought lavender. 'Nothing is planned and occasionally you get something remarkable, like strawberry, grapefruit and mint jam or lemon, tangerine and bitter orange'. They have perfected their jam-making so that it is quick and easy enough for even a bunch of strangers to come away with a pot of something delicious.

When questioned whether a bunch of artists making jam is actually art, they respond, 'It's pretty and it has an aesthetic, but the real thing is getting people, strangers, together to communicate and food is a really good way to do this'. These jam-making events are very public, held in parks or on the pavement, and the smell of the fruit has literally stopped traffic. It's become a bit of an urban legend that when the collective held their first public jam, they didn't actually know how to make jam. 'We learnt fast that you needed to make the jam very quickly to keep people engaged. We ask people to bring the fruit off the maps and we provide the other ingredients.' They do recommend set proportions of key ingredients so that jams set, but they don't suggest specific recipes. 'Often you're hanging out with someone else's grandmother, so people share experiences and skills. We want to encourage everyone to negotiate how to make jam themselves.'

## Handpicked: public fruit mapping

Fallen Fruit's maps are not intended just as shopping lists, they are supposed to be treasure hunts, an exercise in learning how to see a neighbourhood with fresh eyes. Their maps can all be walked within an hour, they can be downloaded for free and neighbourhoods are encouraged to make their own maps. (To download go to www.fallenfruit.org/index.php/media/maps).

Initially, Fallen Fruit offered masses of fruit tours complete with handouts on how to pick fruit. 'At the beginning there was this real anxiety about public fruit, about whether it was safe or legal'. After a couple of years, some of the maps had become so well-known in their neighbourhoods that the fruit was picked clean, so they started to persuade people to plant up the edges of their private spaces so that the trees would hang over into public spaces. 'We started encouraging people to plant up their perimeters and turn their neighbourhoods into a community garden, and suddenly people started adding to the collections.' Their maps are growing.

Impressed by their energy and genuine desire for collaboration, my afternoon with Fallen Fruit left me desperate to get out and find some of this hidden bounty. I printed out a map of Venice Beach and headed off to see what I could find. The treasure hunt analogy is very true. Initially, I couldn't find a single tree, but once I relaxed into just enjoying a tour through an unknown neighbourhood, I was falling over figs, avocados, prickly pears, grapefruit, tangerines, bananas, dates and apples – most, I admit, were not ripe, but if I lived there I could see you'd have fun 'shopping'.

City Fruits

# URBAN FRUIT COLLECTING

**I CONTINUED MY** journey from LA to Portland, Oregon, to see how the Portland Fruit Tree project was distributing tens of thousands of dollars worth of fruit (and some nuts) to those in need of fresh fruit.

Portland is a city so green that it almost overwhelms a visitor. The Pacific north-west climate is kind to plants – hot summers and mild, wet winters mean that the streets tunnel through overgrowth, trees literally drip into the roads. There are so many fruit trees in this city that you can't walk down a street during August and September without seeing a pile of fallen fruit. Katy Kolker is a Portland resident who works in urban agriculture and food security. She was well aware of how expensive fresh fruit is to those on low incomes, so she came up with what seemed a simple idea to connect the fruit that was going to waste with the people who needed it. Five years ago she set up the Portland Fruit Tree Project to bridge the gap. Throughout autumn, the project harvests unwanted fruit from around the city. Some of these trees are street trees, but most are on private properties. Owners can register their tree's fruit to be donated to food pantries (organisations that distribute food to people in need).

'We have a growing harvesting programme which has been doubling every year. We had 50 harvesting events this year and collected over 25,000 dollars worth of fresh fruit', explains Katy. The harvesting parties are simple – the owner of registered trees phones up the project two weeks before they think the fruit will be ripe. Katy or one of her volunteers then liaises a date for the harvest party. There are 10 people per harvesting party and each month the harvesting schedule is put up on the internet. Within days the harvesting parties are full. The volunteers get to take home half of what they harvest, the rest is distributed to the food pantries.

They never harvest windfalls and only pick off the trees to minimise health risks. The fruit varies in quality, so they sort it into good fruit and okay fruit. Generally, at least one volunteer intends to make jam or process the fruit in some way, so they're happy with the lesser quality. One of Katy's biggest challenges from the start has been the popularity of the scheme, and managing expectations. At the beginning, they were offered many more trees than they could easily pick, with more people interested in participating than they could initially involve.

Many of the registered fruit trees are huge old trees where harvesting requires ladders and poles, and clearly sending a volunteer up a ladder has health and safety implications. Each harvesting party now has two harvesting leaders who are volunteers trained to co-ordinate the picking, teach people how to pick safely and generally make sure that it all runs smoothly. There are also tree scouts who find and register new trees for the project, and also a tree care team, who work with owners to teach maintenance and pruning of their trees to keep them in tip-top condition for harvesting. 'If you've got a big tree, then picking all that fruit is hard work and no-one likes to see fruit go to waste, so I think it works because the owners are grateful for the help, the volunteers are excited about harvesting the fruit and taking it home, and, of course, the food program is grateful for the donations. And it's fun, it's about bringing people together.'

TO THE FUTURE

IMAGINE IF WHEN YOU WANTED A FEW APPLES FOR A RECIPE OR MAYBE HALF A DOZEN PLUMS FOR A TARTE, YOU GOT ON YOUR BIKE AND TRAWLED AROUND YOUR NEIGHBOURHOOD. IF YOU KNEW THAT ON ANY GIVEN STREET THERE WOULD BE A TREE OR A PLANTER WITH SOMETHING EDIBLE IN IT? SOME WOULD BE HIGHLY CULTIVATED, OTHERS MIGHT BE A CELEBRATION OF THE FERAL, A WILD DAMSON OR A GREAT CRAB APPLE THAT HAD ESTABLISHED ITSELF THERE. IMAGINE IF YOUR HOMETOWN WAS PLANTED UP FOR PICKING, THEN YOUR PLACE WOULD BE TO PICK.

# UK CASE STUDY
# INCREDIBLE EDIBLE TODMORDEN

*community beans*

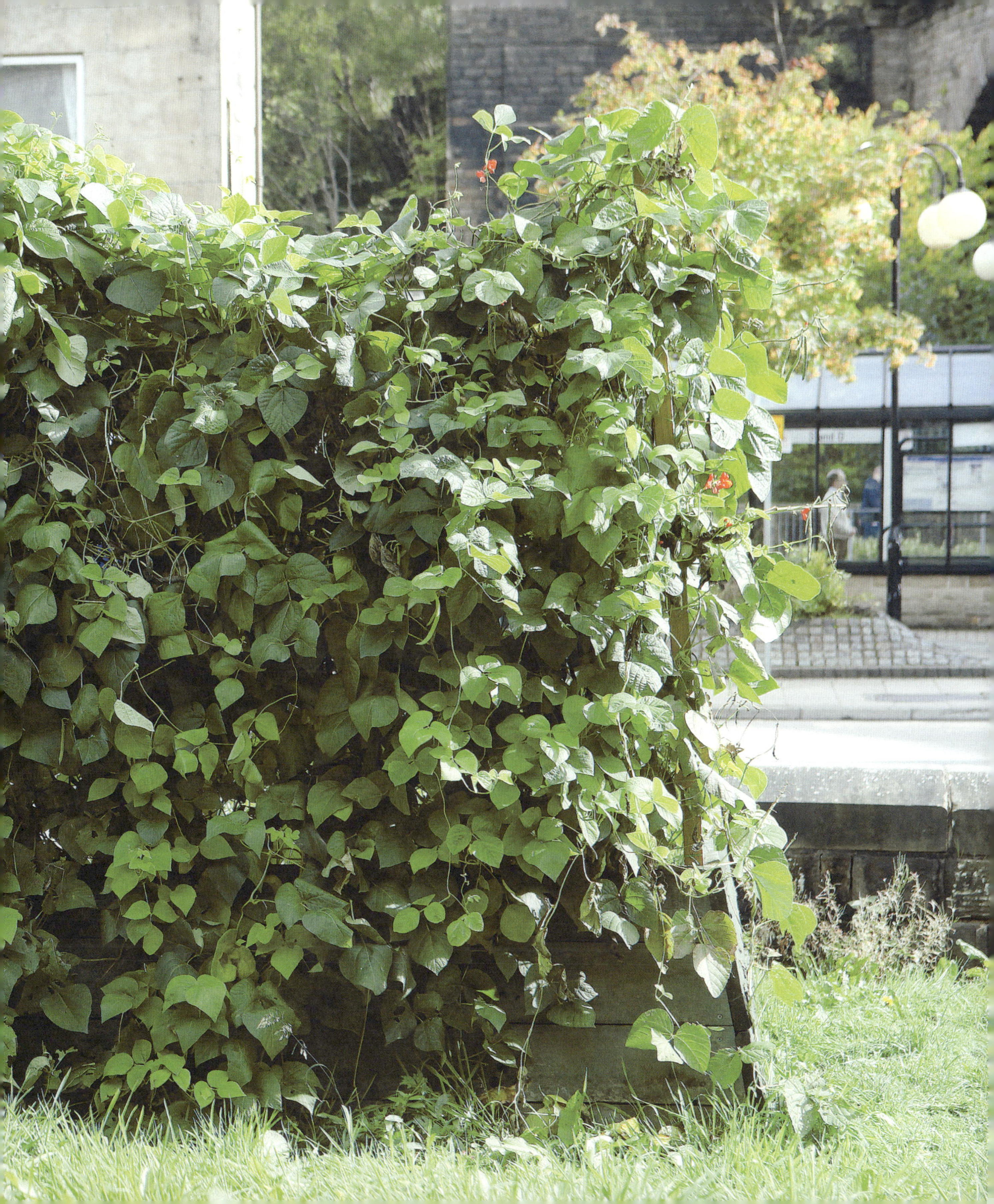

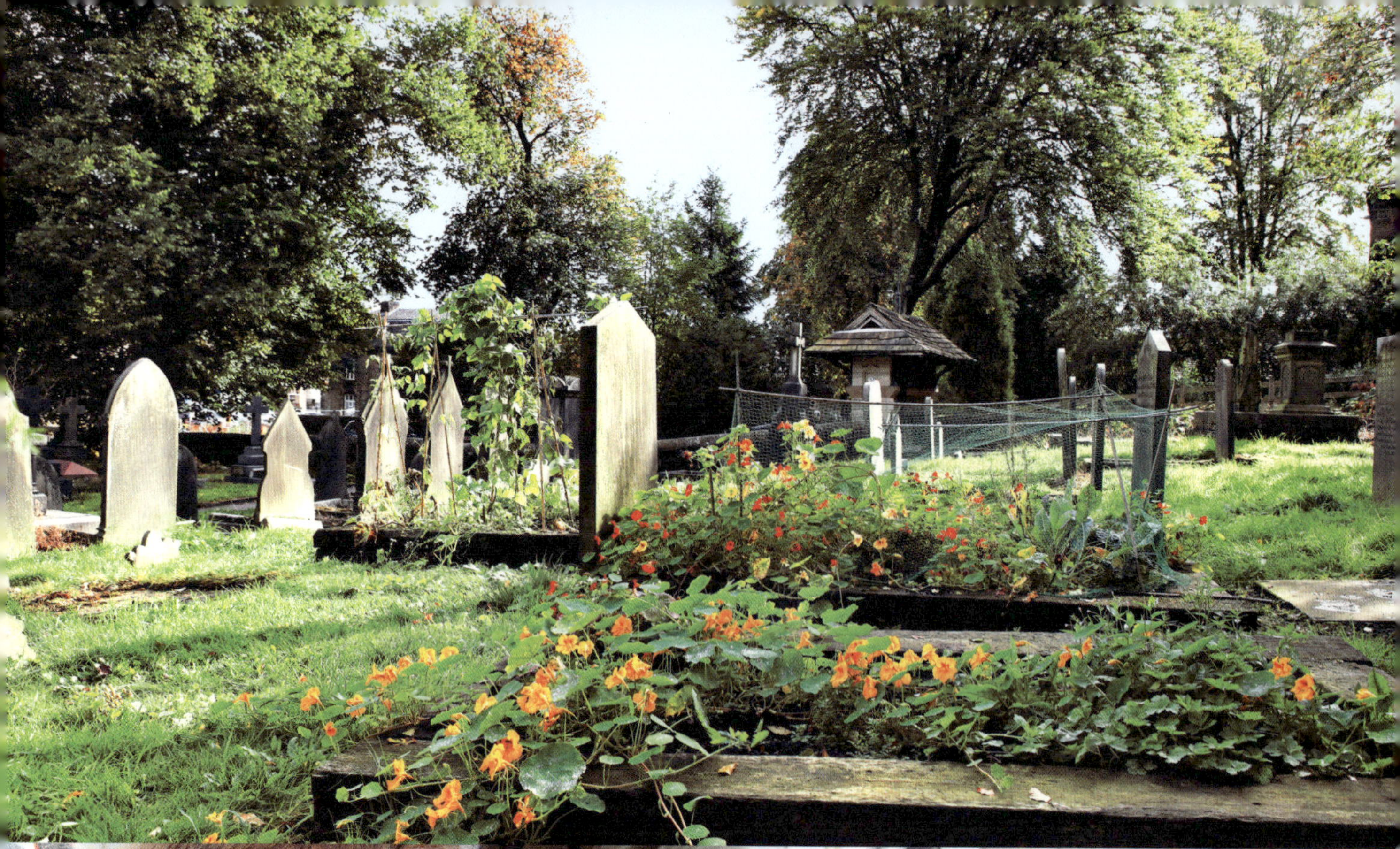
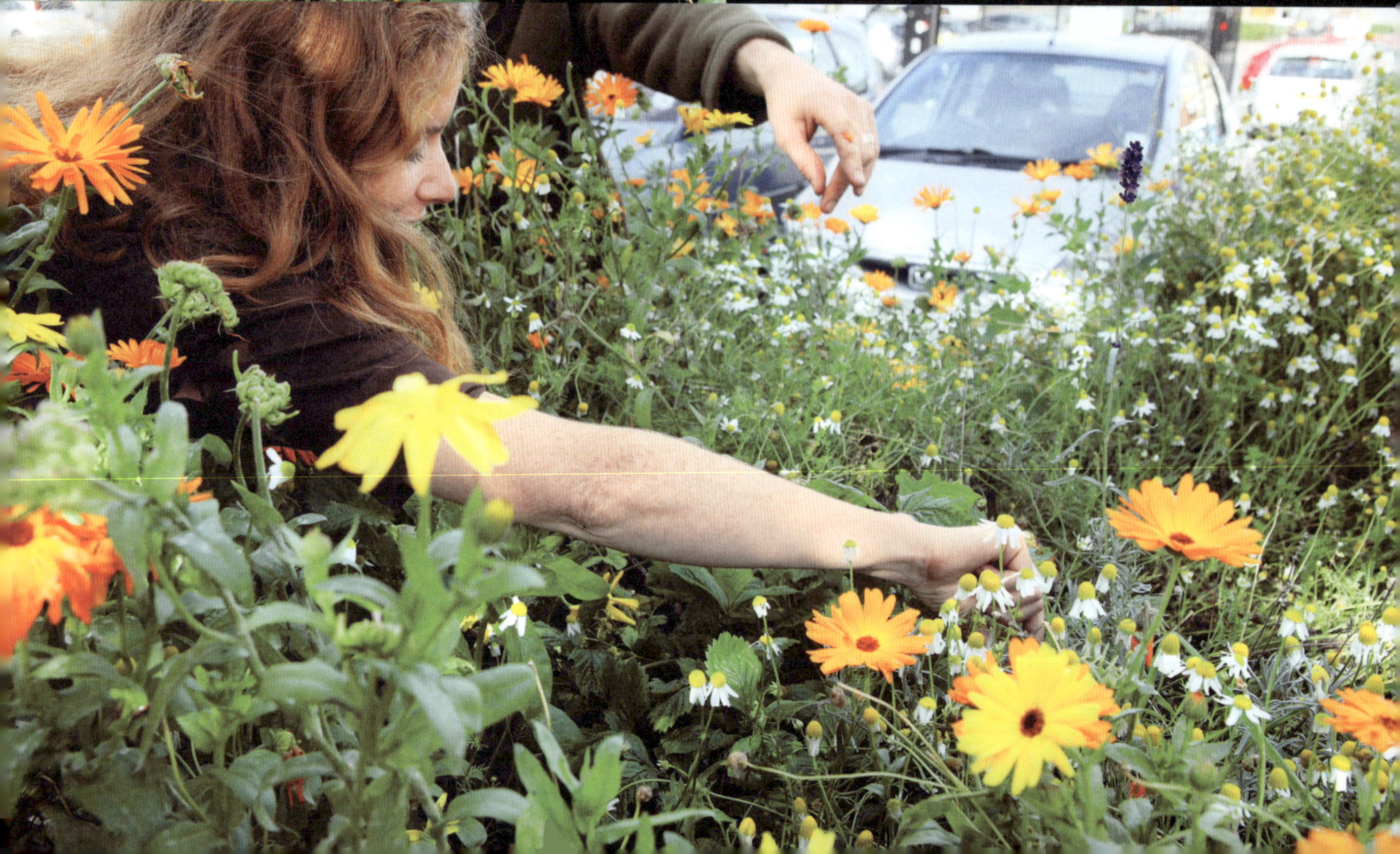

This isn't just some kind of utopian dream. Already there are places where spare land is being planted up with something a little more useful than pansies. Incredible Edible Todmorden (IET) started off as just an idea around a kitchen table. Some local residents, the kind that like to get things done, decided that they needed a movement based around food that 'would pass on a better future to our children'. They chose food because it is our common language.

Todmorden has 150,000 residences and the idea was to increase the amount of land for food growing. But, instead of asking the council for more allotments, they decided to think a little differently. They identified any unused public land around the town and earmarked it for potential growing sites. This used land included everything from a graveyard to a strip outside the police station. Sites included schools, old people's homes, the fire department, National Rail and the NHS health centre. The group sometimes asked permission, but sometimes they just got on and made a raised bed.

They planted up the beds with vegetables, tomatoes and herbs, they found places for fruit trees and soft fruit bushes. Blueberries, raspberries and medicinal herbs now surround the NHS centre, the railway station grows culinary herbs, the fire station produces tomatoes and the police station had a huge crop of courgettes and sweetcorn last time I was there.

The project only began in 2007, and since then, over 500 fruit trees have been planted across the town and residents are encouraged never to leave home without a bag in order to harvest this free resource. There is an edible map for visitors so they too can pick their own, and the idea is spreading fast with people coming from around the world to see this innovative project.

At the heart of IET is the idea that everyone has to be part of the project for it to work. That means including the community, local farmers, schools and businesses in all the decisions. By relocalising the food movement, they have been able to encourage more local food producers. Local farmers now grow directly for the town and there are more local producers at the daily open market.

I think one of the successes of IET is that, although it started off with just a couple of packets of seeds and a lot of goodwill, it's quickly moved on to thinking long term. This isn't just guerilla gardening, it's about addressing how this town can become sustainable long term. It tries to balance the interests of business, economy and education so the project isn't just about building an edible landscape, it's about creating a strong and resilient community. Not everyone in the town has been behind the project, the local newspaper has its fair

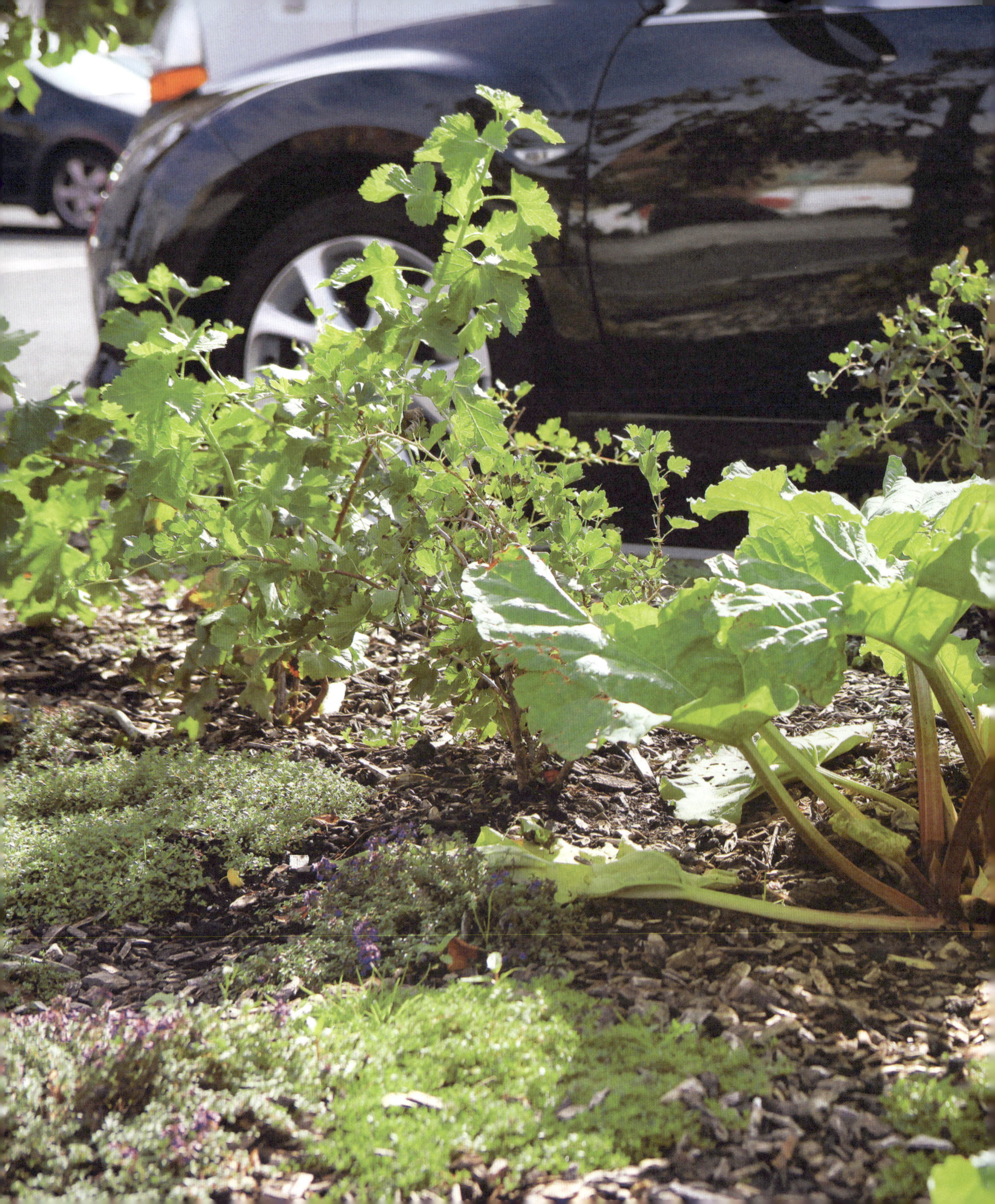

share of disgruntled letters and sceptics but, whatever else has happened, more people are growing their own. Seventy per cent of the residents say that they are now actively involved in growing food, this shows a huge change in perceptions.

Everyone involved will say at some point it's about taking a few risks. They haven't always asked for permission before planting, but they always say thank you. There are now 130 growing spaces around town. The Incredible Edible beds last year harvested 815kg of food, nearly £2,000 worth. Slowly, the beds are being adopted by groups and individuals who are dedicated to looking after their own patches for the community, re-sowing, offering advice and putting up friendly signs when stuff is ready to pick. It's easy to assume that people will know when vegetables are ripe and ready, but it turned out that an awful lot didn't, and were either letting vegetables rot or picking too early. Harvesting is a skill that is now being taught all over Todmorden.

All six schools are involved in growing their own food, up to 30 per cent of high school meals are from locally sourced food. There are free classes on vegetable growing, pruning, healthy eating and grafting. Beekeepers are involved, and there's a map showing where to buy local eggs. There's also a project collecting people's memories and knowledge about local growing. The aim is to make all aspects of food production and plant care sustainable long term by developing and spreading skills locally. Food matters to people, it's the glue that binds us together. Next year, Incredible Edible intends to grow enough potatoes for every person in town to have several kilos. It is also looking to take over a large plot of land, the old municipal landfill tip – putting a membrane over the old polluted soil and growing in raised beds – to be run as a community-supported agriculture project.

The local council is completely on board, it has identified all non-strategic land in their area and registered it on a map. Now any local community can identify land on the registry and apply to grow there. Whether the tomatoes and courgettes will still be grown outside the local police station in 20 years time is still to be seen, but the fact that there are now orchards appearing on housing estates and fruit trees planted in public spaces across the town means future generations in Todmorden won't even question whether fruit is for picking, it will just be another part of the town landscape.

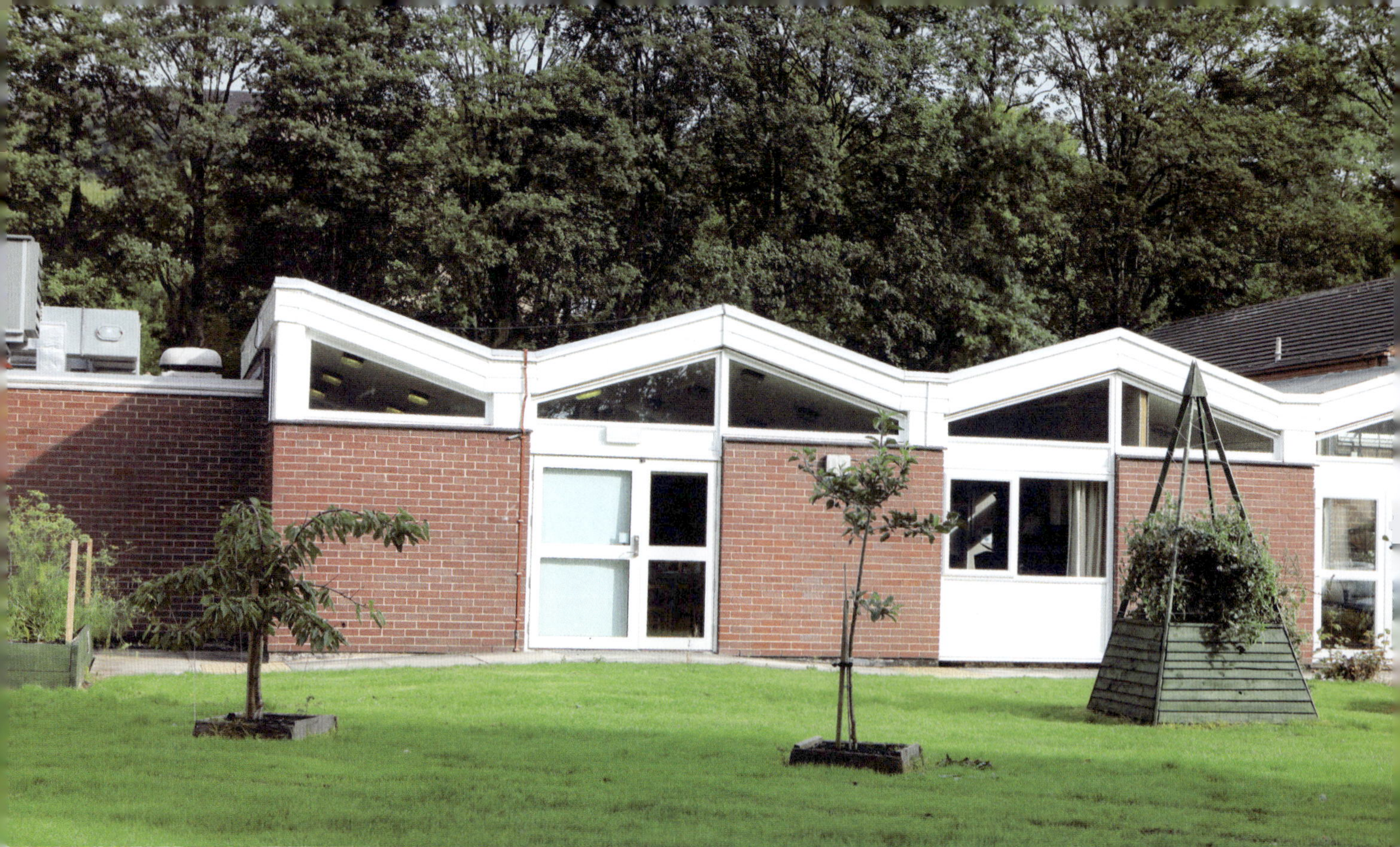

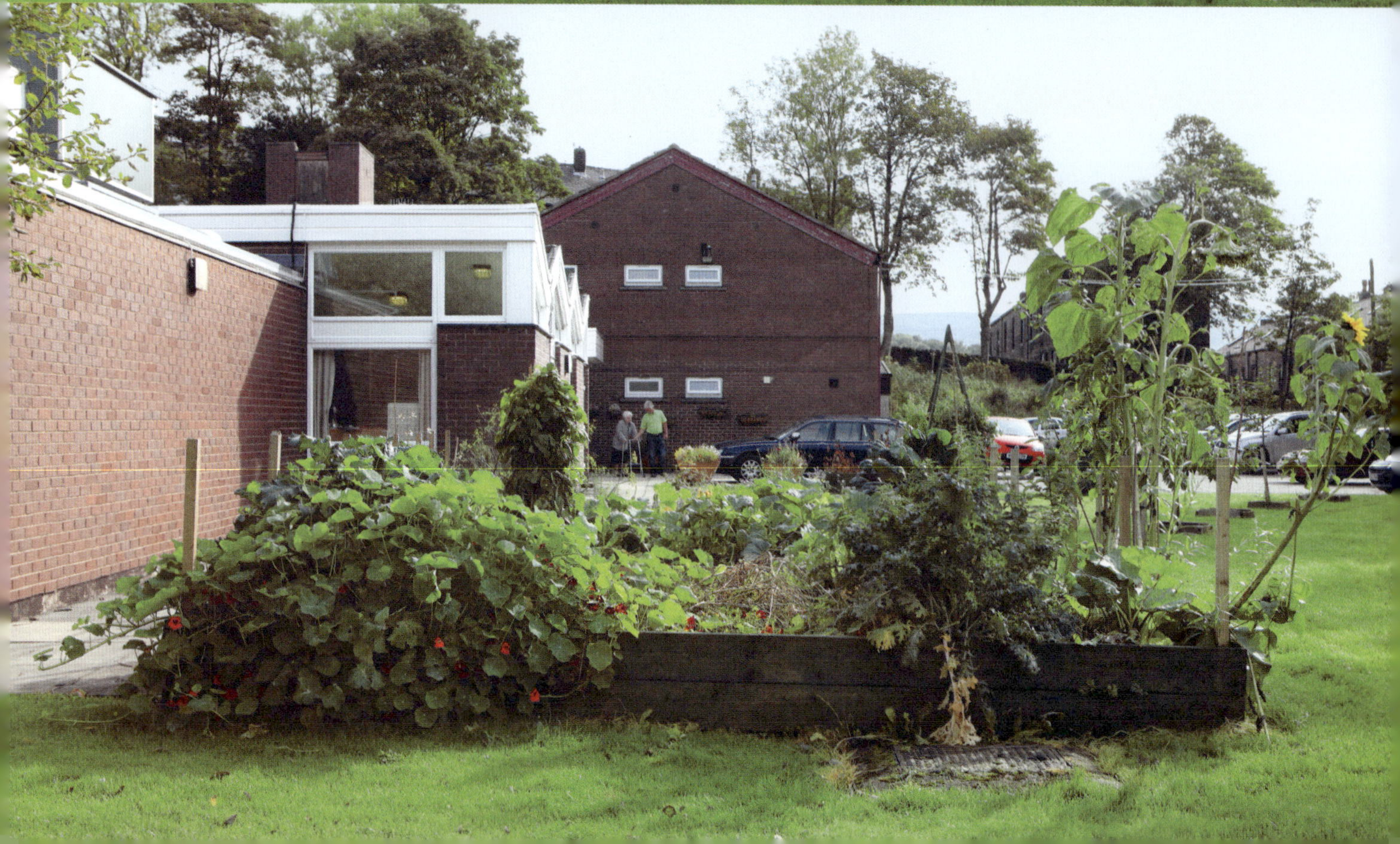

# HOW YOU SET UP A COMMUNITY ORCHARD

**FIRST, FIND A SPACE.** Ask around, there may be hidden spots behind buildings. Trawl around Google Earth. Get on your bike identifying potential spots. Don't get hung up with having a traditional space – you could make a linear orchard, say, along a street, or you might be able to add one to an existing space. My local park has made a fruit patch with picnic benches so that everyone can eat some blueberries. It looks much like any other park bed to the untrained eye. Perhaps you could persuade the local supermarket to plant up its car parks with fruit trees instead of ornamentals.

Once you've found your spot, find out who owns the land. The simplest way is to ask people living or working nearby, someone usually knows. If that doesn't work, then try your local council or parish council. If all else fails, you may have to pay the Land Registry to tell you who owns it.

Decide on the most appropriate way to approach the land owner. For council-owned land, phone first to make sure you'll contact the right person, otherwise your letter will simply end up in the wrong inbox. For a private individual, an old-fashioned letter is most polite. Keep it short, state who you are, exactly what bit of land you want, give a brief outline of what you want to do and why you want to do it, and suggest a meeting.

Have a back-up site in mind, because you may not get your first choice. Keep trying. Someone, somewhere will listen. And when you do get a meeting go well prepared with an expanded plan – be ready to sell your ideas. If you can get letters of support from notable individuals within your community, gather them up. Keep the project small and doable at these early stages, your initial meeting is not the moment to run away with ideas or you may just come across as mad! You will need to agree some sort of access, as you will need formal permission for this, even if it's an open site.

As soon as you've got a spot and a friendly landowner, you need to get your wider community involved. You'll need money, many hands and a lot of love to get an orchard off the ground. Some residents may have reservations about your project that you'll need to address. It's best to start small because if you make a success in the early stages and people see that you are committed, then even the hard-hearted are usually won over.

# THE SITE

**WHEN YOU HAVE** managed to agree on a plot, you must make sure it's the right one for your project before getting stuck in. It's easy to run away with enthusiasm and not look at the wider picture.

First, you must be sure that the site is suitable for food growing – look at how it is used at the moment and, more importantly, how it's been used in the past – you may think it's worth testing the soil to make sure it's not contaminated and is potentially fertile. Make sure that your plans are not going to harm any wildlife or damage the wider aesthetic of the landscape. This orchard is for the community so make sure that any other users of the spaces agree with your plans. If the local lads are going to use your trees as goal posts you might not be in the right spot. Some local residents might not be keen on parking under a fruit tree.

However perfect the location of the site may seem, be realistic. If your chosen area is overrun with problematic weeds, such as brambles, Japanese knotweed or thistles, you need to think about the time and money involved in tackling them. Young plants don't do well if they have to compete with invasive weeds. And you need to be sure that there are no groundworks, such as utility cables or waterpipes, that might prevent you working the soil.

Fruit trees prefer certain conditions, so find out about the soil type and the microclimate. Few fruit trees grow successfully in frost pockets and they don't like sitting with their roots in water. Steer clear of marshy areas, and ditches or streams running through your chosen spot may mean that the area tends to flood. You do, however, need a good source of water nearby, as young fruit trees need a lot of water in their early years. Very sloping or lumpy ground can be a problem, if only because of health and safety issues.

Access is important, there's no point choosing a spot that's away from public transport or car or even bike parking. And watch out for signs of vandalism. It's a bonus if there's a building on site for some sort of tool storage.

**Legalities and insurance** You will, at some point, need legal advice and insurance. As a group, you may need a constitution to avoid group members or trustees becoming personally liable if anything goes wrong. You'll definitely need some sort of legally binding agreement for leasing the land, or a legal licence to manage it. Remember to keep in touch with the landowner about your plans before you even start to put a spade in the ground. Everyone involved should have an idea of where you are heading, as this can prevent a lot of future problems.

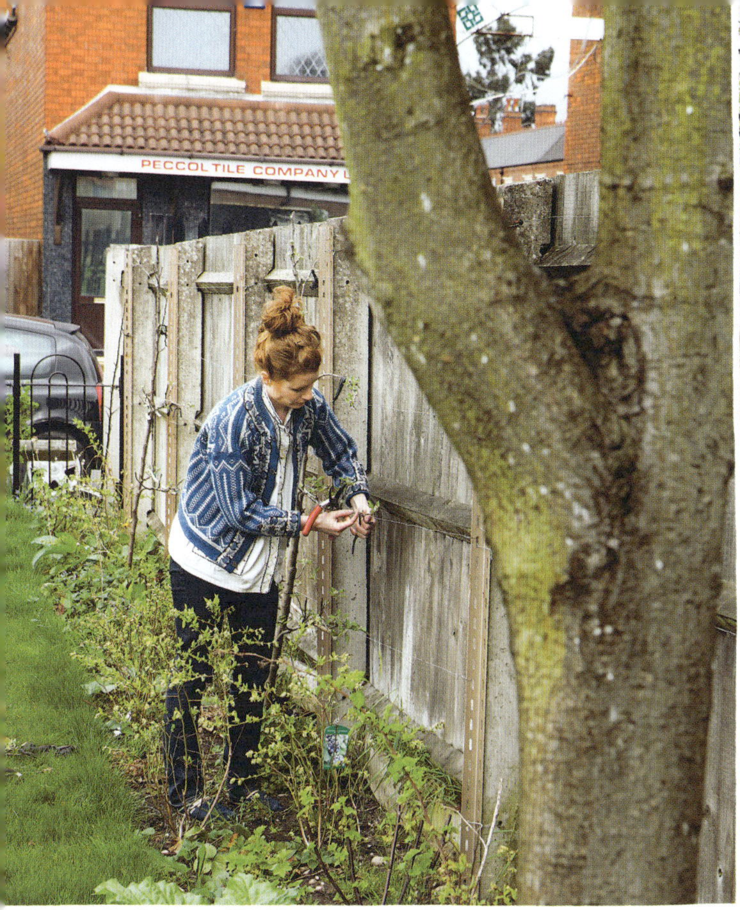
PECCOLTILE COMPANY
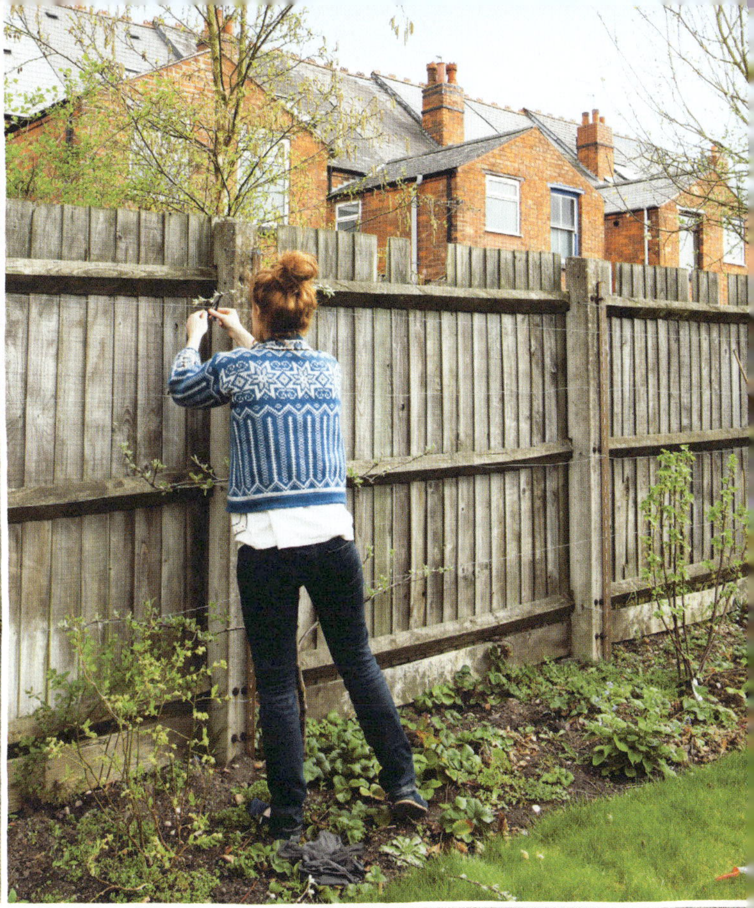
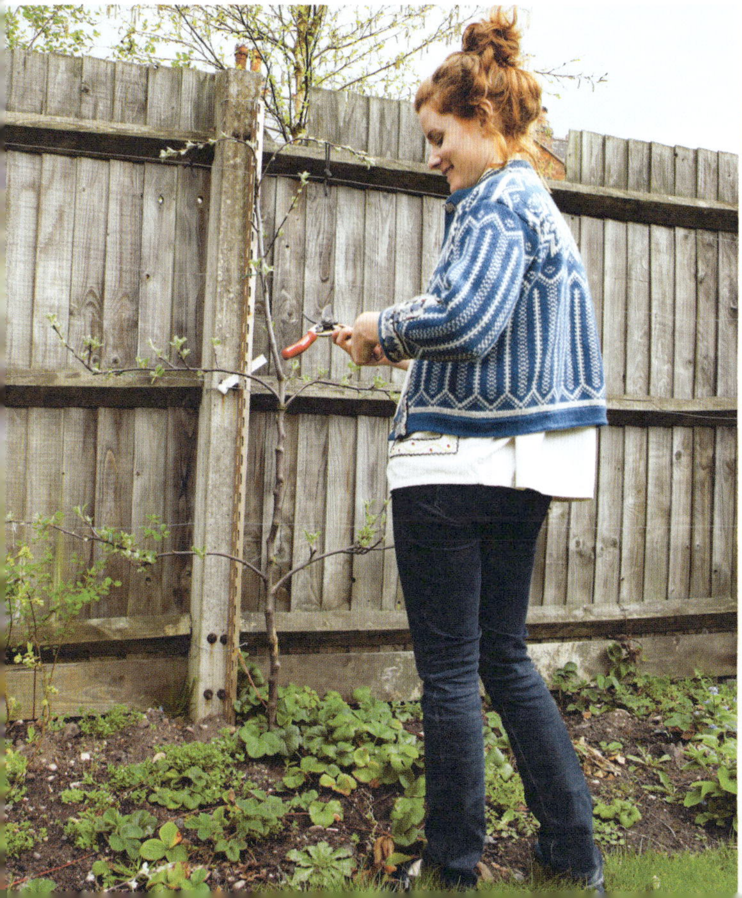
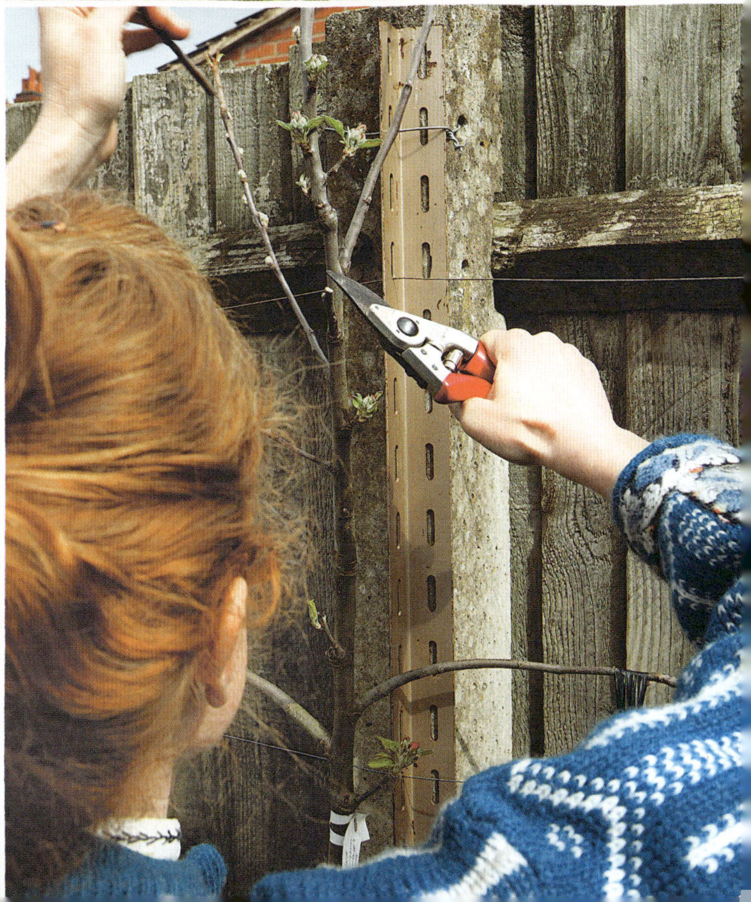

# CREATING A DESIGN

**THERE ARE PLENTY** of books in the resource section (*see page 186*), which will help with layout and design of an orchard, but right at the start you must be very realistic about how much time people can devote to a project; fruit trees need ongoing maintenance and money. The first stage is to gather ideas and consult with your community, and you may decide to ask for expert help at the start. The Royal Horticultural Society and other gardening bodies, such as Garden Organic, may be able to offer advice. A good nursery will be a great help when you are choosing your fruit.

The younger (and smaller) a plant the cheaper it is, but it may be better to have a few more expensive mature plants to make an impact. At my local community centre we used semi-mature trained fruit trees, with immature in between, partly to make an impact and partly as a teaching tool to show people what an espalier looks like. But, most importantly, it gives the garden an air of being established.

Remember to include seating or benches in your design. This is a place for people to come, relax and be part of.

Not all fruit flowers at the same time so, when you choose fruit varieties, consider if there's a partner for pollinating. You need to think about the hardiness of the trees, and how tough they are. Some varieties are more resistant to pests and diseases than others. You may want to use some local or historical varieties, if they are available.

Think about the harvesting time and the keeping qualities of the fruit – you don't want your harvest to be over in a flash and you probably want some varieties that can store well. But, above all, think about taste. There are now hundreds of apple-tasting days around in autumn, so go to your local one and sample all the varieties. There's not much point in growing some beautiful ornamental and historical varieties if they just don't taste great.

When you've decided what to grow, you need to think how you want the orchard to look and how much maintenance it will take. Formally trained fruit, such as espaliers or fans, require a lot more work than untrained trees. But you may have the perfect spot to train a cherry or peach, or some of your group may already have these skills, or be particularly keen to learn. Be sure to match expectations and develop skills so that all the knowledge is not held with just a few people.

Make a big day of the actual planting. The more people you can get interested the more successful your project will be, not just in terms of hands-on support but positive publicity. The more people that get involved in the project, the more responsibility they will feel for it and the less likely you are to suffer from future vandalism. If you don't involve as many people as possible, don't be surprised when your trees are snapped in half. Plus a big planting event means you get to thank everyone, and this is hugely important as everyone likes to feel appreciated.

# FUTURE MAINTENANCE

**YOU'LL NEED SOME** sort of long-term maintenance plan. It is very important that you write things like this down at the start and keep records. People move away, plans change, you need to be able to pass all the relevant information on to future gardeners. Consider how you are going to tackle things like weed control, watering, feeding, pruning, propagating and replacing plants due to losses, and who is going to be responsible for these different areas. At my local community garden I've started a tree care scheme where an individual agrees to look after a tree for a year in return for training in pruning and some of the harvest. The volunteer agrees to train a new person the following year and, before you know it, you've got lots of people who know how to care for the plants.

## ENJOYING THE FRUITS OF YOUR LABOUR

ORGANISE HARVESTING PARTIES, TEACH PEOPLE HOW TO PRESERVE, BAKE YOUR GOODS AND SELL THEM FOR FUNDRAISING, SING, DANCE, MAKE BOOZE, GIVE GUIDED WALKS, IDENTIFY VARIETIES, DRESS TREES, WRITE POEMS, KEEP BEES, TELL STORIES AND INVITE THE LOCAL PRESS. THE SUCCESS OF YOUR PROJECT IS ABOUT MAKING PEOPLE EXCITED, PROUD AND ACTIVELY INVOLVED IN THEIR OWN LANDSCAPE.

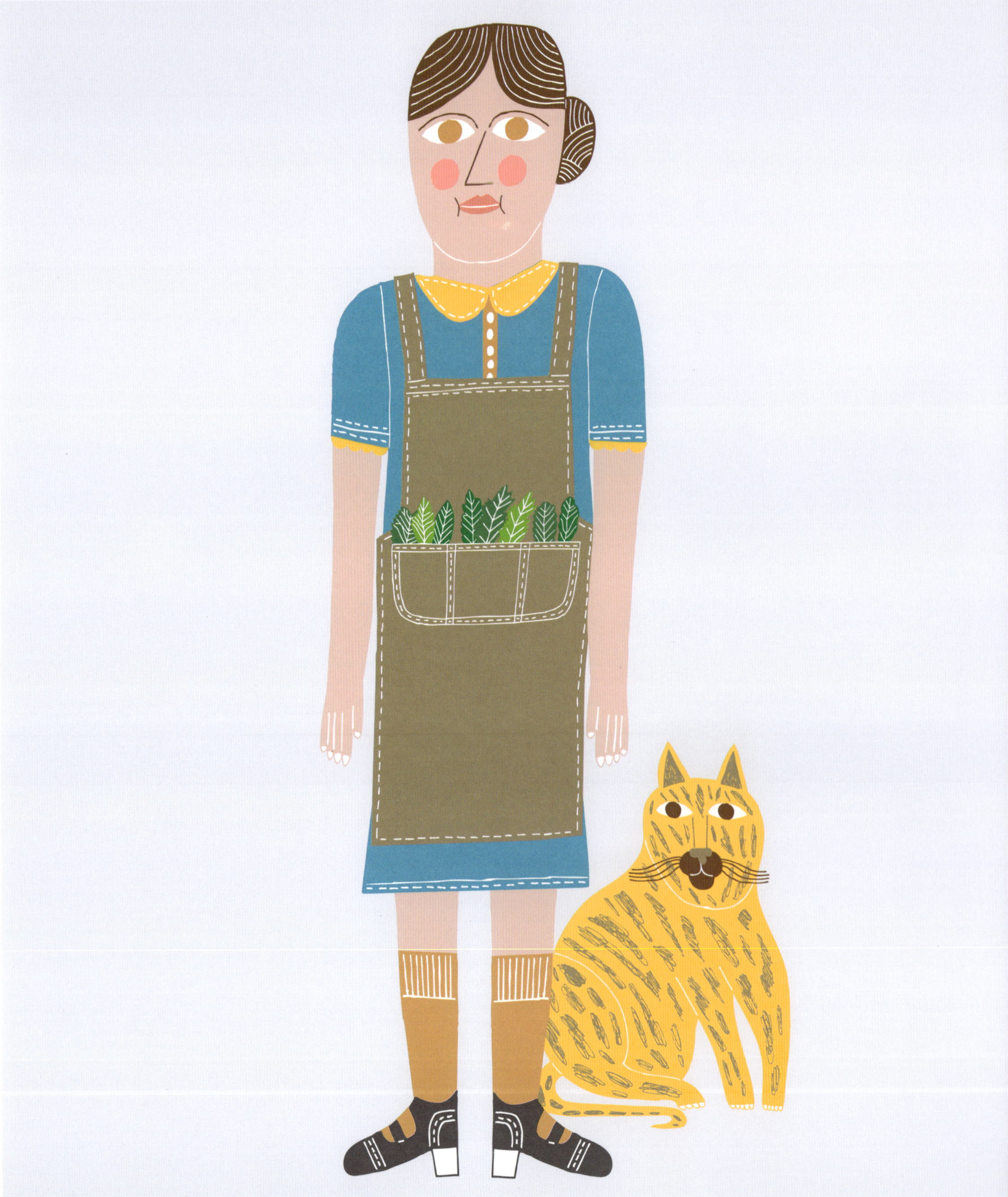

# THE PLANT DIRECTORY

You've arrived at the fun bit of the book. From here on in, it's just plants, plants and more plants. Each entry (*from page 86*) has a botanical description, an idea of ways to eat it and a story here and there to keep you keen. The plants are alphabetically ordered by their Latin name. This is because if you used the common name everyone would be confused, one person calls a plant one thing, another something completely different, the Latin never changes. This is particularly important if you are cross-referencing with other books. The 'at-a-glance' table (*page 64*) is a quick reference so you can see seasonally what to go and hunt for.

Before you wade in, there are one or two things you need to know. The bitter flavours of many wild greens are unfamiliar to our palates that have grown up on bland lettuce and spinach. I love this flavour now, but have learnt to temper its bitter flavour for newcomers to my table.

Make sure you pick only the youngest, most tender leaves. The bitterness is most pronounced in old leaves, it's often there to act as a slug or insect deterrent. Fat (butter or bacon) will coat the greens and calm the bitterness; caramelised onions, chopped chives or spring onions enhance it, and a squeeze of lemon juice or a little sumac will give it a pleasing tang. Tahini makes an excellent sauce for many greens; diluted with a little water and lemon, it coats bitter flavours wonderfully. But, if you just add salt and pepper and serve with good hearty bread, you can persuade many sceptics to enjoy most wild greens.

I find you can lose a lot of bitterness by making a salsa verde to use on meat, fish, cheese or rice dishes. It's great with a really good hamburger or on goat's cheese. You roughly need to mix three-parts bland greens with one-part bitter. Paula Wolfert, in *Mediterranean Grains and Greens*, calls this mixture 'apron greens', the 'wild and garden greens that Mediterranean women gather, tucked in the front pocket of their aprons. Often a woman's apron pocket will be divided into several compartments', for sweet greens and bitter ones.

For bland greens, use fat hen, salad burnet, borage, mallow, nettles or lemon balm. For bitter herbs, try dandelions, good King Henry, sorrel or sowthistle. Blanch, rinse and wring out any excessive moisture from greens and then chop them finely. Mix finely chopped shallots or chives, add vinegar (the best you can get, Champagne white vinegar is really worth paying out for), and perhaps a few capers, a little salt and a touch of olive oil to bind it together. Alternatively you can add anchovies, garlic, or for a German take on things, chopped-up boiled eggs. This will last for several days in the fridge and can be frozen.

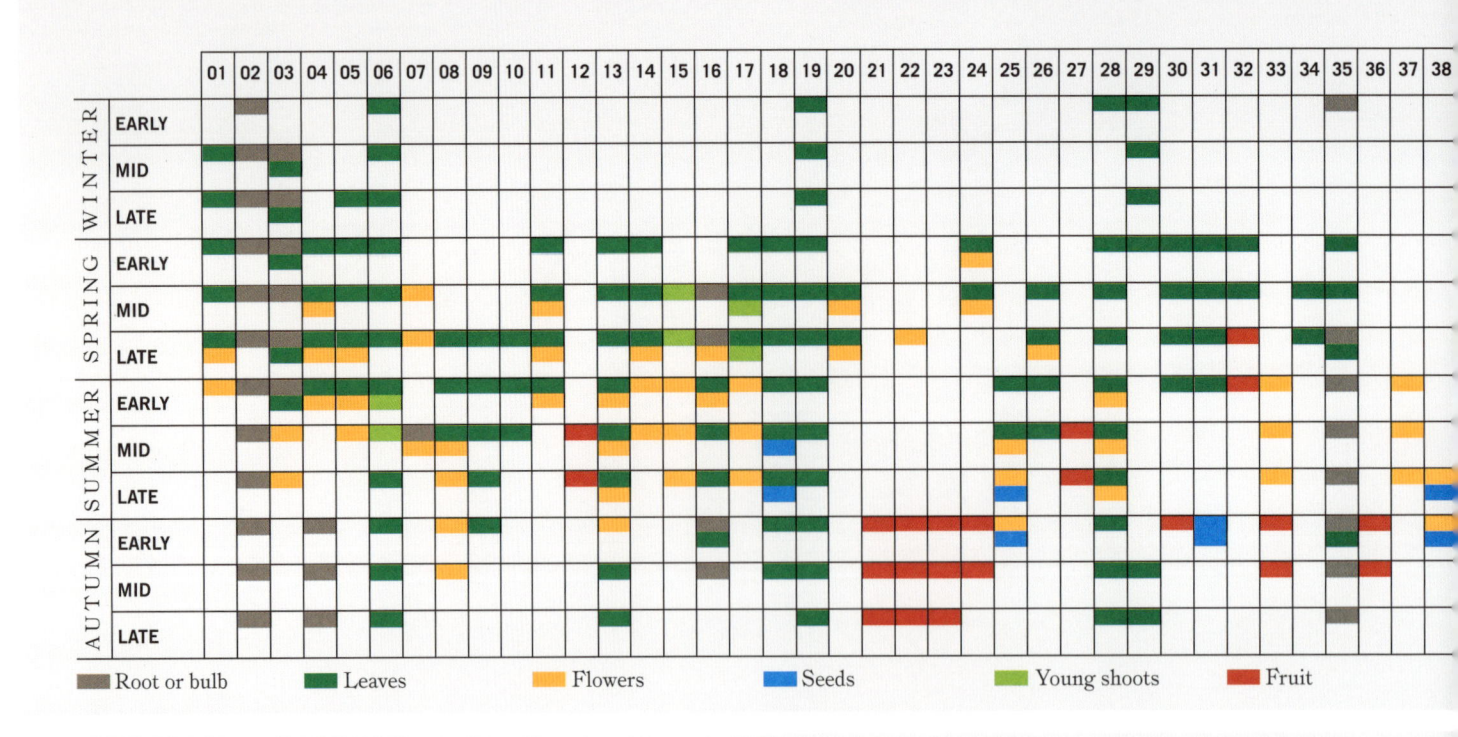

## WHAT TO PICK WHEN

**01** *Aegopodium podagraria*
**Ground elder** Leaves and flowers
**02** *Armoracia rusticana*
**Horseradish** Roots
**03** *Allium ampeloprasum var. babingtonii*
**Wild leek, Babington's leek** Leaves and flowers
**04** *Allium triquetrum*
**Three-cornered garlic** Bulb, leaves and flowers
**05** *Allium ursinum*
**Wild garlic or Ransoms** Leaves and flowers
**06** *Alliaria petiolata*
**Garlic mustard, Jack-by-the-hedge** Leaves and seeds
**07** *Amelanchier lamarckii*
**Juneberry, Service berry** Berries
**08** *Atriplex hastata*
**Hastate orache** Leaves and unopened flower buds
**09** *Atriplex hortensis*
**Garden orache** Leaves
**10** *Atriplex patula*
**Common orache** Leaves
**11** *Bellis perennis*
**Daisy** Young leaves and young flower buds
**12** *Berberis darwinii*
**Darwin's barberry** Berries
**13** *Borago officinalis*
**Borage** Leaves and flowers
**14** *Campanulas*
**Bellflower** Leaves and flowers
**15** *Campanula trachelium*
**Nettle-leaved bellflower** Young shoots and flowers
**16** *Campanula rapunculus*
**Rampion** Leaves, flowers and roots
**17** *Campanula portenschlagiana*
**Dalmatian bellflower** Leaves, flowers and young shoots
**18** *Capsella bursa-pastoris*
**Shepherd's purse** Leaves and seeds
**19** *Cardamine species*
**Bittercress** Leaves
**20** *Cardamine pratensis*
**Lady's smock** Leaves and flowers
**21** *Chaenomeles species*
**Flowering quince, Japanese quince** Fruit
**22** *Cydonia oblonga*
**True quince** Fruit
**23** *Castanea sativa*
**Sweet chestnut** Fruit
**24** *Crataegus species*
**Haws, hawthorns** Leaves, unopened young flower buds and fruit (not seeds)
**25** *Chenopodium album*
**Fat Hen, lamb's quarters** Leaves, flower heads and seeds
**26** *Chenopodium bonus-henricus*
**Good King Henry** Leaves and young flower shoots
**27** *Corylus avellana, Corylus maxima*
**Hazelnut, cobnut, Filbert** Nuts
**28** *Diplotaxis tenuifolia*
**Wild rocket, perennial wallrocket** Leaves and flowers
**29** *Epilobium montanum*
**Broad-leaved willowherb** Leaves
**30** *Ficus carica*
**Common fig** Fruit
**31** *Foeniculum vulgare*
**Herb fennel** Leaves/foliage and seeds
**32** *Fragaria vesca*
**Alpine strawberry** Fruit and leaves
**33** *Fuchsia species*
**Fuchsia** Flowers and fruit
**34** *Galium aparine*
**Goosegrass, sticky willie, cleavers, scratch tongue** Stems and leaves
**35** *Geum urbanum*
**Herb Bennet, avens, clove-root** Roots and leaves
**36** *Ginkgo biloba*
**Maidenhair tree** Nuts
**37** *Hemerocallis species*
**Daylil** Flower buds – unopen, open or dried
**38** *Impatiens glandulifera*
**Himalayan balsam** Flowers and seeds
**39** *Juglans regia*
**Walnut** Nuts

64 | The Thrifty Forager

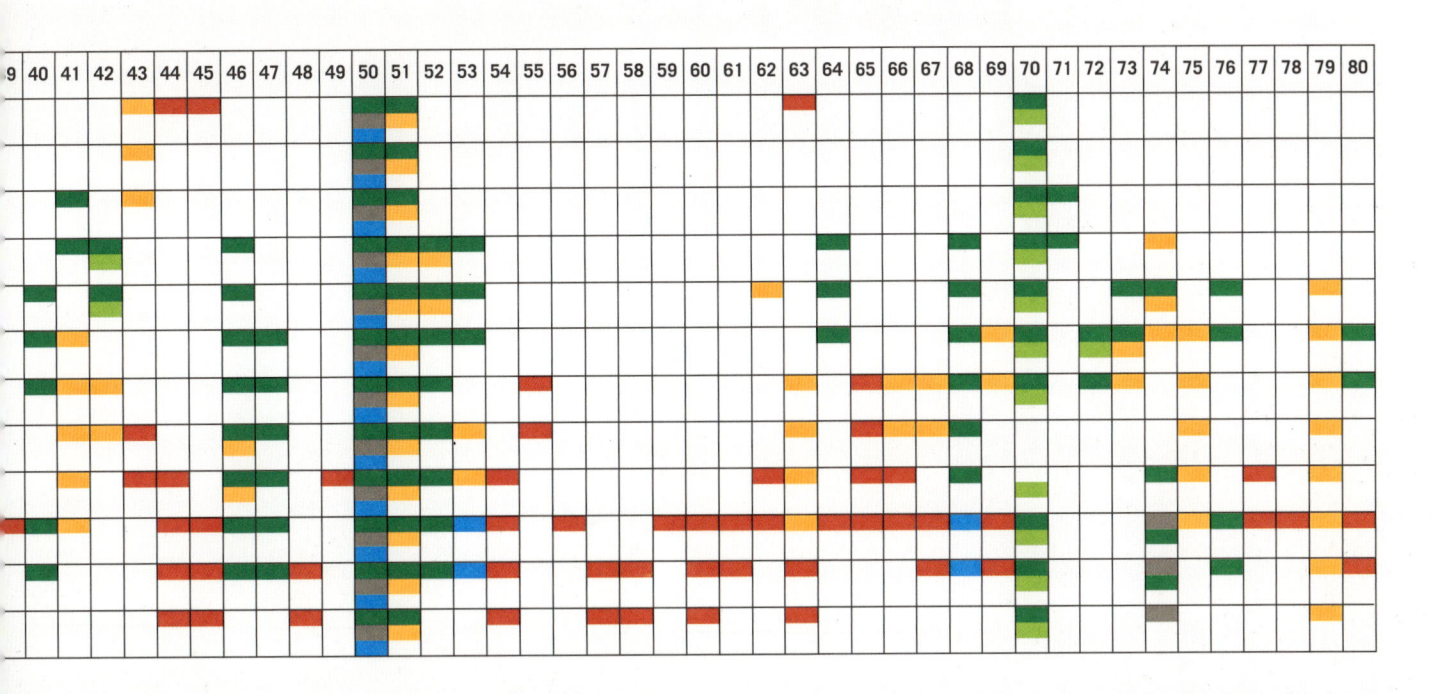

**40** *Lamium species*
**Archangel, deadnettle**
Young leaves
**41** *Leontodon hispidus*
**Rough hawkbit**
Young leaves and flowers
**42** *Leucanthemum vulgare*
**Marguerite, ox-eye daisy**
Young leaves, young shoots and flowers
**43** *Mahonia aquifolium*
**Oregon hollygrape, Holly barberry**
Berries and flowers
**44** *Malus species*
**Apple** Fruit
**45** *Malus sylvestris*
**Crab apple** Fruit
**46** *Melissa officinalis*
**Lemon balm** Leaves
**47** *Mentha aquatica*
**Water mint** Leaves
**48** *Mespilus germanica*
**Medlar** Fruit
**49** *Morus nigra*
**Black mulberry** Fruit
**50** *Myrrhis odorata*
**Sweet cicely**
Leaves, roots and seeds

**51** *Origanum vulgare*
**Oregano, pot marjoram**
Leaves and young flowers
**52** *Oxalis acetosella*
**Wood sorrel** Young leaves
**53** *Papaver rhoeas*
**Field or common poppy**
Leaves, petals and seeds
**54** *Prunus species*
**Cherries, plums, bullaces, damson and sloes** Fruit
**55** *Prunus avium*
**Wild cherry** Fruit
**56** *Prunus cerasifera*
**Plums** Fruit
**57** *Prunus spinosa*
**Sloe or blackthorn** Fruit
**58** *Prunus domestica subsp. insititia*
**Bullace** Fruit
**59** *Prunus domestica subsp. insititia*
**Damson** Fruit
**60** *Pyrus communis*
**Common pear** Fruit
**61** *Rhus typhina*
**Stag's horn sumach, velvet sumach** Berries

**62** *Ribes odoratum*
**Buffalo currant**
Fruit and flowers
**63** *Rosa species*
**Rose** Petals and hips
**64** *Rubus fruticosus*
**Blackberry, bramble**
Young leaves and berries
**65** *Rubus idaeus*
**Wild raspberry**
Young leaves and fruit
**66** *Rubus tricolor*
**Chinese bramble** Fruit
**67** *Sambucus nigra*
**Elberberry** Flowers and berries
**68** *Sisymbrium officinale*
**Hedge mustard**
Leaves and seeds
**69** *Sorbus aucuparia*
**Rowan** Berries
**70** *Sonchus species*
**Sowthistles** Leaves and stems
**71** *Stellaria media*
**Chickweed** Young leaves
**72** *Silene vulgaris*
**Bladder campion**
Young leaves and shoots

**73** *Tilia cordata, Tilia platyphyllos*
**Small-leaf lime**
**Large-leaf lime/linden**
Young leaves and flowers
**74** *Taraxacum officinale*
**Common dandelion**
Young leaves, unopened flower buds, young flowers, roots and crown of new leaves
**75** *Trifolium pratense*
**Red clover**
Young leaves and flowers
**76** *Urtica dioica*
**Stinging nettle** Young leaves
**77** *Vaccinium myrtillus*
**Bilberry, whinberry, whortleberry, huckleberry**
Berries
**78** *Vaccinium vitis-idaea*
**Cowberry, red whortleberry**
Berries
**79** *Viola species*
**Violets** Flowers
**80** *Vitis coignetiae*
**Crimson glory vine**
Leaves

What to pick when | 65

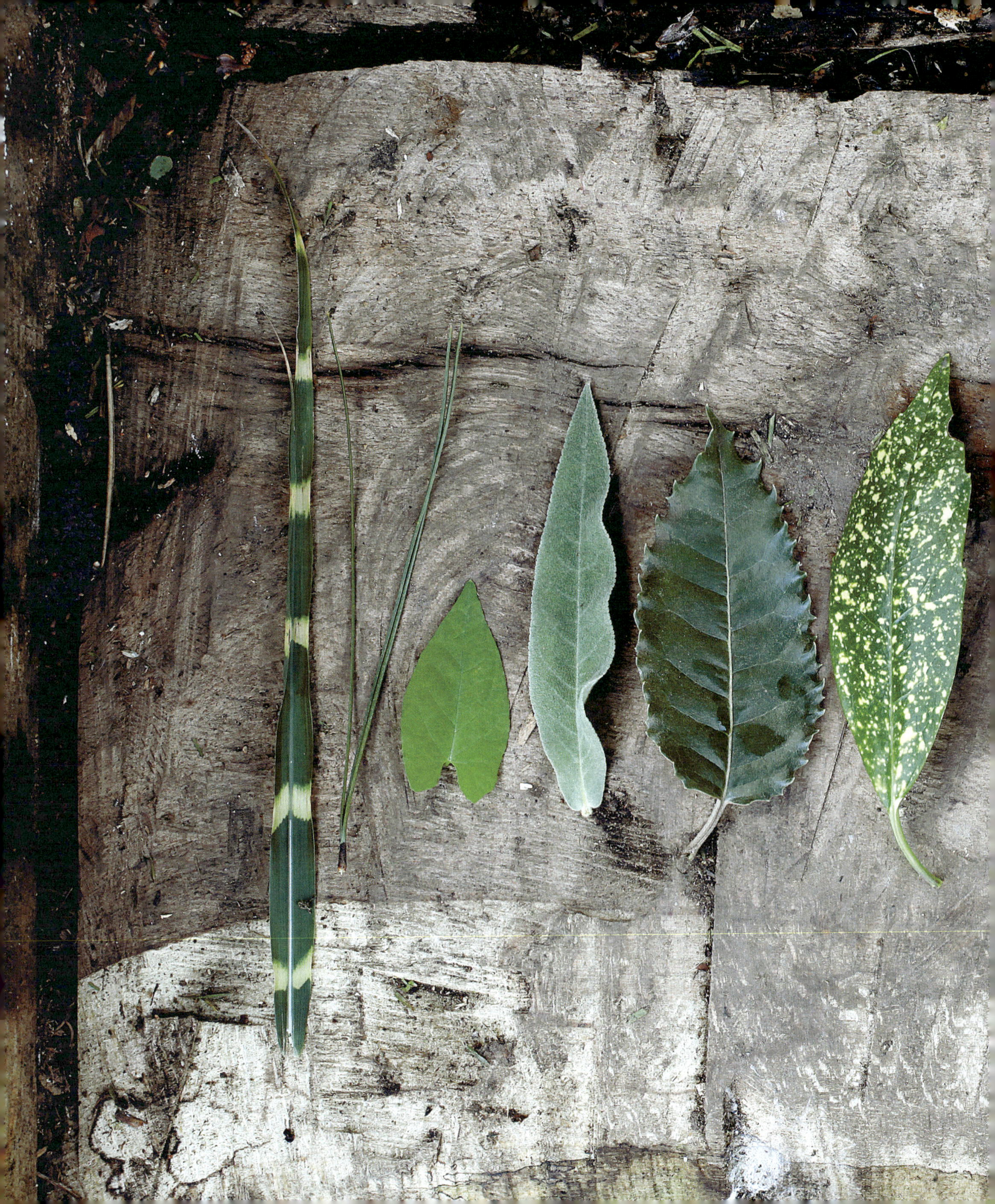

leaf shapes

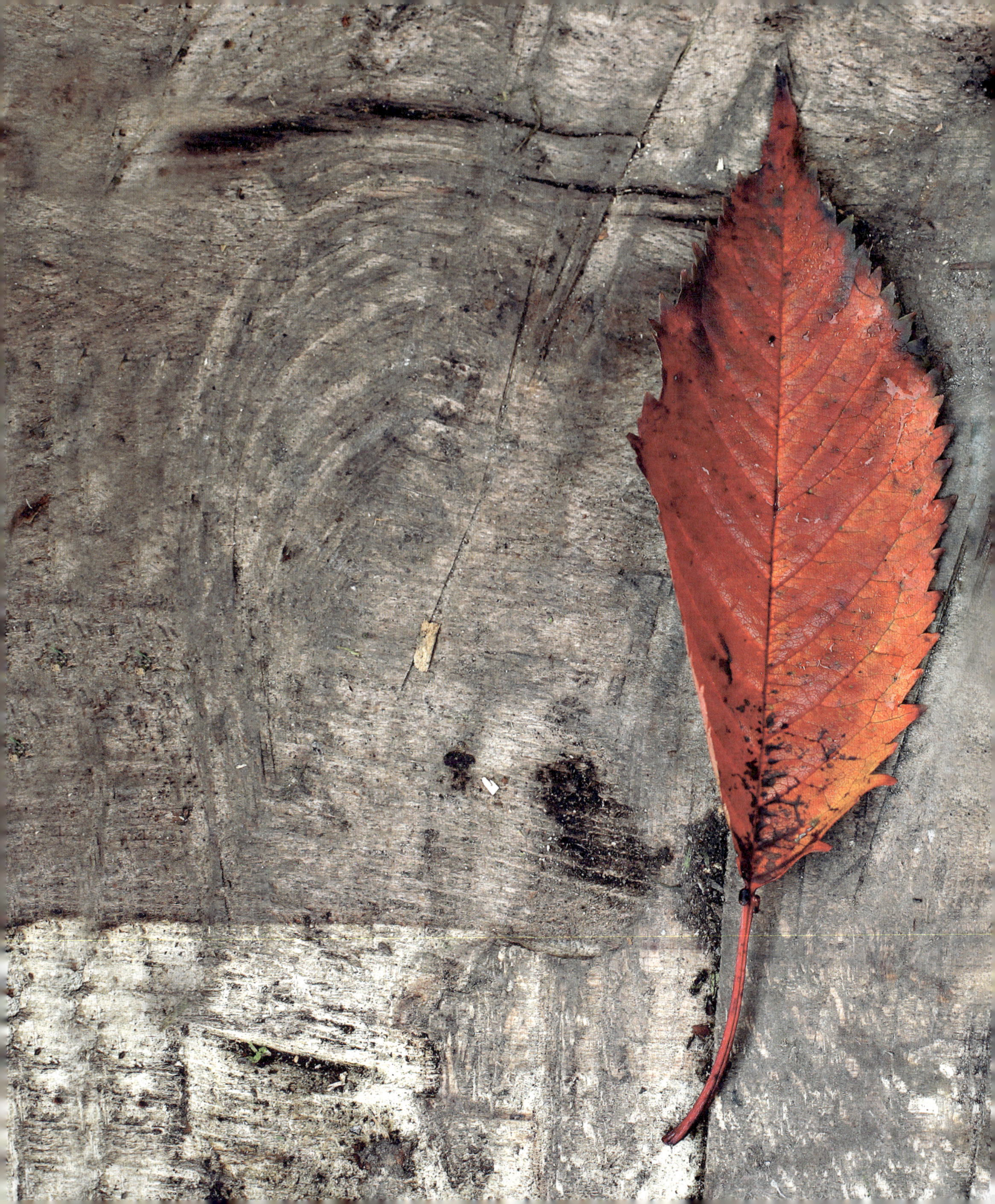

leaf margins

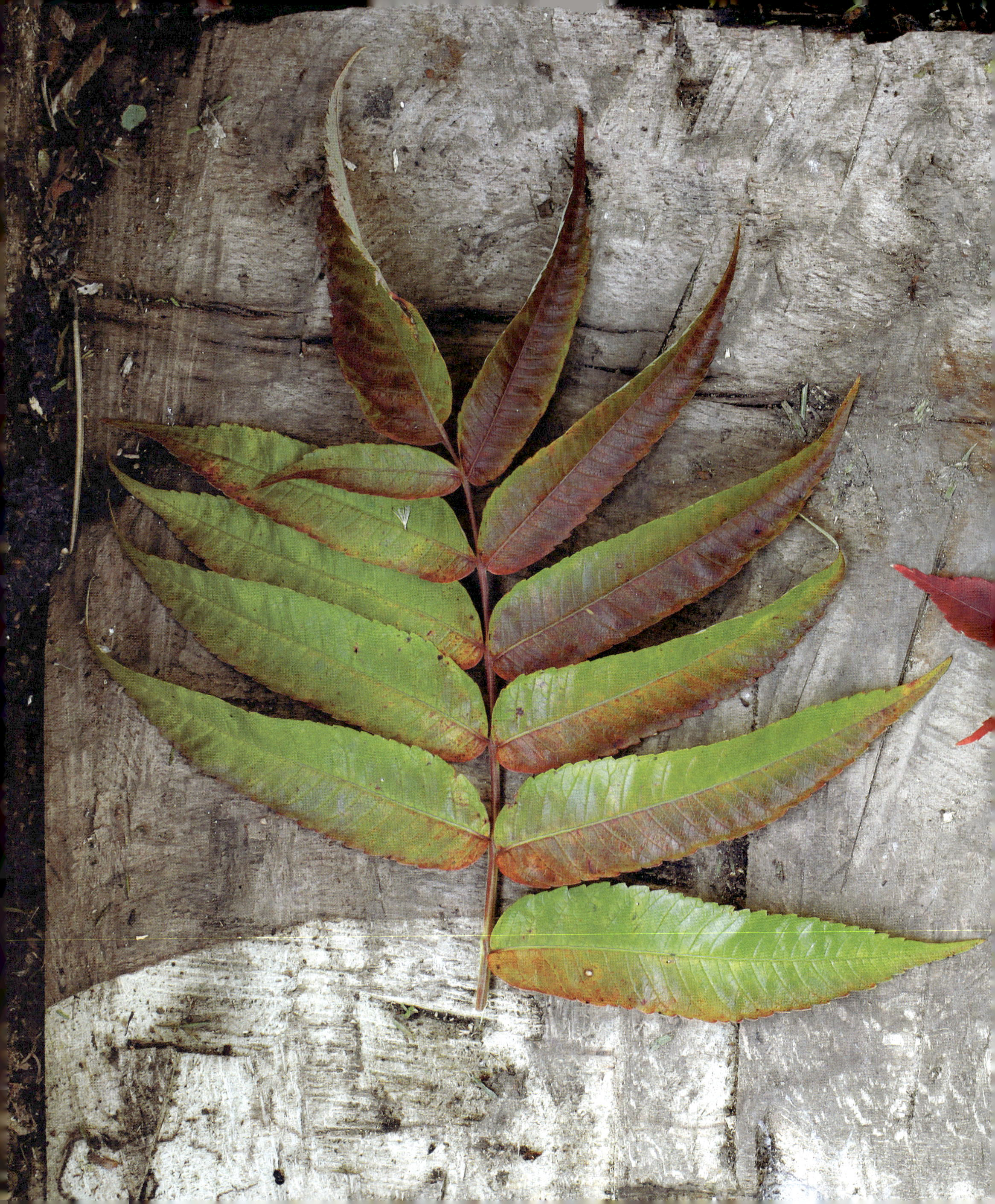

leaf arrangements

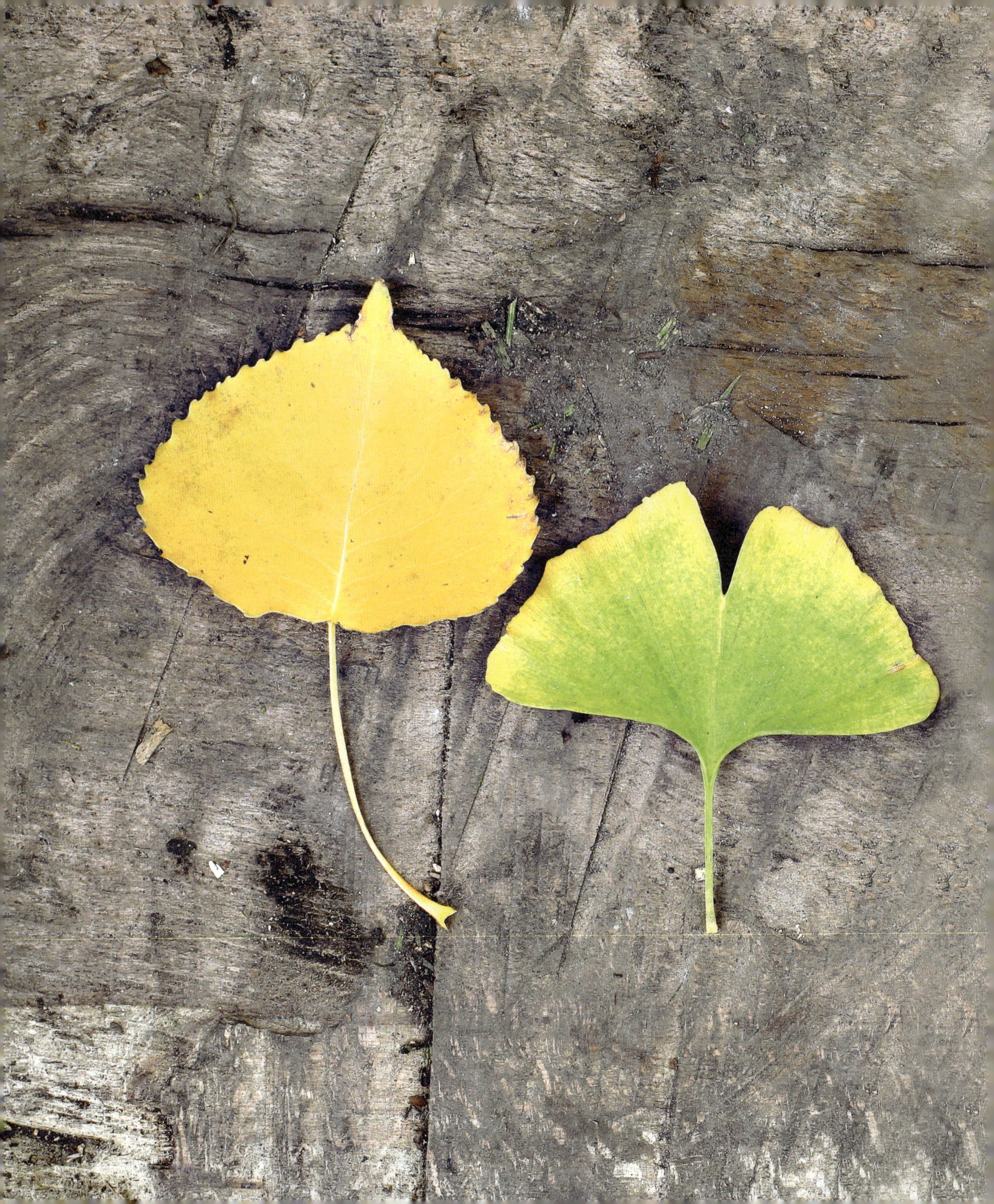

leaf tips

leaf pairings

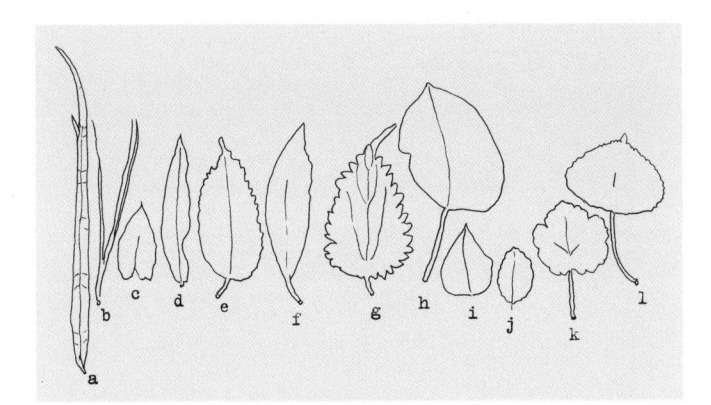

**LEAF SHAPES**  a. Strap-shaped  b. Linear/needle
c. Ovate  d. Lance  e. Ovate (broadest part near stalk)
f. Elliptic (widest in the middle, pointed both ends)
g. Diamond shaped  h. Cordate or heart shaped
i. Diamond/cuneate shaped  j. Ovate  k. Lobed  l. Ovate

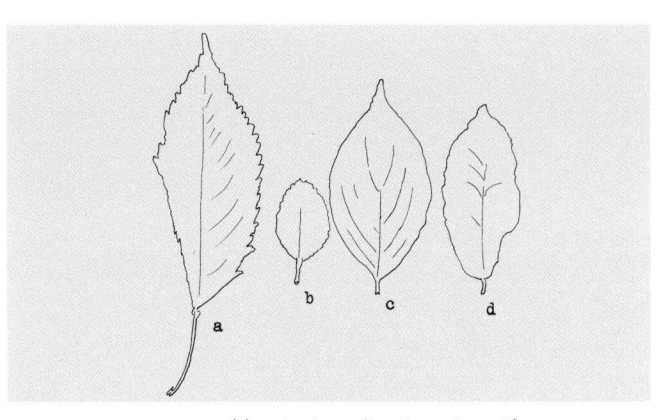

**LEAF MARGINS**  a. Toothed  b. Scalloped  c. Entire
d. Wavy

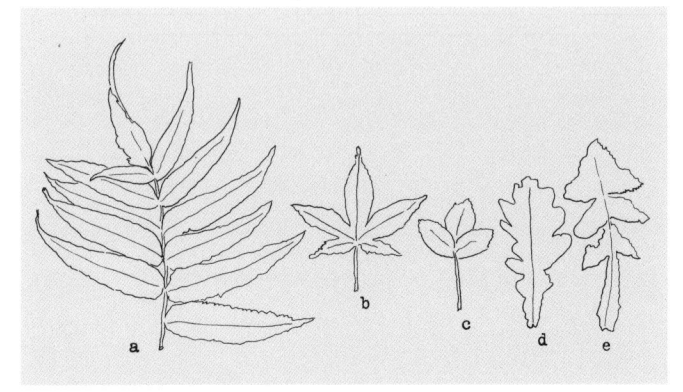

**LEAF ARRANGEMENTS**  a. Pinnate (2 rows of leaflets, one on either side)  b. Palmately lobed (a whole leaf with 4 or more lobes arising from a single point)  c. 3-palmate  d. Pinnatifid (deeply cut lobes)  e. Pinnatisect (deep cut lobes that are opposite each other)

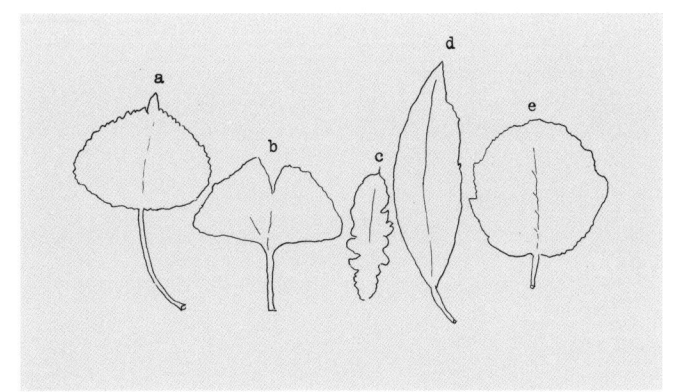

**LEAF TIPS**  a. Pointed  b. Notched  c. Blunt  d. Sharply pointed  e. Blunt

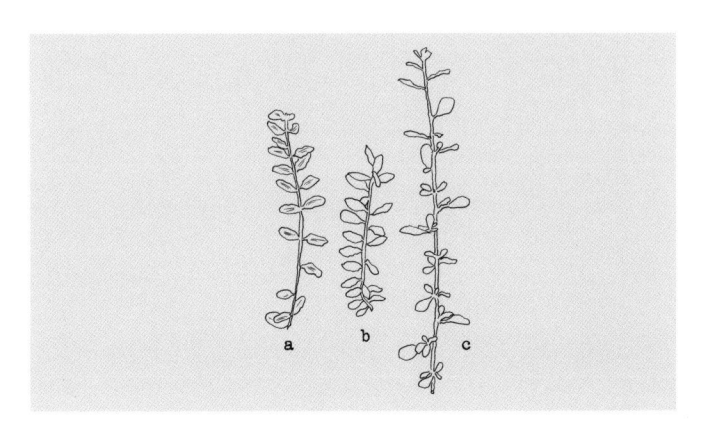

**LEAF PAIRINGS**  a. Opposite  b. Alternate
c. Alternate and whorled (meaning spiralling around the stem)

Leaf Descriptions | 75

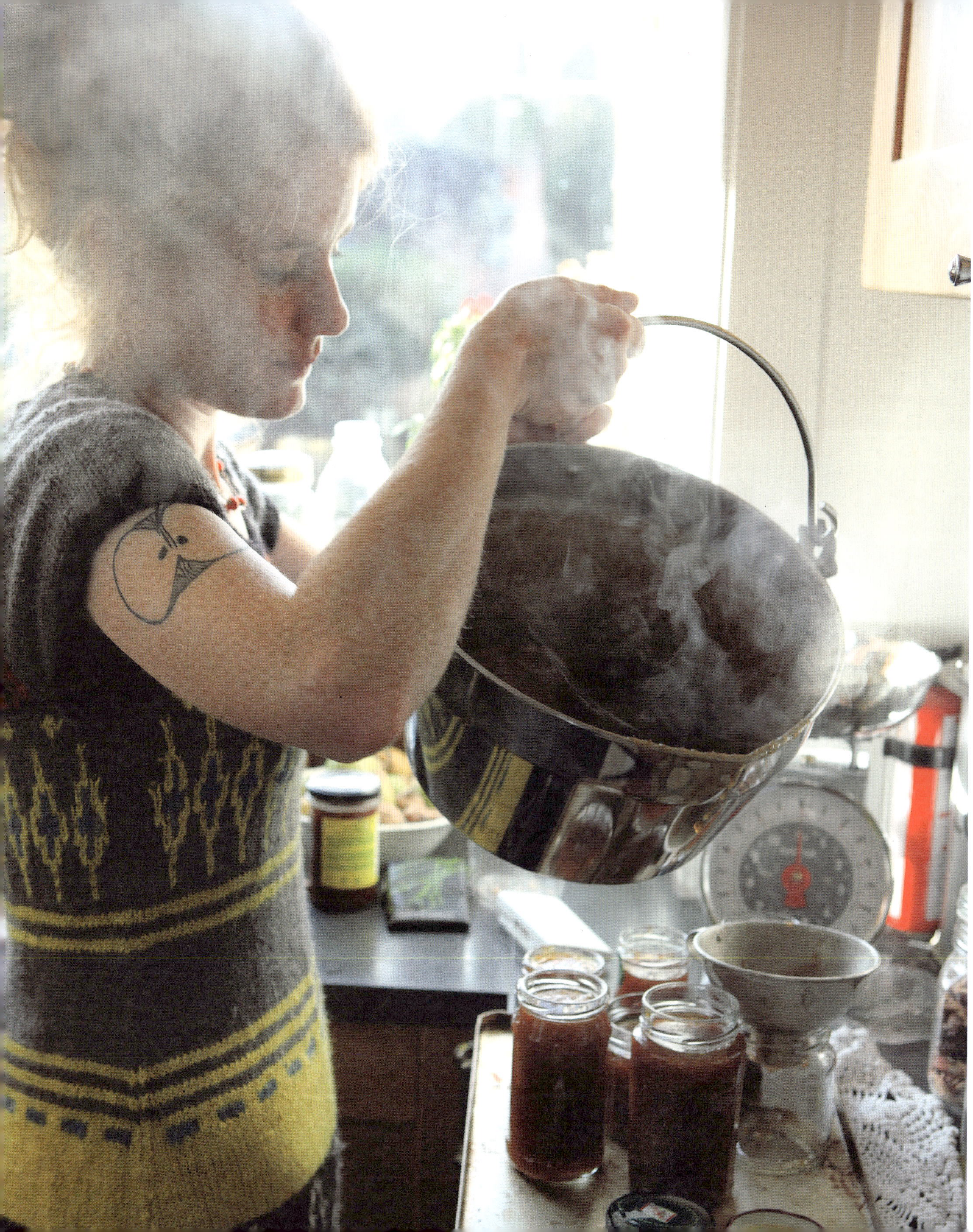

# HOW TO PRESERVE FRUITS

**MANY FORAGED** berries and fruit will not store well, so you either have to freeze them or process them into some sort of preserve. Jams, jellies, cheeses and fruit leathers are some of the best ways to preserve fruit. They make wonderful presents and there is nothing like seeing rows of the jewel-coloured pots, knowing the contents were mostly free!

## JAMS

Jam preserves fruit through the combination of boiling the fruit to sterilise it and then adding enough sugar to inhibit the growth of bacteria. The sugar content needs to be 60 per cent of the weight of the fruit – that's a lot of sugar – you can use less sugar but low-sugar jam won't store very long and will need to be kept in the fridge.

> You'll need a heavy-based pan. It's worth investing in a preserving pan if you're going to make a lot of jam.
> Sieve, preferably nylon, or a mouli food mill
> Wooden spoon
> A stack of clean saucers stored in the fridge while you make the jam
> A plastic jam funnel
> Clean, sterilised jars

**Basic jam method** Wash the fruit and remove any stalks.

The fruit needs to be soft before the sugar is added. I usually add just enough water to cover the fruit and then simmer very slowly until the fruit is soft.

Don't overboil the fruit at this stage or you lose the flavour.

Take the pan off the heat and remove any stones (say, plums) with a slotted spoon, sieve out the pips if they're not your thing (I can't stand blackberry or elderberry pips in anything), and remove any spices you may have added. Return the pulp back to the pan and add the granulated sugar. The general rule is for every 600ml (1 pint) of fruit (before cooking) you need to add 450g (1lb) of sugar. I work by this method: for every pint of pulp, I add a pound of sugar. My jam pan has pint measures up the side which makes it a whole lot easier.

At this point, you need to bring the jam to a rapid boil. The fruit is not going to cook any further so, if it's hard at this point, it's going to stay hard. The rapid boil is merely to get the jam to set.

Overboiling the jam makes it dark, spoils the flavour and causes what's known as sticky jam (i.e. you're on your way to making fruit toffee). Underboiled jam will be runny and will not keep, it may also ferment – you can tell if this happens, as it will change colour and smell gassy.

To determine the setting point, get your clean saucers ready.

Fruit for jam is best when slightly underripe. If it's overripe, you may have to add extra pectin – the wild fruit solution is to add some crab apples (apples are a second-best choice). Plums, currants, damsons, tart apples and gooseberries are all high in pectin, so they should set well on their own. Cherries, rhubarb, strawberries and blueberries are all low in pectin. You can buy commercial liquid pectin, made from apples and crab apples, in most supermarkets. If I need to add pectin and don't have crab apples or underripe apples handy, I use this rather than jam sugar which tends to make the jam set too hard. The pips, cores and skins of fruit tend to be high in pectin, so if you cook the fruit whole and then strain it through a sieve, you get a better set.

I don't like runny jams, I think it should stay in place on the toast, but a little skating across the butter is nice. How I determine this is to drop a little of the jam on a clean saucer and let it cool. If it's set, it will wrinkle when you push your finger into it. When you're testing the jam for setting point, turn the heat down. If you leave it on a rapid boil and wait for your test dollop to cool, then you may overboil your jam.

If you have scum on the jam, now is the time to remove it with a spoon or add a tiny fingernail's worth of butter to dissolve it. If you keep constantly skimming off the scum as it cooks, you waste a lot of jam.

Ladle the jam into clean, sterilised jars – a funnel makes this much easier. The best way to sterilise jars is to wash them and dry them off in an oven at 60°C/really low oven for 10 minutes or so (they will be very hot when you remove them). Sterilise their lids in a pan of boiling water for about 5 minutes.

You can fill the jam right up to the top of the jar, as it will shrink as it cools. When cool, there should be 1cm or so between the jam and the top of the jar. A wax disc (you can buy them ready cut) helps stop mould growing on the jam.

Put lids on the jars, label (date and type) and store somewhere cool, dark and ventilated. And enjoy!

**Juices** Strain softly cooked fruit (don't squeeze) and then add the desired amount of granulated sugar to make a cordial concentrate. If you want a slightly tart cordial, use less sugar. However this won't store for more than two weeks in the fridge so I find it best to store this in small water bottles, which freeze well so you can have an ongoing supply. I often make blackberry cordial this way.

**Basic juice method** Wash the fruit, place in a large pan and just cover it with cold water. Simmer gently until the fruit is soft then sieve the fruit and strain it as for jelly, through a jelly bag, muslin or a clean pillow case. Then add granulated sugar: the quantity varies to taste and whether you want the cordial to store, but roughly use 340g (¾lb) to 600ml juice (1 pint). Don't heat this mixture, just stir to dissolve the sugar and you should then strain the cordial again through muslin once the sugar is dissolved.

The pulp left behind from jelly or juice making can be rubbed through a sieve and used for fruit leather (*see page 80*).

**Jellies** To make a jelly, you cook the fruit up as for jam and, before adding the sugar, you let the pulp strain through muslin, a jelly bag or a clean pillowcase (iron it first to sterilise it). Never squeeze the bag, as this makes cloudy jelly. Usually, jelly is left straining overnight. Unless you have a custom-made device, you'll need to make something to suspend the jelly bag over a bowl. I use a chair to support the bag on a bamboo cane. Once all the juice has drained from the pulp, you add granulated sugar and proceed as for jam, using 450g (1lb) of sugar for each 600ml (1 pint) of juice.

## FRUIT CHEESE

*Fruit cheese is a firm type of intensely flavoured jam, a bit like a cross between jam and jelly. It is a brilliant way of processing fruit with tough skins, such as medlars and quinces, or when you don't want to take the stones out of damsons or other fiddly fruit, and is also good for fruit with annoying pips, such as brambles. Fruit cheeses, such as crab apple and quince, are particularly good with cheese and cold meats.*

Start the fruit cheese in the same way as making jam, but when the fruit is soft put it through a sieve before boiling it with granulated sugar. Then add the same amount of sugar as the weight of the fruit pulp and boil the mixture until it is stiff enough to leave a clean line when you draw a spoon across the bottom of the pan. Pour the hot cheese into clean, sterilised jars and cover and store as for jams. Traditionally, the cheese is bottled in wide-necked jars or moulds so that you can turn the cheese out whole and cut it in slices.

## CHUTNEY

*Before we get lost in the land of jam (a place I'm most happy to be in), we should talk chutneys. Chutneys are the savoury alternative to jams. Essentially, they are chopped vegetables and fruit cooked with spices, sugar and vinegar. There is considerably less sugar in a chutney than jam, and the fruit and vegetables are preserved by the acidic conditions of the vinegar that stop the growth of bad micro-organisms.*

*I prefer to use cider vinegar (for a fruity flavour) or white wine (sharp for sweeter fruits). You can also use malt vinegar. It is best to add the vinegar towards the end of cooking as this economises on how much you use. Brown sugar is often used to give the chutney a darker colour. You can use a variety of spices, but the most common ones are mustard seed, chilli, ginger, nutmeg, paprika, cinnamon, cloves, mace, allspice and peppercorns. Whole spices should be tied loosely in a muslin bag so you can fish them out before bottling – no-one likes to bite down on a clove!*

**Basic chutney method** For every 4kg (9lb) of fruit and vegetables, you need roughly 400g (14oz) of sugar, 15g (3 teaspoons) of salt and ½–1 litre (1–2 pints) of vinegar, depending on how moist your vegetables are. You can use virtually any sort of fruit, or firm vegetable, in chutney.

Wash and chop up your fruit and vegetables. Nearly all chutneys have onions and garlic in them; apples, tomatoes and raisins and dried fruit are often included too. The addition of sweet dried fruit allows you to cut down on sugar.

Place all the fruit, vegetables, salt, sugar, spices and vinegar in a large pan, which must not be copper or iron, as those react with vinegar. Cook slowly until the vegetables and fruit are tender – this can take anything from 30 minutes to several hours depending on the ingredients, but a good chutney is cooked slowly. If you use very hard fruit, soften it by cooking in a little water in a separate pot with a lid, then transfer it into a large pan to make the chutney.

Bottle up in clean, sterilised jars whilst the chutney is still hot, place the lids on tightly and store in a cool, dark place. Most chutneys improve with age, so wait at least a month or so before eating.

How to Preserve Fruits

## FRUIT LEATHERS

*Fruit leathers are puréed fruit, spread out, dried and then rolled up to store. They never stick around for long, as they're just too delicious – a perfect snack to be made as healthy or as sickly sweet as you fancy. They're a great way to use up a lot of left-over fruit bits – a handful of this, some of that, a ripe banana, and suddenly you have something good to eat.*

**Method** Wash your fruit, discarding any damaged or bruised bits. Chop into large pieces and, for every four cups of chopped fruit, add one cup of water. Add any spices (cinnamon, vanilla, Herb Bennet roots, cloves and ginger all work well), and simmer until the fruit is soft.

You may need to strain the pulp of seeds, so either rub it through a sieve with a wooden spoon or use a mouli. Return the pulp to the pan and decide whether it needs sweetening. Drying naturally preserves fruit leathers, as this inhibits moulds and bacteria from growing, rather than sugar, so you don't necessarily need to make them too sweet. I use medlars (incredibly rich in natural sugars), honey and apple juice concentrate as alternatives to sugar. You may want to add a little lemon juice too. I like it when the leather tastes like those fizzy sour sweets, so I'm always hunting after that balance between tart and sweet. If you do add sugar, add it a little at a time and keep tasting.

Pour the mixture onto baking trays lined with parchment paper. You want the mixture to be no more than 1cm thick, otherwise it will take too long to dry out.

Next you need to dry the leather. Either do this in your oven at its lowest setting, below about 60°C, preferably with the fan on and the door open. At this temperature it will take 4–8 hours to dry the leathers. This is clearly not very economical so, if you make a lot, you might consider investing in an energy-efficient dehydrator, which can dry slowly at much lower temperatures. Fruit leathers are dry when they no longer feel sticky and peel away from the paper, usually with their edges curling slightly.

*Storing fruit leathers* I like to dust my leathers in icing sugar, which absorbs any excess moisture and stops them sticking together. Fruit leathers store very well in the fridge for several months in an airtight container or you can freeze them. I keep mine in an old tin at room temperature (not an airtight container or they sweat) and they will store like this for roughly 30 weeks, but I defy you to keep them that long, they're just too moreish.

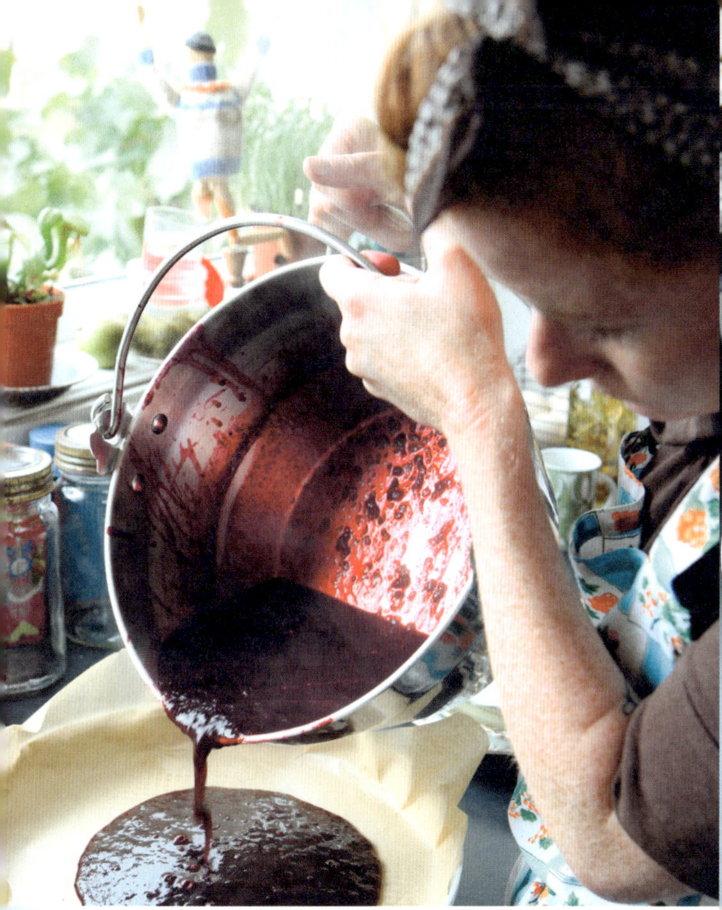
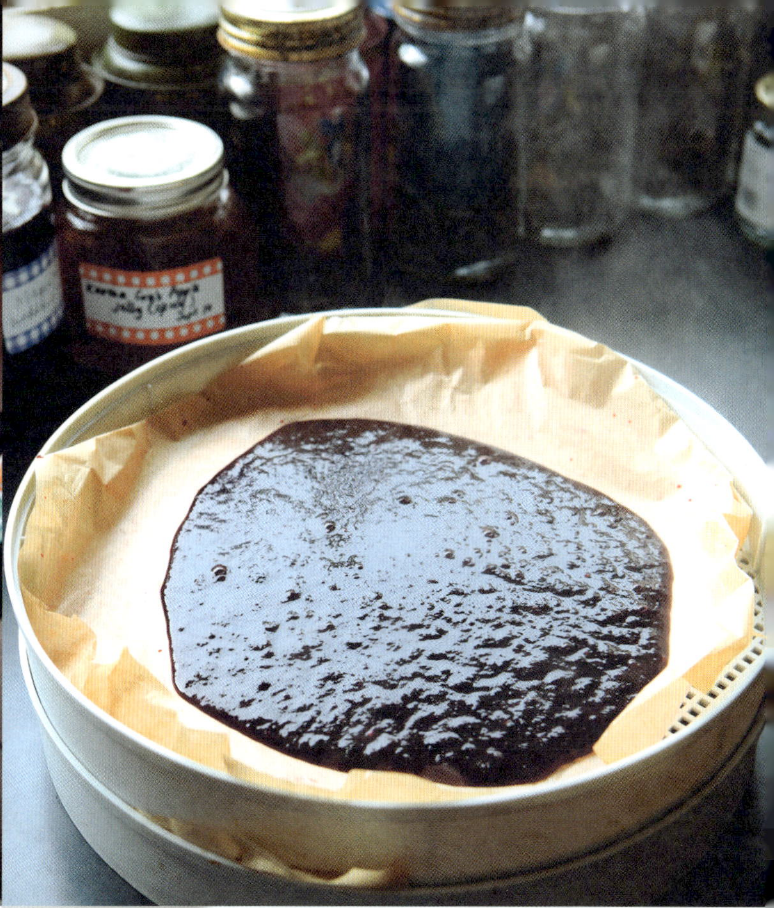
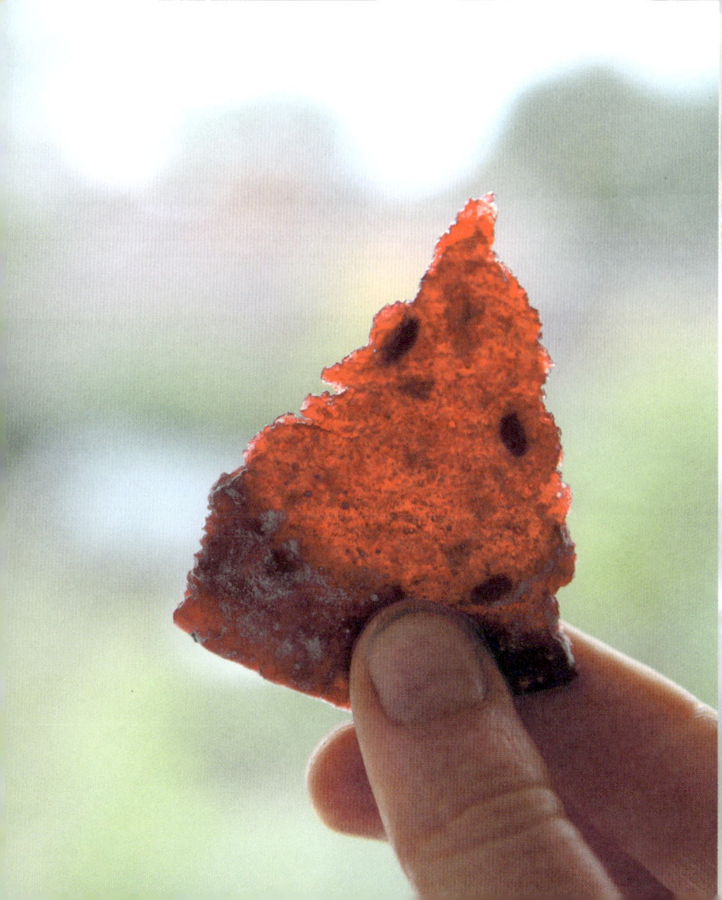
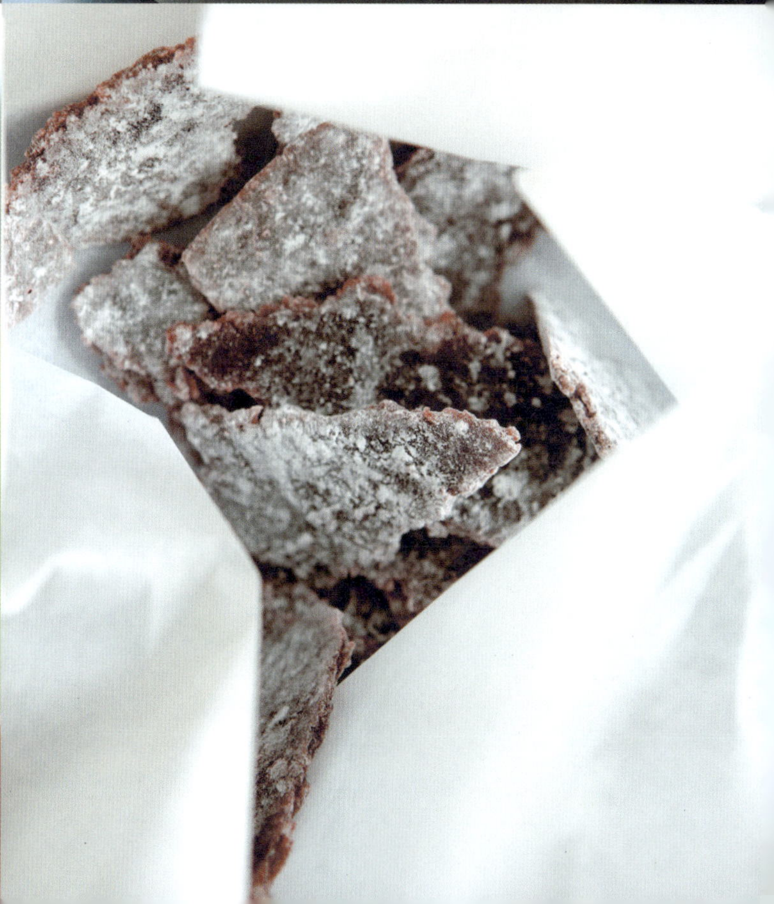

# BIRGIT'S KITCHEN

**BIRGIT AND I** met on at a community gardening programme. She didn't bat an eyelid when I suggested we eat the weeds we were removing. She also willingly came on afternoon-long hunts for ingredients. Our friendship was forged on these long walks.

Birgit is a cook, not a chef, a good wholesome cook. When I was confused about how to make a certain green more palatable or easier to cook with, I'd drop some off at Birgit's house and, a few hours later, a text would appear with a delicious recipe.

## BIRGIT'S STONE SOUP

*Stone soup comes from an old folk story found in many parts of the world about making something out of nothing. Birgit is quite used to me turning up at her house with a handful of this or that and staying long enough for them to be whipped into something nourishing for lunch. Her version of the soup is excellent for instant positive results after foraging, and ideal when coming back cold from a long foraging walk. This is a warming soup that takes just 30 minutes from bag to bowl.*

Serves 4 as a starter or 2 as a main course

**2 medium onions**
**Garlic (2 cloves or more to taste)**
**3 big potatoes**
**2 big handfuls of mixed foraged herbs: stinging nettles, wild garlic, chickweed, lemon balm, sow thistles, ground elder, bladder campion, three-cornered leeks, Herb Bennet leaves, sorrel, dandelions, dead nettles, mallows (though these make for a mucilaginous soup if you include too many), fat hen, oraches or borage. Or just a single green, such as sorrel or stinging nettles**
**Butter or good frying oil, such as rapeseed oil**
**Good-quality vegetable stock cube or powder**
**Good-quality salt (such as Himalayan rock salt or sea salt) and freshly ground black pepper, to taste**
**Bread of your choice, to serve**

Chop the onions and garlic finely.

Peel and chop the potatoes into fairly small cubes.

Roughly chop the herbs.

Heat the fat in a heavy-based pan over a medium heat. Add the finely chopped onions and stir until they start to glaze, then add the garlic and fry until just golden. Add the potatoes and cook for 5 minutes, stirring to stop them from sticking to the bottom of the pan. Cover with boiling water, add a little vegetable stock (cube or powder) and cook for a further 7–10 minutes. Add the roughly chopped herbs and cook until just tender (say another 4 minutes) – do not overboil the herbs or they'll lose their goodness. Season to taste. Serve with chunky bread.

If you prefer a smooth-textured soup, whizz it through a blender. This will also fuse the flavours together, particularly if you've used a lot of bitter herbs, and make it more palatable to those who may be a little wary of wild things.

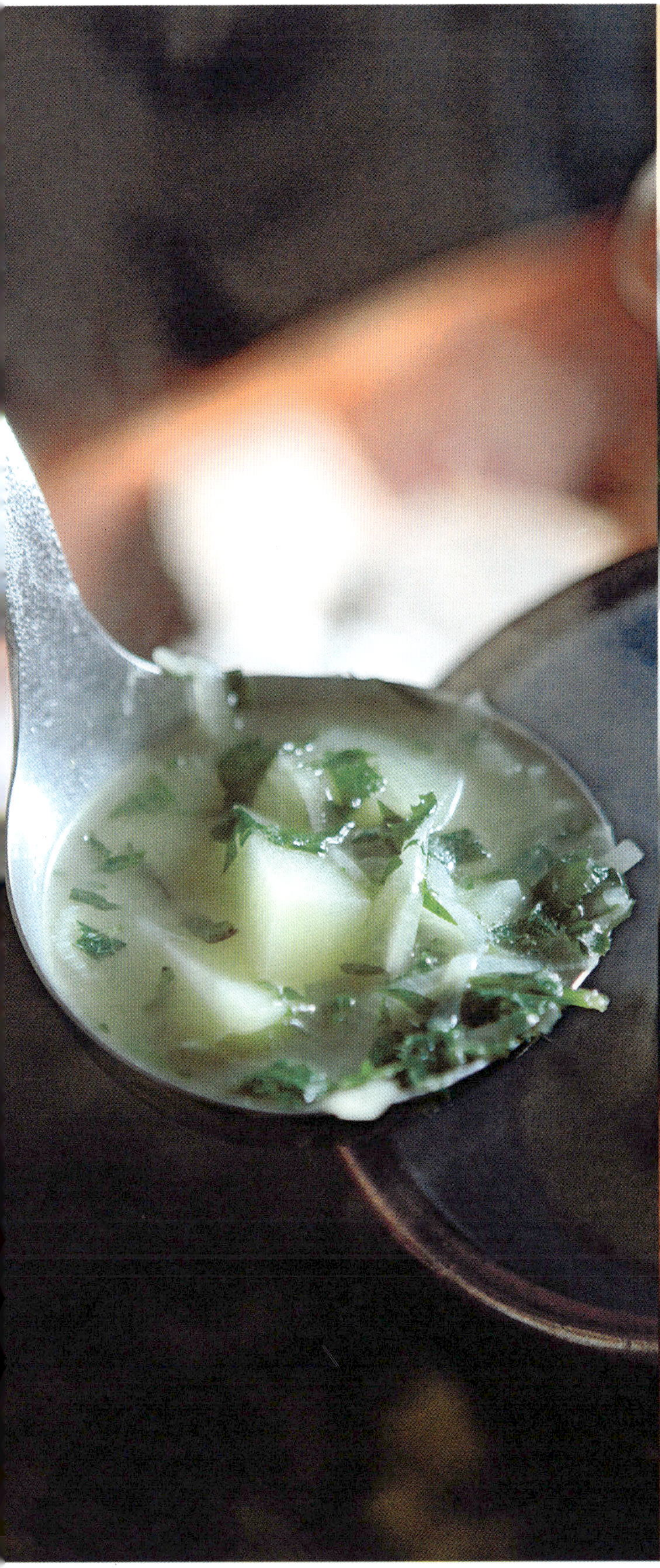
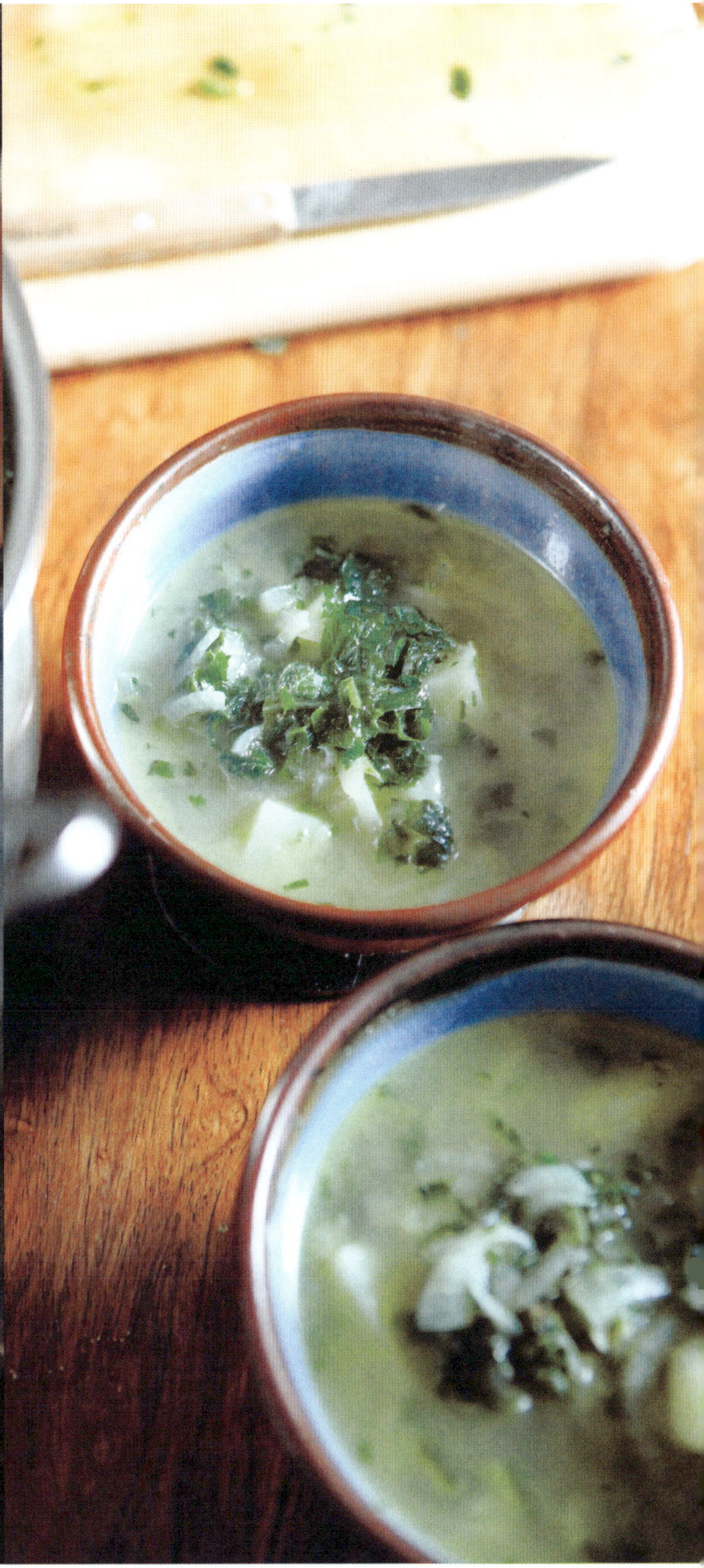

# WILTED GREENS

**ONE OF THE** most delicious ways to use wild greens (and the easiest) is just to wilt them and serve them as a side dish. Wash the leaves thoroughly and add them to a shallow pan with melted butter, the water on the leaves is all that is needed to wilt them. Cook briefly until tender over a gentle heat or they'll lose their colour. They'll take 5 minutes max. The very bitterest greens need to be soaked in salt water and rinsed several times before cooking. The cooking water needs to be discarded and the greens rinsed again. If they are just too tough, you can rub salt into the leaves and let them rest for half an hour (in much the same way as you treat aubergines) and then rinse. This will make the leaves tender and less bitter. Borage works well this way. Then you can wilt or steam and cook as usual.

## SALSA VERDE, GERMAN OR HESSIAN GRÜNE SOSSE

- 2 handfuls of mixed wild herbs, including bitter ones (you can steam the herbs first, but I think it tastes a lot less exciting)
- 2 dessertspoons of olive oil
- 2 dessertspoons of white balsamic or sherry vinegar
- Pinch of good-quality salt
- 2 dessertspoons of Greek yogurt
- 1 raw shallot
- 2 boiled eggs

Wash the herbs well, discarding any damaged bits and tough stems. Mix all the ingredients together using a blender. Traditionally, this would be served with boiled potatoes – salad varieties work best, such as Pink Fir Apple or Charlotte. It's equally good with a dark rye bread.

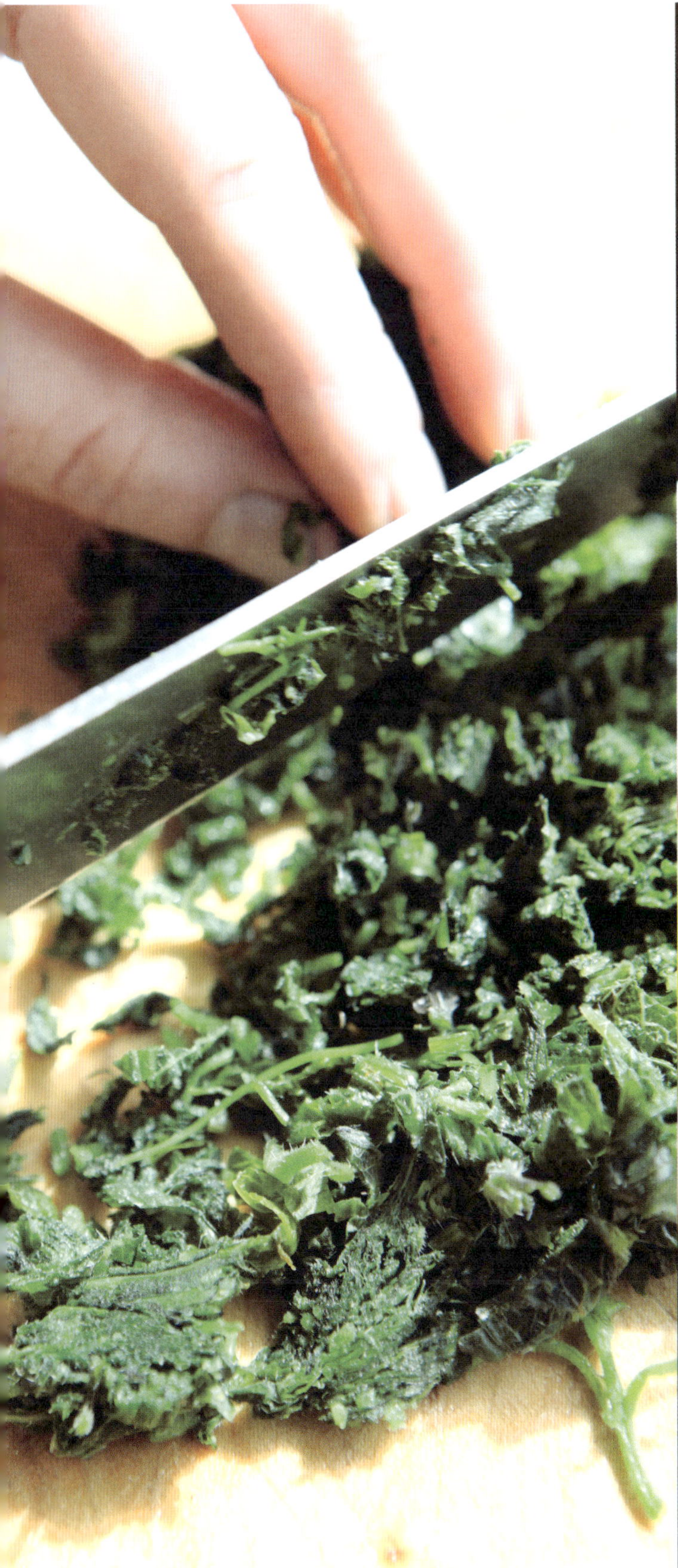
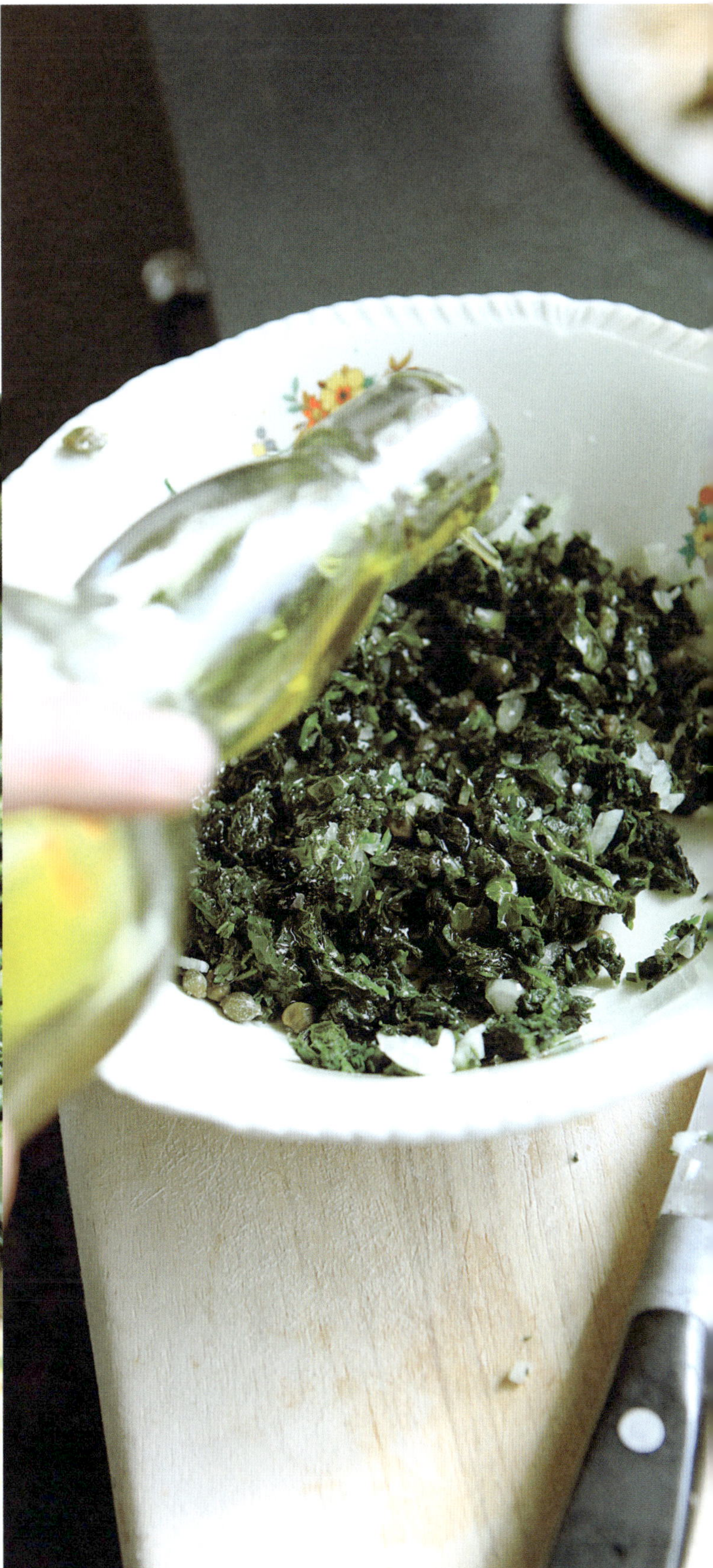

### AEGOPODIUM PODAGRARIA
## Ground elder
Late spring to mid summer flowers, mid winter to late spring leaves

*Ground elder was introduced to the UK by the Romans as a food source and has been the scourge of gardeners everywhere ever since. I don't think you'd ever want to introduce it specially, but if you've got it you might as well try to harvest it into submission. It was a common vegetable in medieval Britain and used to be known as gout weed, as its high vitamin C levels meant it was an excellent cure.*

**How to recognise** Ground elder is a perennial that doesn't mind sun or shade and has traditionally been found around human habitations. It has hollow, pale green, grooved stems up to 1m tall, though it mostly grows to around 30–50cm. Roots are long strap-like rhizomes and the plant is always found in spreading clumps, never singly. The leaves are 8–22cm long and a dark glossy green. They are triangular shaped in groups of three leaflets, ternate (so each leaf has 9 leaflets), often with an uneven base and irregularly shaped, toothed margins. Flowers are very pretty umbels of white or sometimes pink-tinged flowers that last a surprisingly long time in the vase.

**What to eat** The very young leaves and shoots can be used in salads and have a slightly lemon flavour – you either love them or hate them. On the whole, the leaves are better earlier in the year before flowering. Older leaves are good cooked, but their texture is oddly papery so use them shredded in soups or stews. You can use them in pasta sauces or in mashed potatoes. I like to bake trout on a bed of them.

---

### ARMORACIA RUSTICANA
## Horseradish
Roots all year round, as long as the soil is not frozen

*Horseradish has a long history of being eaten; it is mentioned in Greek mythology and the Romans used it medicinally. Although not native, it has naturalised widely through Britain and you often see stands of it growing alongside motorways. It looks essentially like giant dock weed and loves damp places, wastelands and banks.*

*The roots of wild specimens are often pretty raggedy and forked, but it's potent stuff and gives a proper kick to a Bloody Mary. Although it grows pretty much everywhere, it is not legal to dig it up unless you have the landowner's permission. Apparently you should not eat large doses of horseradish as it's not good for you, I don't know why, but I do know it's a good idea to wear goggles when peeling it, as this plant has the devil inside it!*

**How to recognise** It's a large perennial herb with numerous large leaves that arise straight from the taproot. Leaves are bright green with a prominent vein and wavy margin. When crushed, they smell distinctly of horseradish. The flowers are surprisingly small, on slender stalks up to 1m tall. The seed is not viable and it propagates via its spreading roots, which is why you often see great stands of the stuff.

**What to eat** The good thing about horseradish is that it reproduces from tiny bits of root so, as long as you leave some behind, it's very hard to dent a population. The bad thing is that it's actually quite tough to dig up. Some of my earliest foraging memories are of being sent off with a trowel to dig up horseradish for a roast beef dinner – it can take a while to get a decent bit. If you find plants growing near water, in sand or very free-draining soil, you'll have a better chance.

**Note** In some herbals a horseradish preparation is recommended for rheumatic pain or inflammation. However it should be noted that the mustard oils (glycosides) can cause blistering and irritate the skin.

86 | The Thrifty Forager

ground elder

## ALLIUM AMPELOPRASUM VAR. BABINGTONII
### Wild leek, Babington's leek

Mid winter to early summer leaves, mid to late summer flowers

*Native to the UK, the wild leek is mainly found by the coast and sometimes on wastelands, believed to grow on the site of old habitations, such as monasteries. If you do come across any in the wild – I never have – please don't harvest it because it's very scarce, but you can get plants for your garden from mail-order suppliers. Elephant garlic is a cultivated variety grown for its huge cloves. The good thing about this leek is that it's perennial so, once you've got it established, you'll always have something to pick.*

**How to recognise** They look much like a cultivated leek, but the leaves smell of garlic when crushed. It has a large, loose, irregular round head with lilac to deep purple flowers and bulbils can reach up to 2m tall. Leaves are flat, hollow, and greyish green with a keel running down the underside of the leaves.

**What to eat** You can eat all parts, but it's most prized for its leek-like leaves. The bulb is often very deep so the stem is naturally blanched. It has a mild, garlic flavour. Flowers are similar in flavour, and you can eat the small bulbils, which are best cooked but a bit of a fiddle to eat.

**How to grow** It is quite tolerant of heavy soil, as long as it gets full sun. In well-drained soils it doesn't mind a bit of shade. Remember to plant wild leeks fairly deep. They are easy to propagate through division in late summer or early autumn – just dig up the plant and remove the small bulbils around the base of the large bulb and repot these into individual pots. This gives better results than planting straight into a permanent position. Plant out the following spring. Or you can sow seed in spring or when ripe in autumn into pots, which you should keep in a cold frame over winter. Then plant out as well-grown young plants in early summer.

## ALLIUM TRIQUETRUM
### Three-cornered garlic

Late winter to mid summer leaves, mid spring to early summer flowers, early to late autumn bulbs

*This is a garden escapee, but one I welcome into the wild (or at least into my local park) as it is so tasty, but it would be wrong to introduce this into areas of natural importance. It is much sweeter than wild garlic and can be used raw in salads, or cooked. I'm particularly fond of eating the flowers.*

**How to recognise** It does best in well-drained soils in semi-shade and can be found along roadsides, verges, woodlands and wasteland, often in the places where you might find bluebells. It is distinguished by its triangular leaves and stem – this is most obvious in the flower stem. It has very pretty white, bell-shaped flowers, which have a green stripe down each petal. You could easily mistake this for a white bluebell or a very large snowdrop, but the distinctive garlic smell of the leaves gives it away.

**What to eat** All parts are edible – the small 20mm diameter bulbs have a mild, sweet garlic taste. Dig these up in autumn and use leaves from autumn through to winter as a leek substitute. The summer flowers are particularly sweet in salads. If you want to cook with the leaves, add them briefly at the end of cooking to preserve their flavour.

**How to grow** Three-cornered garlic is not completely hardy, so it needs a sheltered, well-drained shady spot – under a tree is perfect. Bulbs need to be planted fairly deep. Seed should be sown ripe in a pot in autumn or stored and sown in spring, and seedlings need to be kept somewhere frost-free for their first year. The easiest way to propagate is to divide plants in summer, once they have died down, water them in well and label or you won't remember where you planted them.

*wild leek*

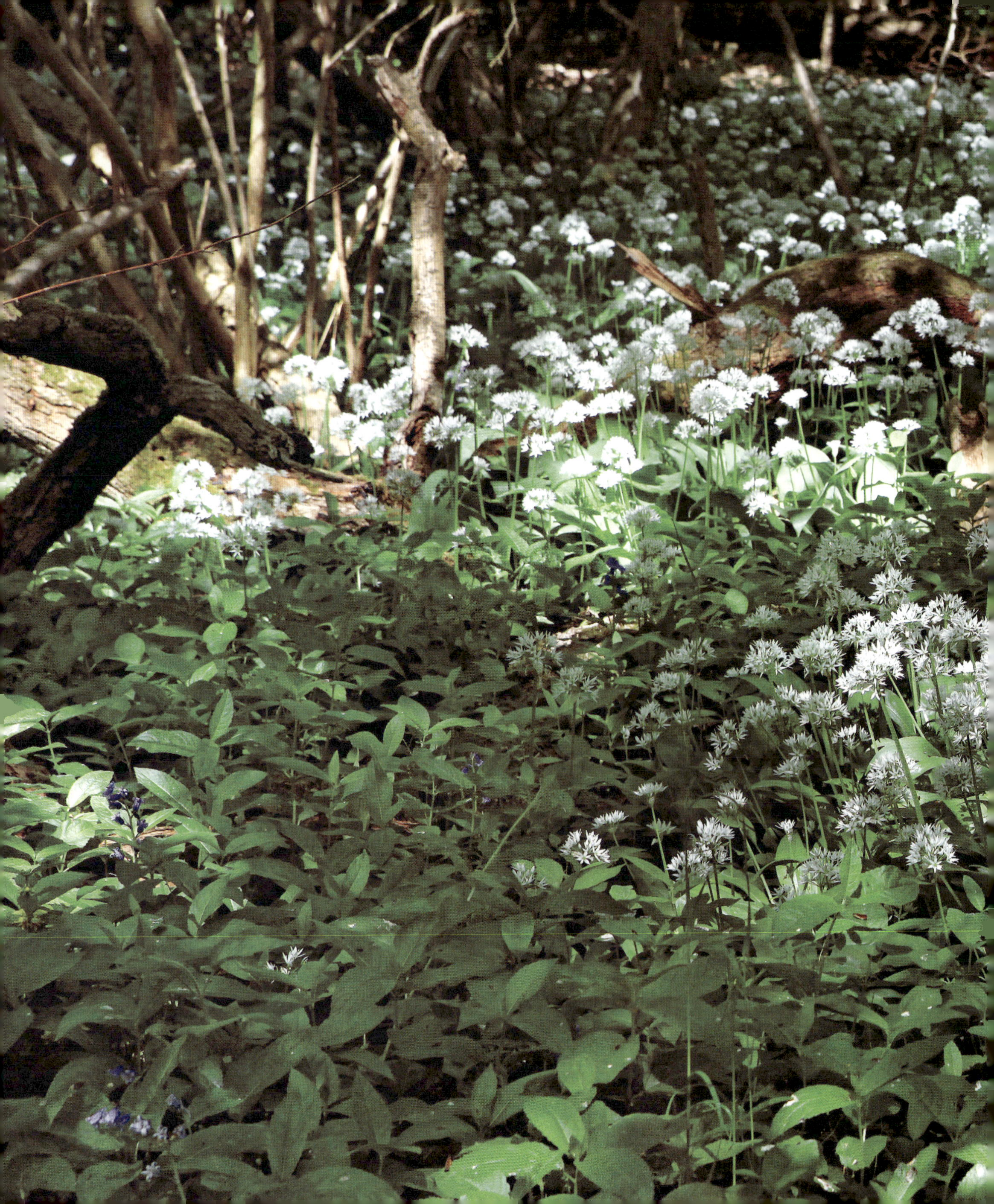

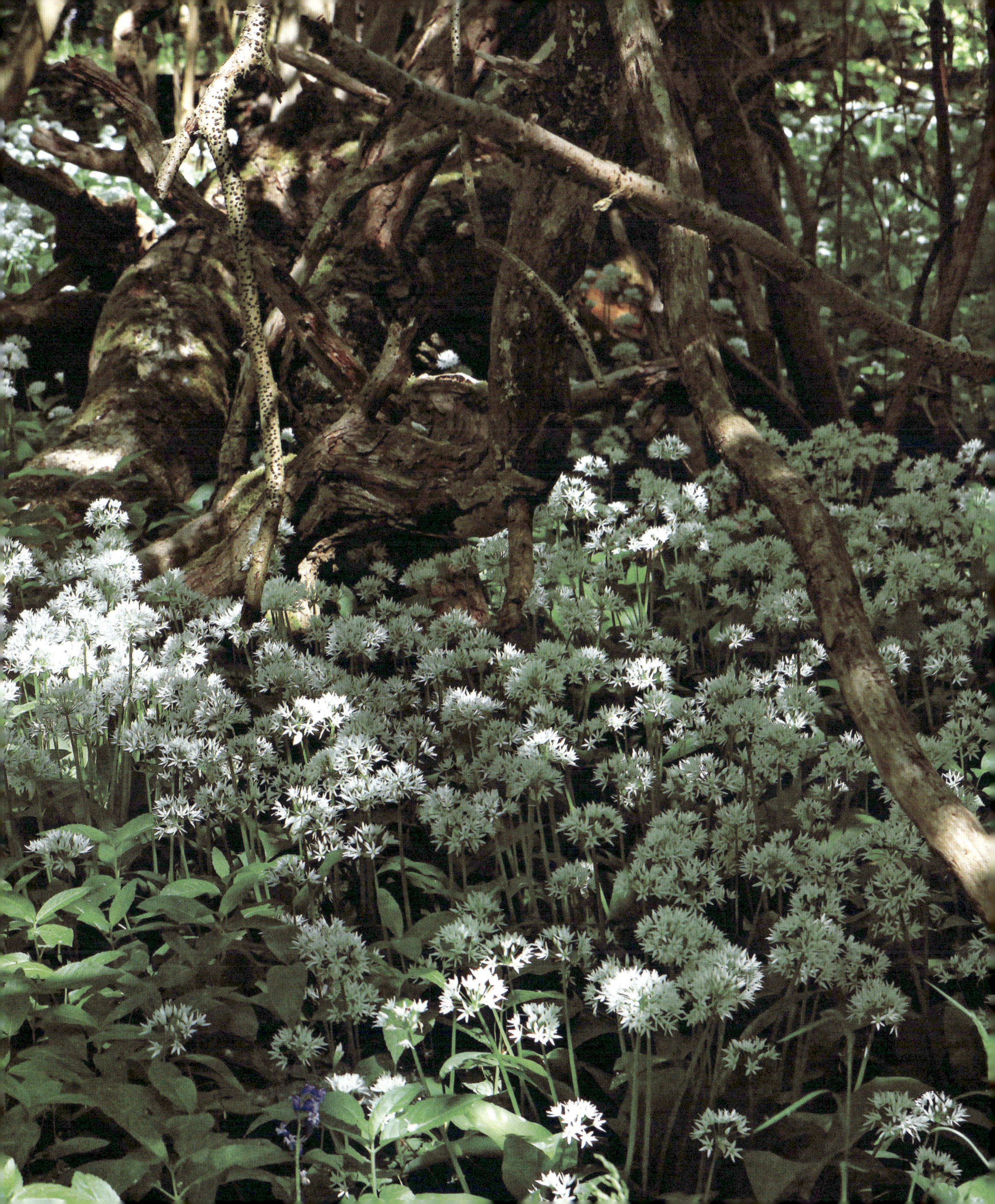

ALLIUM URSINUM
## Wild garlic or Ransoms

Late winter to early summer leaves, late spring to mid summer flowers

*This is one of the first plants I learnt to identify. Whenever my mum and I would drive past the great stand of garlic that covers Hampshire woodlands, she'd shout 'wind down the windows and smell the garlic' and we'd whistle through that lovely smell.*

**How to recognise** Wild garlic haunts dappled shade and woodlands, though just a few trees are enough for it to make itself at home. It likes damp soil, but can thrive in all sorts of soil types, from chalk to clay. It can and will grow in full shade. It is an indicator of ancient woodland.

Firstly, it is given away by its distinctive smell, so strong when in flower it is unmistakable. It has broad, shiny green leaves up to 25cm long and tapered towards the end. They look similar to lily-of-the-valley leaves (not edible) and colchicum (poisonous), but you can easily tell wild garlic because the leaves smell so distinctly of garlic when you crush them. In early summer, it has lovely star-shaped white flowers held in a loose round cluster.

**What to eat** All parts are edible, but the immense popularity of this plant these days, particularly as a must-have restaurant food, means, I think, that you should only eat the leaves and flowers if you are harvesting from the wild. Yes, there is a lot of it out there, but if we all go and dig it up, there won't be. However, you can probably harvest as many leaves as you desire and do very little to dent a population.

This is a strong garlic flavour, one I can't get enough of when it appears, but I'd caution eating it raw (at least if you were thinking of going on a first date). I like to use wilted leaves on top of pizza or pasta and make a pesto with leaves, olive oil, and Parmesan. You can use it in omelettes, soups, stir-fries and stuffed in bread. If you have it growing in your garden, you can thin plants (encouraging more for next year) and pickle the young bulbs.

**How to grow** You'll need space as it can quickly become invasive, but if you've a wild woodland of a garden it has to be the perfect plant. Sow ripe seed on bare ground in early summer or in pots in a cold frame, but it's easiest to spread by dividing plants in late summer when the leaves have died back. The bulbs needs to be planted fairly deep and will colonise quickly in damp soils.

**Note** *Allium sphaerocephalon*, the roundheaded leek, is protected by law under the Wildlife and Countryside Act and should never be harvested from the wild, due to its scarcity.

ALLIARIA PETIOLATA
# Garlic mustard, Jack-by-the-hedge

Year round leaves,
mid spring to early summer flowers,
early to late summer seeds

*Garlic mustard is a Willy Wonka wild food. It starts off with a powerful blast of mustard and then, with a bit more chewing, you're hit with a wave of garlic. It's fantastic eaten in moderation: if you eat too much, you'll stink.*

**How to recognise** Its name gives it away, it is mostly likely to be found in hedges or the edge of woodland or growing in the shade of walls and fences – it basically likes to hug something. It is a biennial with a long, thin taproot that has a distinct strong, mustard smell. In its first year, it produces a rosette of kidney or heart-shaped yellow-green leaves with wavy or toothed margins. The plant, when in flower, can be anything from 15–120cm tall, depending on how rich the soil is. The flowers are white, with four petals, arranged in a terminal cluster – they look much like many other brassica flowers. The seed pods are long and thin, up to 6cm long, containing dark black seeds.

**What to eat** I think it's best shredded up in winter salads to add a spicy note, and is good with a heavy balsamic vinaigrette. If you want to cook with the leaves, I like it in nettle soup, added at the very end of cooking so they just wilt, otherwise they'll make the soup taste bitter. Young seed pods can be eaten.

**How to grow** If it likes you, you'll have plenty, but as it's your supper it is not a hardship. It needs damp soil and shade to be happy. Sow seeds *in situ* in spring or autumn, but do think hard before you do so as it will take over.

The Plant Directory

## AMELANCHIER LAMARCKII
### Juneberry, Service berry

Mid to late spring flowers, mid summer fruits

*Juneberries are somewhere between a blackcurrant, blackberry and blueberry but grow on trees rather than bushes, which is probably why everyone misses them. Amelanchier are much loved ornamental North American trees planted in car parks, around offices and new builds, in parks and in gardens. They have clusters of pretty pink and white flowers in spring and quite spectacular autumn colour. The fact that very few people have so far cottoned on to the lovely berries is an added bonus, although they are foraged for in their native habitats. There are several quite common edible ornamental species,* Amelanchier canadensis, A. lamarckii, A. x grandiflora *and* A. x grandiflora 'Ballerina'. *The Saskatoon,* A. alnifolia, *is a shrub grown in Canada for berry production, but it's a pretty rare find outside of Arboreta.*

**How to recognise** They are deciduous trees, up to 8m tall, or upright shrubs, with five-petalled, star-shaped, flat white or pinkish white flowers appearing from late spring to summer, up to 2cm across. The leaves are alternate, ovate to oblong, often a bronze colour when young and appear at the same time as the flowers. The fruit is blue-black, round and sometimes pear-shaped, up to 9mm long, and very attractive to birds, but there's always plenty to go round. Fruits have chewy seeds.

**What to eat** They are best eaten straight off the tree, as they are fairly time-consuming to pick. On young trees or hedge specimens, the picking is easier so you can then pick as many as you can to dry or freeze. The berries are very sweet, so there is no need to add sugar – they work well in muffins, pies and jams, and the seeds have a slightly almond taste, which adds to the flavour. Stephen Barstow (*see pages 26–41*) dries his berries (he has rather a lovely hedge of the stuff) and then rehydrates them to sweeten breakfast cereals.

**How to grow** Amelanchier make a wonderful tree for the garden and prefer lime-free fertile, well-drained soil in either full sun or partial shade. 'Ballerina' is a shrubby tree suitable for smaller spaces, with wonderful large white flowers (up to 15cm long) in spring and, subsequently, large fruit (sometimes up to 1.5cm wide) that starts off red and ripens a dark purplish blue. By autumn, the leaves turn the most wonderful purple and red, so you get three seasons of interest and something for breakfast too.

juneberries

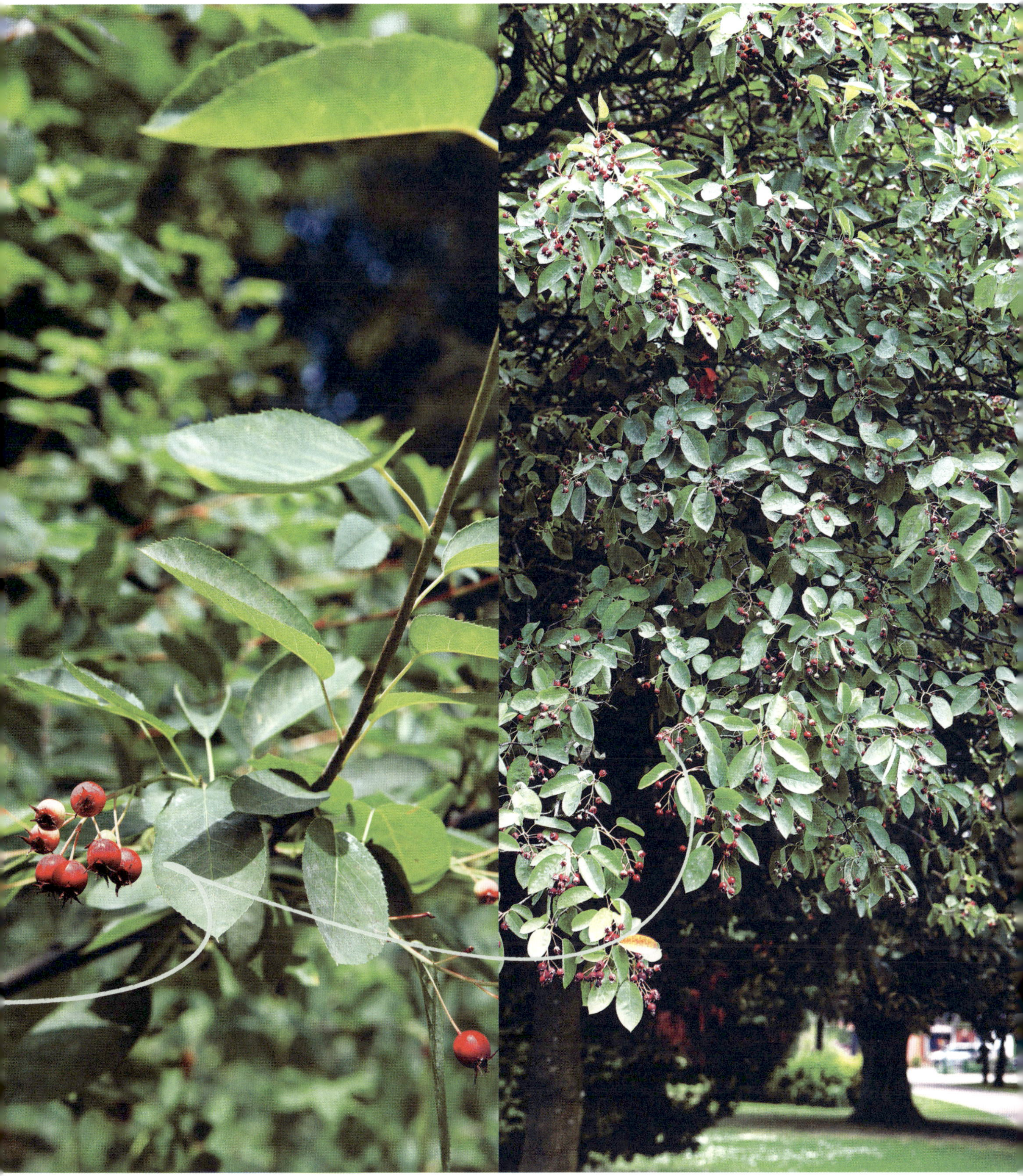

*garden orache*

## ATRIPLEX HORTENSIS
### Garden orache
Mid spring to early autumn leaves

*This is mainly a garden escapee. It used to be widely cultivated and the purple or red form,* Atriplex hortensis var. rubra, *is seeing a bit of a renaissance. It's one of my favourite spinach substitutes and, as the red form keeps its colour when cooked, it's a wonderful way to get kids to try their greens.*

**How to recognise** It's found in arable land, waste and disturbed land, near or around gardens and allotments. It can grow 30–100cm tall with green leaves often tinged red when young. The purple form is now used in some annual flower mixes. Young leaves have a mealy surface (on green, blonde and red forms). It is an upright plant, lower leaves are heart-shaped, the middle ones are triangular with coarse-toothed margins, and the upper leaves are elongated with almost no serration to the margins. The flowers appear up the entire stem and the seedheads have a distinct papery bract circling the seed.

**What to eat** The tip is most tasty and can be used in salads or steamed, lightly boiled or fried and is especially good in omelettes; young leaves are also good to eat. When the plant is about 10cm high, pinch out the tip to make it bushier, so it will offer more tender young leaves.

**How to sow** Choose the highly decorative red or blonde forms, sold as Purple Orache and Gold and Green varieties, and sow in mid or late spring. In the first year don't harvest but let the plant go to seed, then you shouldn't have to sow again as it is a prolific seeder. Weed out and eat any unwanted seedlings.

## ATRIPLEX HASTATA
### Hastate orache
Mid spring to mid summer leaves, mid summer to mid autumn unopened flowers

*I found this growing in Norway along the shore, and you'll spot it on a number of seaside coasts. Like many salt-tolerant plants it is naturally seasoned, so just add pepper. It looks very similar to fat hen,* Chenopodium album, *but the leaves are thicker, with the tell-tale white mealy look to them.*

**How to recognise** This weed can be found along roads, canals and neglected spaces, on mud and shingle – as long as it can smell the sea. It is an annual and can grow to 80cm tall, though it's more likely to be around 20-30cm, branching from the base.

**What to eat** Cook leaves like spinach from late spring to mid summer and, from mid summer to mid autumn, the unopened flower buds and stalks can be steamed like broccoli. Seeds are edible and can be mashed up to thicken soups, but you'd have to be really hungry to want to do that as they are so small and fiddly. **Note** Any orache grown with artificial fertilizer may accumulate harmful amounts of nitrate in their leaves.

BELLIS PERENNIS
## Daisy
When in leaf, eat leaves, when in flower, eat flowers

*'When you can put your foot on seven daisies summer has come.'*
*Now I'm not saying you can ever live on daisies alone, to be honest the flowers don't taste of much, but they do look lovely. A lawn isn't a lawn for me without daisies.*

**How to recognise** Daisies only grow in mown or grazed lawns. Clearly, make sure you pick from herbicide-free areas. They are perennial herbs with stout roots, which is why they don't mind being mown. The leaves are arranged in a basal rosette and are paddle or spoon-shaped. Classic daisy flowers are terminal with white ray florets, often tinged pink, and yellow disc florets.

**What to eat** You can eat young leaves in salads or sandwiches – some people love them, some don't. They can also be cooked in soups or stews, and the young flower buds can be preserved as a rather poor caper substitute – they only resemble capers because of the vinegar.

**What to grow** There are loads of cultivars, such as 'Tasso', 'Strawberries and Cream', 'Pomponette' or 'Blushing Bride', which have double flowers and pink variations so they make for interesting decorations. The leaves of these cultivars tend to be larger, but eat with caution if you've bought them from a garden centre as they may contain pesticide residue. I think it's best to grow them from seed – it's cheaper and safer. Sow late summer to early autumn in pots or trays of moist seed compost in a cold frame. Do not exclude light, as it helps germination, and keep the seeds moist.

## BERBERIS DARWINII
### Darwin's barberry
Mid to late summer fruits

*This was one of the fruits Darwin sent back to England from his trip on the Beagle. It's native home is South America, from Chile through to Patagonia, and it was a food source for indigenous Patagonians. The berries are very sweet, a little blackcurrant-like, with rather large, chewy pips.*

*It's a bit of a cottage garden staple and you're likely to find it as hedging in car parks, parks and municipal plantings.*

**How to recognise** It is a small, upright, evergreen shrub with glossy dark green obovate, spine-toothed leaves between 2–4cm long. Very bright, almost neon-orange flowers in spring contrast rather well with the dark foliage. They are followed by dark-blue, black fruit, up to 7mm long, sometimes glaucous with a greyish bloom.

If you don't like the chewy seeds, you'll have to process the berries through a sieve (or mouli). You can do this with cooked and raw berries. They are good dried, in puddings, stews, summer puddings, jams, fruit leather, or just straight off the bush as a snack before heading into the supermarket.

## BORAGO OFFICINALIS
# Borage
Late spring to early autumn leaves and flowers

*Borage is a wonderful plant, though some might say it's a little too wonderful as it quickly self-seeds and, before you know it, you have rather a lot in your garden. However, if you know how to eat it, there's no such thing as too much, just too little time to cook it all. It doesn't mind dry, difficult soils and the bees go nuts for the nectar and pollen.*

**How to recognise** This annual has distinctly bristly leaves that are unpleasant to handle when large (and a very useful way to make sure you're picking borage and not young foxgloves that look surprisingly similar, but foxgloves are smooth to touch). Stout-looking, plants will grow to 60cm but are more usually about half that height. Mature, lance-shaped leaves are up to 25cm long, stalkless and clasped around the stem. Flowers are five-petalled, star-shaped and typically bright blue, though there is a less common white form, *B. officinalis* 'Alba'. It flowers all summer long.

**What to eat** Very small (no more than 3cm long), young leaves are delicious raw in salads where you can taste the clean, cucumber flavour. Larger leaves can be used like spinach and have a buttery flavour. If the leaves are too tough for your liking, rub salt into them until they release their juices and then rinse and soak several times and you'll find they are much better. Once the leaves are 10cm long, they tend to be too hairy, so eat the young plants and allow some to flower, as the flowers are edible. Use the flowers in salads or freeze them in ice cubes for Pimms and other summer drinks. The blue flowers will also dye vinegar blue – in case you ever feel the need to do that.

**Note** The leaves contain alkaloids that can cause liver damage. You would have to eat an awful lot of leaves, but as a precaution, if you suffer liver problems, do not eat the leaves or flowers.

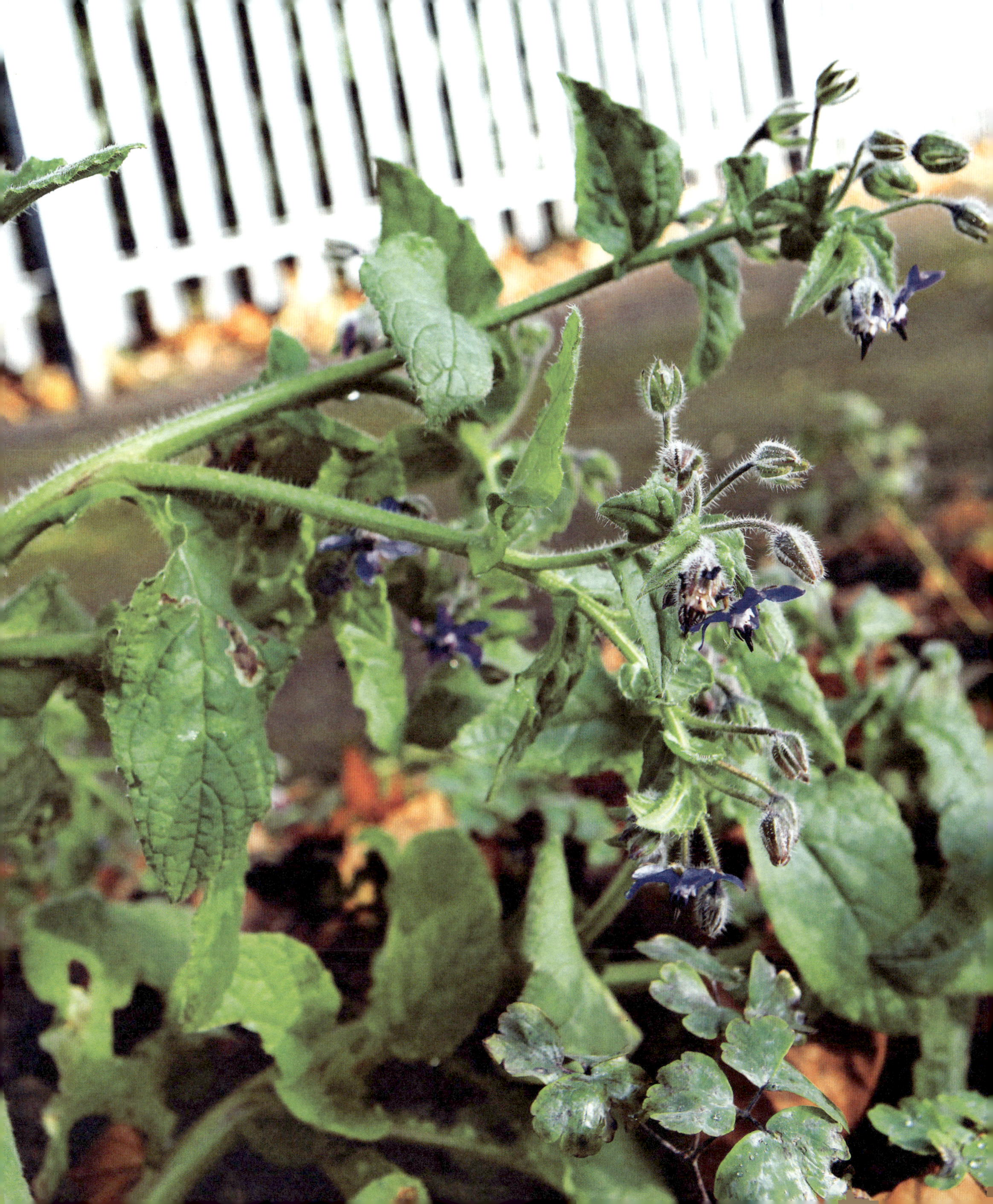

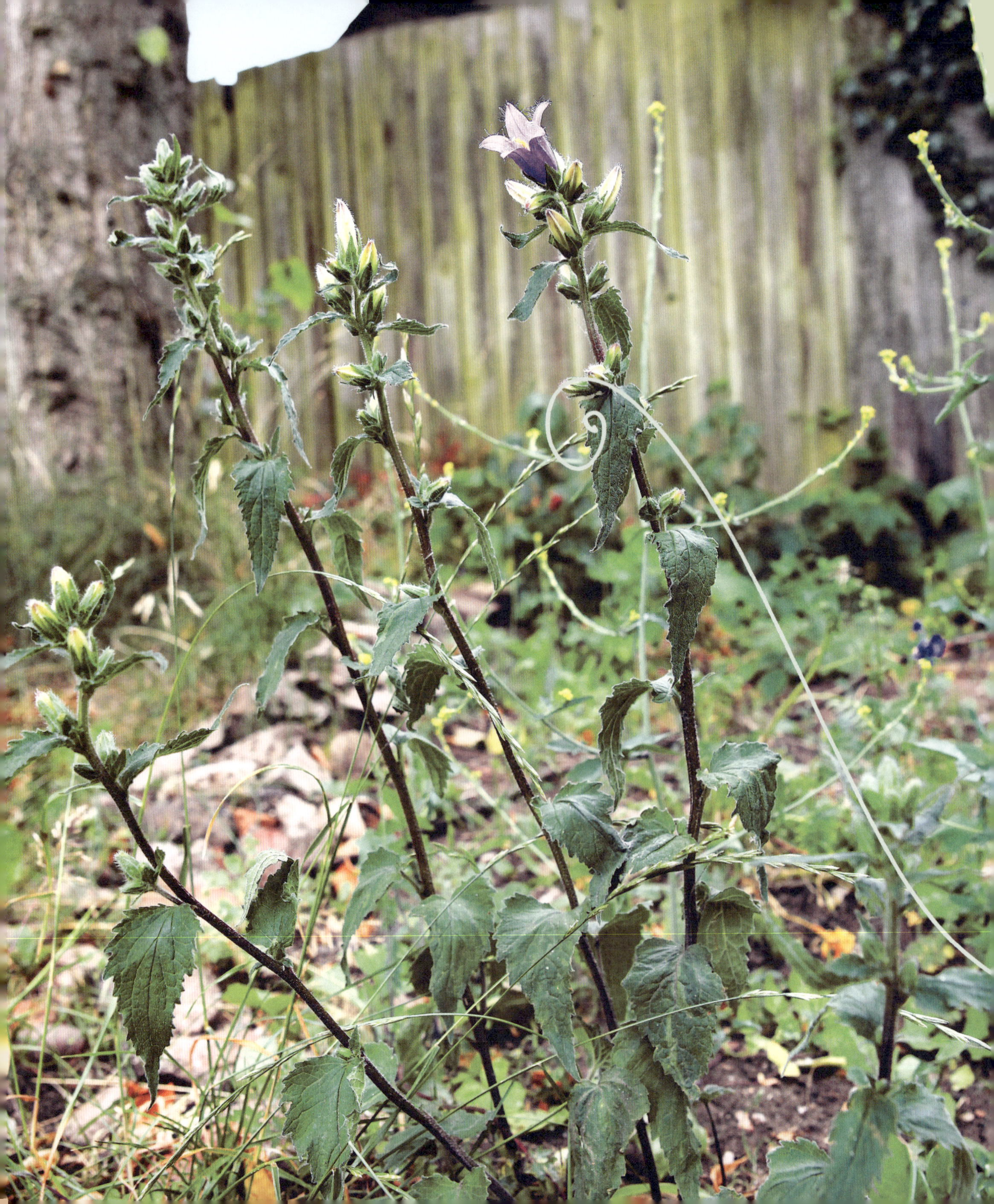

## CAMPANULA SPECIES.
### Campanulas, Bellflower
Late spring to mid summer flowers, leaves all year round

*All campanula flowers are edible and delightfully pretty, so they make excellent garden plants. Hardy perennial species, such as* C. cochlearifolia, C. portenschlagiana, C. poscharskyana, C. persicifolia *and* C. lactiflora *are all worthy candidates and will also bring plenty of bees into your garden. They will tolerate some shade and need little maintenance. The large flowers of* C. persicifolia *or* C. lactiflora *can be stuffed with sweet ricotta cheese, the smaller flowers of the other species are lovely sprinkled through salads. You can eat young leaves before the plants come into flower.*

---

## CAMPANULA TRACHELIUM
### Nettle-leaved bellflower
Mid to late spring young shoots, early to late summer flowers, leaves all year round

*The nettle-leaved bellflower is a lovely wild thing – you'll find it bringing a bit of cheer to the driest of places.*

**How to recognise** This hardy perennial lives in dry soil, often in woodland margins or similar shady spaces. Found throughout Europe, Turkey and Western Asia, plants are up to 1m high, often branching from a woody base. The leaves are 5–12cm long, dark green, hairy and distinctively nettle-shaped. The stout stems are often tinged red, topped with a series of tubular white, blue or lilac flowers from mid- to late summer.

**What to eat** The young shoots are good cooked or steamed. They are a little too hairy for salads, but a few leaves can be used sparingly, blanched, steamed and wrung dry and mixed with shallots and vinegar. The flowers are lovely in salads or used in jellies.

---

## CAMPANULA PORTENSCHLAGIANA
### Dalmatian bellflower
Mid to late spring young shoots, early to late spring leaves, early to late summer flowers

**How to recognise** This is a spreading plant, most at home in the crack of a wall or pavement. It is a mound-forming, tough perennial with small toothed-edged, mid-green leaves, 2cm long, that are kidney to ovate heart-shaped. Funnel-shaped deep purple flowers appear from mid summer – the more you pick, the more they come.

**What to eat** Young leaves and flowers in salads. Young shoots can be steamed.

**Similar species** *Campanula poscharskyana* grows in a similar habitat but has star-shaped lavender flowers with white centres. It has the same spreading nature, but the stems are less robust.

*nettle-leaved bellflower*

## CAPSELLA BURSA-PASTORIS
### Shepherd's purse
Early spring to mid autumn leaves, mid summer to early autumn seeds

*I like the fact the Latin name of this plant translates quite literally, 'bursa', meaning purse, and 'pastoris', meaning shepherd. It is found everywhere, from gardens to rubbish tips and fields. It's very small and no one is going to suggest that you will dine well off it but, sprinkled among salads, it makes a lovely peppery addition, particularly satisfying if it's one of your garden weeds.*

**How to recognise**  An annual, 3–30cm tall, shepherd's purse is upright and slightly hairy with basal leaves that are usually deeply lobed and bright green. The small leaves have a distinct arrow shape at their base and clasp the stem. Tiny flowers are white with four petals, but it's the tiny seed pods that are the giveaway – they're distinctly heart-shaped, 6–9mm long and 4–9mm wide.

**What to eat**  Young leaves are peppery with a slightly cabbage-like overtone – scatter them through salads or steam them, wring them dry and use as greens. The seed has a very strong mustard flavour, but you'd only think of collecting it if you have a large patch. In China and Japan, you can find cultivated forms.

*shepherd's purse*

## CARDAMINE SPECIES
### Bittercress
leaves all year

*Bittercress have small peppery leaves that are most useful in winter.*

## CARDAMINE FLEXUOSA
### Wavy bittercress
Mid spring to early summer flowers, leaves all year

*This species is very similar to hairy bittercress (see page 106), but has large leaves and tends to be found in damp places, woodlands, shady and boggy areas and by rivers and streams. It grows to 50cm tall and the flower stems are slightly wavy, hence the name. The four-petal flowers are white and the stems and leaves are slightly hairy. The overall plant is larger than hairy bittercress and there are more leaves.*

*wavy bittercress*

The Thrifty Forager

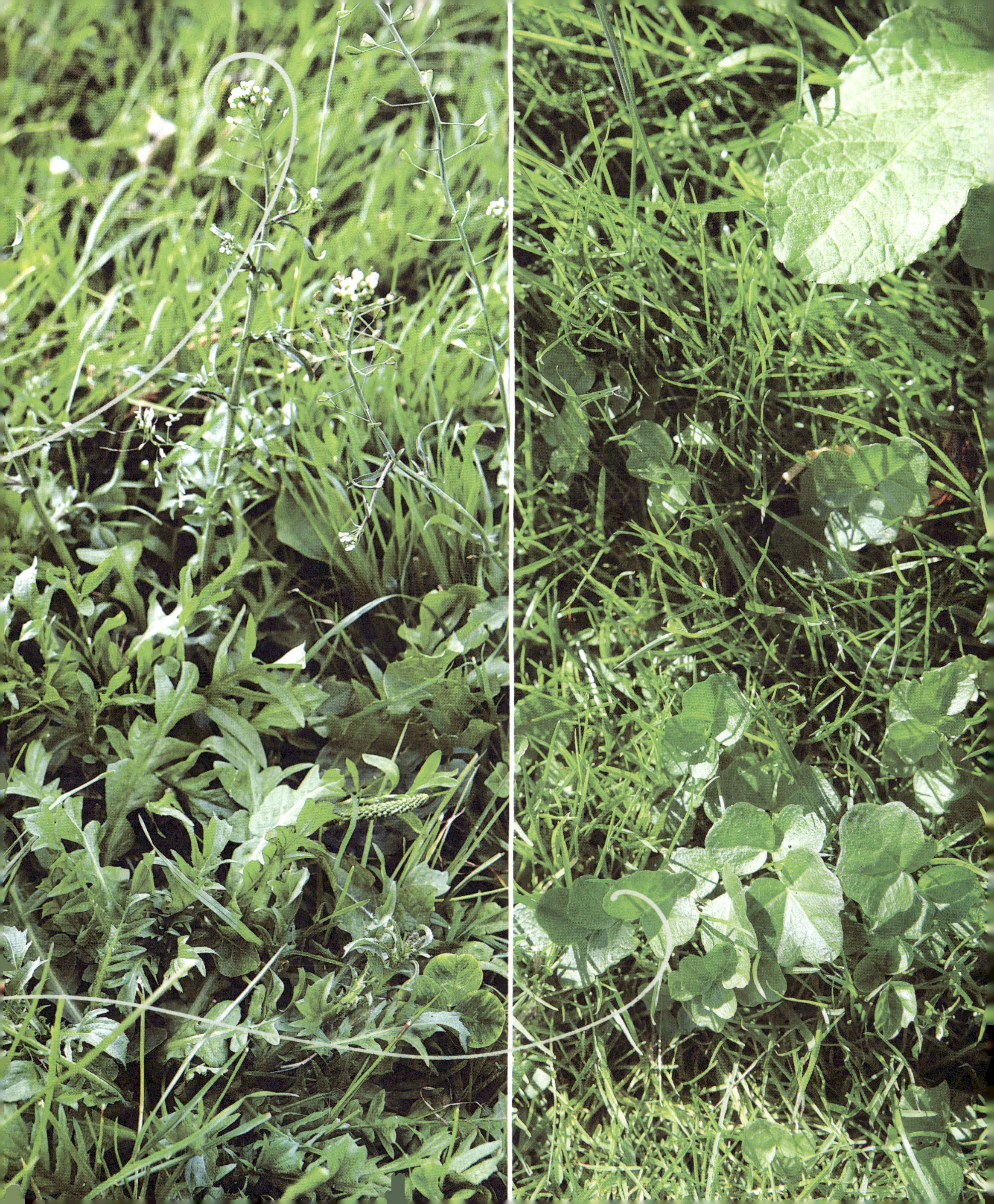

### CARDAMINE HIRSUTA
**Hairy bittercress**

Leaves all year

*You're most likely to find this as a garden weed. It's that small rosette of leaves that takes hold on any bare spots of soil, however thin. As it overwinters particularly well, it's best to see this not as a weed, but as an excellent salad plant that you don't have to cultivate. It's a coloniser of bare soil that is quickly outcompeted by other more vigorous plants in a bed. It can survive in dry soils, but prefers moist ground and will happily appear in pavement cracks.*

**How to recognise** It has a basal rosette of deep green leaves made up of rounded pairs of leaflets; upper leaves have very distinctive hairs. In winter, they often take on a pretty purplish tinge. The white flowers are tiny, 1–2mm. It has a particularly effective seed capsule that catapults seeds in all directions at a mere brush so, once you've got it you'll never be rid of it.

**What to eat** It's best to pick the whole young rosette before it flowers, as the individual leaves are very small and fiddly to pick. The flavour is somewhere between rocket, cabbage and watercress – it starts off hot and then calms down to a cabbage-like tang. It is good in salads, hot or cold, it works well with strong flavours and fats, such as bacon. It can be cooked and used in soups. I like it with couscous, tabouleh or quinoa salads.

---

### CARDAMINE PRATENSIS
**Lady's smock, Cuckoo flower**

Mid to late spring leaves and flowers

*'When daisies pied and violets blue*
*And lady-smocks all silver-white*
*And cuckoo-buds of yellow hue*
*Do paint the meadows with delight.'*
FROM LOVE'S LABOUR LOST

*I used to work next door to Shakespeare's Stratford-upon-Avon home and, there, lady's smock (so-called because the flowers resemble an old-fashioned skirt) flowered in great profusion, which seemed fitting.*

**How to recognise** This is a herb of wild meadows, wet, damp grassy places, common in parks where they don't mow too regularly. You often find it growing along streams. It's a perennial with a basal rosette of leaves; each leaflet is rounded and the end one is kidney-shaped and much larger than the rest. The flowering stem is 10–60cm long (the damper the conditions, the taller it grows). Pretty four-petalled flowers are 12–18mm wide, in shades from delicate pale pink to lilac or, occasionally, white, cupped at first and eventually flattening out.

**What to eat** The leaves and flowers taste somewhere between horseradish and watercress and pack a punch. The flowers are slightly milder in flavour, but you don't need many to make an impression. Sprinkle them through salads, use them with cottage cheese or garnish dishes with them. I think it marries particularly well with beetroot.

**How to grow** This is such a pretty thing that if you have a damp lawn that is more wild than green, it would seem the perfect addition. Seed should be sown in mid spring into trays and kept damp and out of direct sunlight. Mature plants will often produce babies around the base of the rosette which can be divided in spring or autumn and potted on.

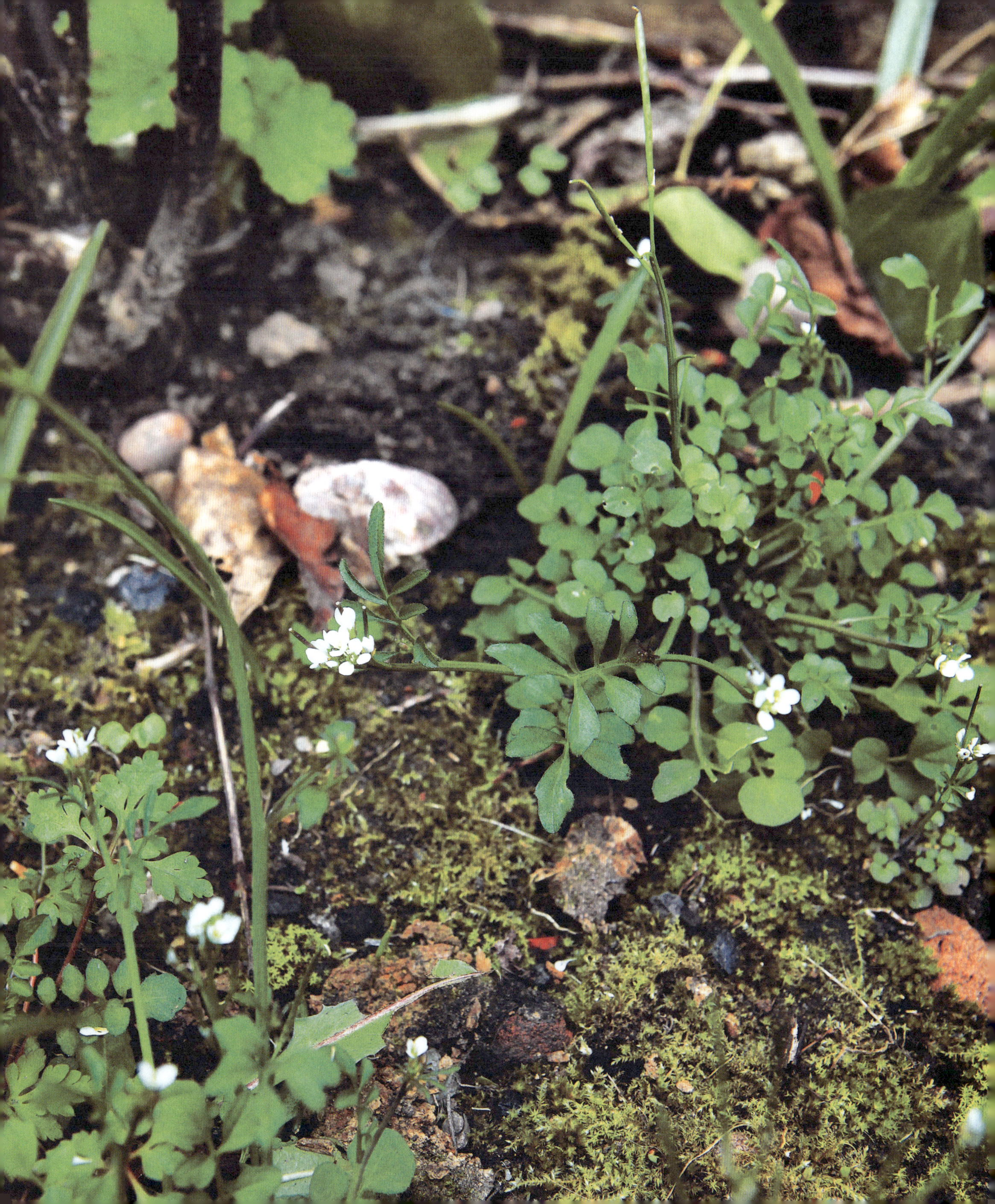

CASTANEA SATIVA
## Sweet chestnut
Early to late autumn fruits

*The sweet chestnut is a very large tree, so you're most likely to find one in a park. There's a lovely double line of them running along the south side of Hyde Park in London that, on a good year, offers more chestnuts than you could possibly know what to do with. Occasionally, you'll find them along streets and roads.*

**How to recognise** Up to 30m tall, the wide trunks of sweet chestnut trees typically have wonderful spiralling fissured bark. The leaves are very distinct, alternate, up to 30cm long, lanceolate with a wedge-shaped base, a prominent spiny margin, shiny and hairless on top and hairy below. They turn a lovely butter yellow in autumn. Male and female trees both produce yellow catkins, and the fruit is enclosed by a very prickly coat. Some trees produce groups of one or two round nuts (good for eating) others three or four flat nuts (not good for eating).

**What to eat** First, you must remove the chestnut from its prickly overcoat. Don't use your fingers, as the spikes have a canny knack of getting under your nails: instead gently tread on the coat and you'll be able to pop the nuts out. You'll quickly get good at spotting the plump ones, but it's always a race against the squirrels. If you want to eat them raw, I suggest you peel as much of the thin, brownish white skin off as possible, as it does make your mouth pucker.

You can boil chestnuts, but it's far better to roast them in the their brown husks and then peel them. Roast them at about 200°C/gas mark 6 for about 10 minutes, but keep an eye on them as smaller chestnuts will roast very quickly. Once they have cooled, it's easy to peel off both the tough outer skin and the inner white skin. You can then boil them for a further 10–15 minutes and add to dishes, use them for stuffing or combine them with Brussels sprouts. Chestnut purée is also very good – for this, you should boil the roasted nuts until tender and then sieve them, mouli them or mash them with a liquidiser.

I made very good flour one year by roasting the nuts, then drying them for a couple of days and whizzing them through a coffee grinder. I kept the flour in an airtight container and it stored for several months (it should smell just like roasted chestnuts – if it smells rancid, it's gone off). Chestnut flour is a speciality of the Umbrian region of Italy, where it is used in numerous recipes from biscuits to pasta. A good starting point is castagnaccio, a flat, dense cake containing little more than chestnut flour, pine nuts, rosemary and olive oil.

## CASTAGNACCIO

**Chestnut flour**
**Warm water (perhaps half and half with warm milk)**
**Pine nuts**
**Walnuts (optional)**
**Raisins**
**Sprig of rosemary**
**Salt**
**Olive oil**
**Honey (optional)**

Sieve the chestnut flour and mix with enough water to make a batter similar to the consistency of pancake batter. To this, add a handful of pine nuts, chopped walnuts, raisins, a sprig of chopped rosemary (must be fresh) and a pinch of salt. Mix together with a good slug of olive oil and, perhaps, a little honey.

Lightly oil a flat ovenproof dish. Spread the batter to the depth of about 2cm (this cake doesn't rise). Bake at 180°C/gas mark 4 for 30 minutes or until the batter is firm and slightly cracked. Cut into squares to serve. This will keep in the fridge for a couple of days, at least.

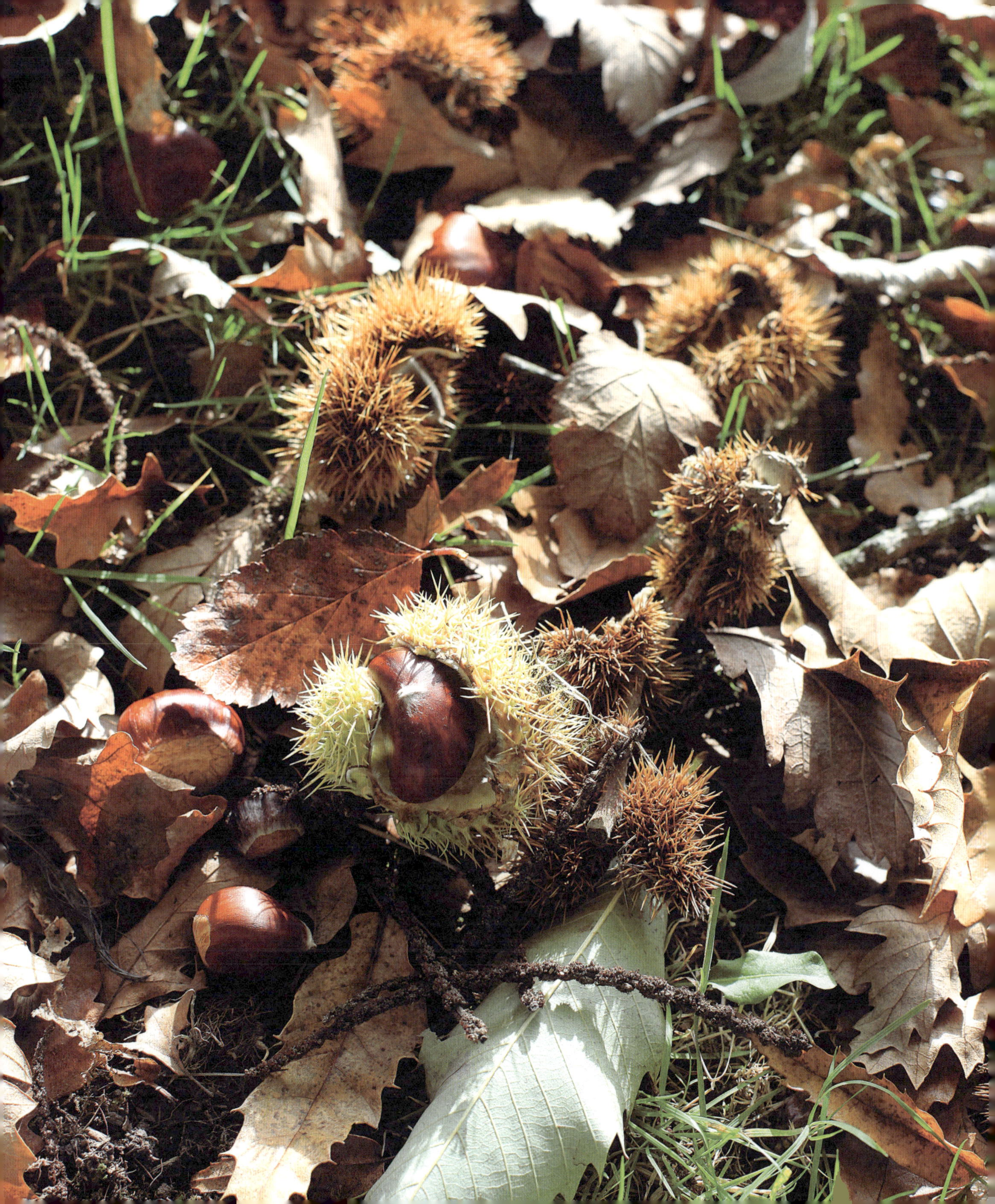

### CHAENOMELES SPECIES
## Flowering quince, Japanese quince, Japonica

Early to late autumn fruit

C. x californica, C. cathayensis, C. japonica, C. speciosa, C. x superba *and cultivars are often car-park bounty. It is a low-growing shrub that can be clipped into a hedge thorny enough so that people don't tend to walk through it. My best harvests have been in car parks or local municipal plantings and it's also common in front gardens. It's got a reputation for being a 70s plant, partly because of the front garden thing, but perhaps it's time for a garden revival as the fruit is certainly worth searching out?*

**How to recognise** Chaenomeles are deciduous, low-growing spiny shrubs from the mountains of China and Japan – occasionally they'll grow into a very small tree about 3m tall. They are grown for their attractive, five-petalled saucer-shaped flowers that appear very early in spring, clustered or singly, and seem to grow straight from the stem as they sometimes appear before the simple alternate leaves. These are followed later in the year by fruit that are highly aromatic, often waxy, yellow to green or purple-green and a similar shape to the true quince, *Cydonia oblonga*.

**What to eat** I've mainly experimented with making *membrillo* (Spanish quince paste) and jelly (*see page 113*). Martin Crawford, author of *Creating a Forest Garden*, has a recipe for quince lemonade that looks good and makes use of frozen fruit, but I'm a sucker for something really sweet. You can bake the fruit whole, use in crumble, cobblers and pies. I make a lovely stewed apple and quince mush that is wonderful with vanilla ice cream or yogurt. You can also use the fruit with lamb in a tagine.

**How to grow** Chaenomeles are fully hardy shrubs ranging from 1.5–3m high and 2–5m wide. They prefer well-drained soil but are not fussy about fertility and can survive in all sorts of rubbishy ground, as long as they don't get flooded in winter. They tolerate shade and can be grown against a shady wall, though fruit that has ripened in the sun tends to taste better. They fruit from a young age and are very low maintenance, unless you want to clip them into a hedge.

quince

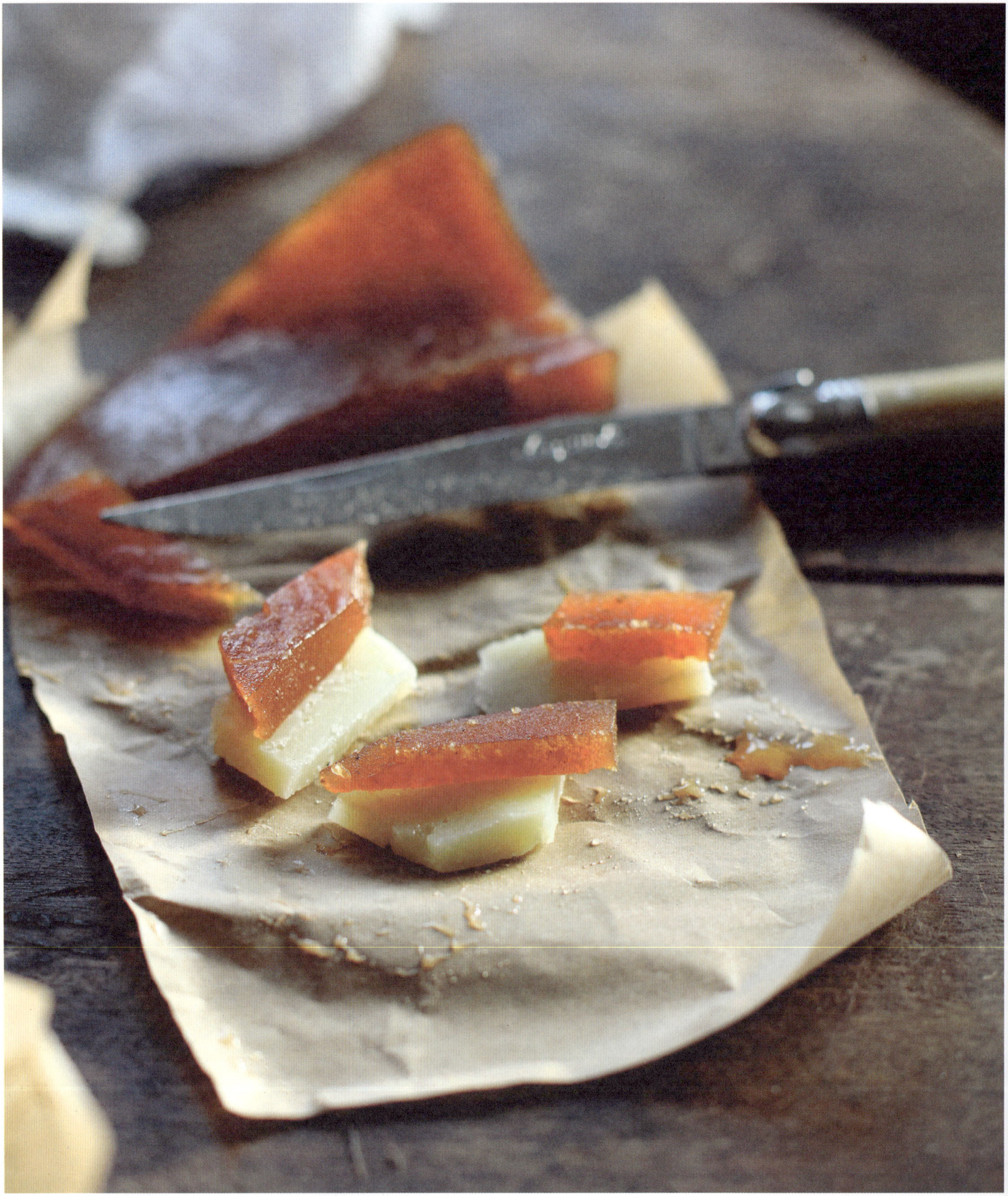

## CYDONIA OBLONGA
### True quince
Late spring flowers, early to late autumn fruit

*I've yet to find a true quince growing in a public place, other than the one I planted in Kings Heath community centre's garden, but I dare say there is one out there. The fruit ripens in late autumn and is the source of authentic membrillo (a Spanish quince paste). Use quinces the same way as their ornamental namesakes (see page 110).*

**How to recognise** This is a round tree or shrub, 5–8m, tall crowned with many crowded branches bearing dark green, broadly ovate leaves up to 10cm long with distinctly downy undersides. The flowers are solitary, shallow, bowl-shaped beauties appearing in late spring, white tinged with pink. The highly perfumed fruit is pear-shaped and very downy (this turns brown with age); they are pale green when young and ripen to a deep golden colour.

## MEMBRILLO

**Quinces or flowering quinces**
**Water**
**1 vanilla pod, split**
**Lemon juice and rind of 1 lemon, cut into strips**
**Granulated sugar**

Wash the quinces well, as they have a sticky coating that attracts all sorts of dirt, then chop them into quarters and remove all their pips – like many other rose family plants, the seeds contain nitrites that are converted into hydrogen cyanide in your stomach. Too many seeds can be toxic and result in death.

Place fruit in a large pan, adding just enough water to cover the fruit. Bring to a gentle boil and simmer until tender. This takes 20–30 minutes.

Strain the juice overnight to use for jelly (see opposite) and put the remaining pulp through a sieve or mouli, then add the vanilla, lemon juice, rind and sugar (the same weight of sugar as pulp). Return the pan to the heat and bring slowly to a boil, stirring constantly so that the sugar melts. Bring this to a rapid boil until it reaches setting point, when the paste will feel thick and scrape clean away from the sides of the pan. This takes between 30–45 minutes. Then take the pan off the heat and pour the paste onto greaseproof paper on baking trays to air-dry. If you have a dehydrator, use it at this stage.

The paste should be about 2cm thick. After several days, it should be slightly shiny and sticky to touch, but not moist. Wrap the paste in greaseproof paper and store it in an airtight container in the fridge. It will last many months kept like this.

### *Quince jelly*

To make jelly, you use the juice from the cooked quinces before processing the pulp for membrillo. Strain the juice through a jelly bag or muslin hung over a bowl overnight to drip. In the morning, measure the amount of juice and, for every 600ml (1 pint) of liquid, allow 450g (1lb) sugar.

Return the juice to the pan and add the sugar, stirring constantly until it has dissolved, then boil rapidly for setting point. Pour into clean, dry, hot jars, cover when cool and store. I like to add a little lemon rind to each jar to make a pleasing looking jelly. This jelly is good with meat or cheese.

## CRATAEGUS SPECIES
### Haws, hawthorns

Early to mid spring leaves and flowers,
early to mid autumn fruits, but do not eat the seeds

*Hawthorns grow in many parts of the globe. You find them wild in woodlands and planted as ornamental trees in parks and gardens, grown for their pretty spring flowers and attractive autumn fruits. Many are far larger than our native* Crataegus monogyna *which is, frankly, not the best to eat. Look out in parks for the much larger American haws* Crataegus arnoldiana *with red fruit or* C. missouriensis. *Other good species include* C. ellwangeriana *with crimson fruit, the tansy-leaved* C. tanacetifolia *with orange-yellow fruit and the red-fruited Midland hawthorn* C. laciniata.

**How to recognise** Hawthorns are mostly deciduous trees, 3–6m tall, but some are semi-evergreen, often with spiny stems. The leaves are alternate, simple or lobed and mid to dark green; some species have spectacular autumn colour. The spring flowers are pink or white, shallowly cup-shaped, appearing either singly or in clusters at the end of short, leafy shoots. Autumn fruits can be 6mm–3cm long, usually tones of red though they may be pink, yellow, black or bluish green. They have a fleshy exterior and bony, hard seeds that hang in small tight clusters and resemble nuts.

**What to eat** The leaves and young unopened flower buds of the hawthorn *Crataegus monogyna* are eaten in spring and known colloquially as 'bread and cheese' – they taste of neither but are pleasant enough. The fruit is rather more pleasing and is reputed to do wonders for the heart – some species taste lovely, others are just bland, you'll have to sample and see. None of the fruit will do you any harm, but don't eat the seeds as they may cause stomach upsets. The flesh is quite dry and dense and fruits should be picked when soft and slightly squishy. I mainly use the fruits in jams, fruit leathers and smoothies to bulk out supplies. They taste much like apples, sometimes a little more exotic. I mainly pick *C. laciniata*, which has deeply lobed diamond shaped leaves and bright red fruit.

## CHENOPODIUM ALBUM
## Fat hen, lamb's quarters

Early to late summer leaves, mid summer to early autumn flowers and seeds

*If you are going to start anywhere, start here. Fat hen is the easiest foraged food to love. It is delicious, and ancient with it. It was found in Tollund Man's stomach from 400 BC, and was superseded comparatively recently by cabbage and spinach. It is rich in vitamin A and C, far more nutritious and easier to grow than spinach, and still cultivated in Europe, India and parts of Africa.*

**How to recognise** You find fat hen in sunny sites on recently exposed ground, so it appears all over allotments, newly cultivated land and wasteland. It's usually growing in patches rather than scattered about, as this is how the seed falls. It loves recently fertilised ground and fresh manure.

Fat hen is an upright plant, from 40–100cm tall, with short branches of alternate leaves. Its distinguishing characteristic is the bright green fleshy leaf particularly prominent on the young foliage with a white mealy bloom that is water repellent. The underside of the leaves has a whitish coating and leaf shape is variable, but often goosefoot-shaped (which is how its gets its Latin name) with toothed margins. When you rub the leaves they have no smell, whereas the inedible species of this genus smell horrid. Flowers are small, nondescript and greyish-green and the plants often bow over with the weight of the seed.

**What to eat** Use young leaves just like spinach from early summer. I think it tastes best lightly cooked, allowing the leaves to wilt for around 4 minutes. It can also be steamed. In late summer, the flower heads can be used as a broccoli substitute. From late summer to early autumn, the seed can be collected and milled for flour, but you'd have to be really hungry!

Don't overdo it, if you harvest fat hen that has been growing on dung or other recently fertilised land, be particularly cautious about how much you eat as it can hold too much nitrogen and you'll get an upset stomach. Fat hen could possibly be confused with henbane, *Hyoscyamus niger*, which is a deadly poisonous plant, so take note of three important differences – henbane stinks, it's fetid-smelling; in summer, henbane will have lurid yellow purple-veined flowers; and most important as an indicator, henbane is sticky to touch and the stem and leaves are covered in hairs.

The Plant Directory

## CHENOPODIUM BONUS-HENRICUS
### Good King Henry
Mid spring to mid summer leaves, late spring flowers

*Good King Henry is good, really good, yet it's another plant we're more likely to ignore than acknowledge. It was once a cottage garden essential along with kales and cabbages, but now it's considered a weed. It may be a plant introduced by the Romans.*

**How to recognise** It's a perennial plant that gets around. You'll find it on neglected wasteland and in nitrogen-rich pasture, in farmland and by roadsides, along fences and in ditches. It is also associated with old sewage works (because the seed can persist in the soil for many years).

Large leaves 5–11cm long are distinctly triangular with wavy margins. The leaves are covered in characteristic mealy white bloom when young, and deepen to dark green with age. The flowers are lighter green and appear in clusters up the stem terminating in a leafless flower stalk covered in flowers.

**What to eat** In spring and early summer young flower shoots can be prepared and served like asparagus. From mid spring to mid summer you can treat the leaves like spinach. They keep their shape when cooked and can be used as wraps or stuffing. I think they are better cooked than raw, but a few young leaves in salads are acceptable. If you find the leaves too bitter soak them in salt water and drain and wash them before cooking, this will remove quite a lot of bitter flavour. Tempering them with a sweeter green, such as nettles or goosegrass, will also help.

**How to grow** Sow seeds in spring, in rich, well-drained soil in full sun. It's a handsome plant that can get to 120cm wide and 60cm tall.

## CORYLUS AVELLANA
### Hazelnut, cobnut
## CORYLUS MAXIMA
### Filbert
Mid to late summer nuts

*First, a little taxonomy: hazelnut is the term used for any species in the* Corylus *genus, cobnuts is an English name for* Corylus avellana. *A filbert is the cultivated species,* Corylus maxima, *grown for its larger nuts, but all those hazels that make up vast tracts of hedging and woodlands can also produce small, delicious hazelnuts. They usually do, but it's a battle to beat the squirrels to them. The best bet is to head into the city where the squirrels have yet to claim territory. I've been picking hazelnuts, or more correctly filberts, from* C. maxima 'Purpurea' *growing in my local cinema car park and I think I'm the only bit of wildlife to notice them.*

**How to recognise** *Corylus avellana* is a large, deciduous shrub with smooth reddish-brown peeling bark and young twigs covered in dense reddish, glandular hairs. The leaves are up to 10cm long, broadly heart-shaped, round tipped, toothed and mid green. Yellow catkins appear from late winter to early spring. Nuts are roundish, 2cm wide, and surrounded by a lobed green papery bract, clustered in twos, threes and fours.

*Corylus maxima* is an upright shrub or tree with heart-shaped, mid-green leaves, up to 14cm long; yellow catkins hang down in late winter and nuts in early autumn. The bract surrounds the entire nut with the lobes spreading past the shell. 'Purpurea' has dark purple foliage and purple-tinged catkins and fruit husks.

**What to eat** The nuts should be picked as soon as they look big enough. I chop them up and enjoy them in granola or on desserts.

**How to grow** *C. maxima* 'Purpurea' is probably the most attractive and fairly productive, though it grows up to 6m tall and 5m wide, so it needs space. You can coppice branches for hazel rods and pea sticks for plant supports, making it a useful addition to allotments and larger gardens.

Hazelnuts, cobnuts

## DIPLOTAXIS TENUIFOLIA
### Wild rocket, perennial wallrocket

Early spring to early winter leaves, early to mid summer flowers

*Wild rocket is perennial so, once you find a patch or get one established in your garden, you'll have greens pretty much all year round, particularly if you cover your rocket with a cloche between early winter and early spring, as its natural habitat is scrubland in the Mediterranean.*

*This rocket has a much stronger, spicier flavour than salad rocket and, towards the end of year, it can taste slightly bitter. I love it on top of a sourdough pizza.*

**How to recognise** I first came across this, walking along Regent's Canal in central London where it grows along the base of the walls. There's enough there to supply a small supermarket. It has widely naturalised around the British Isles and, now that more people are growing it in gardens, expect to see even more. It has much thinner and more deeply lobed leaves than salad rocket, they are usually dark green, sometimes grey-green. Pretty, pale-lemon yellow flowers are up to 20mm wide, cup-shaped when first opened. As the plant matures, it has a woody basal rosette, but the young leaves just sprout from the ground.

Don't confuse it with ragwort and groundsel that can look similar when mature, but they both have an unpleasant smell when crushed.

**What to eat** The leaves become tougher as the year goes on. I tend to use them in soups when they get older, added at the last minute and cooked briefly or they're bitter. The flowers are a pretty addition to salads.

**How to grow** If you leave it, you'll have it forever as it self-seeds everywhere. Or sow seed *in situ* or in seed trays in spring and thin seedlings to 20cm apart. Give it a shear in mid summer to keep it in shape or it will flop all over the place.

---

## EPILOBIUM MONTANUM
### Broad-leaved willowherb

Mid autumn to early spring leaves

*Several willowherbs are edible, including hoary and square-stalked forms, but I only rate the taste of the broad-leaved. It tastes, to all intents and purposes, just like corn salad, which I grow masses of for winter salads. Willowherb tastes almost the same when young so, once again what can be found naturally trumps all my efforts as a gardener. You can find it all over the place – in gardens, allotments, on bare ground, growing in cracks of pavements, on old walls and covering wasteground.*

**How to recognise** It is a perennial weed that grows 30–60cm tall in flower. Gardeners will recognise it from its extensive spreading horizontal white roots. In early stages, the basal growth is fleshy, glossy and dark green and the leaves are in opposite pairs, 4–10cm long, sometimes in whorls, oval-broad to lanceolate with a short stalk and a round base. The flower stem is erect and the 6–9mm wide four-petalled flowers are rosy pink.

**What to eat** The very young growth is surprisingly hardy and these leaves make a good addition to winter salads. Once the leaves get older in late spring, forget them as they become unpleasantly bitter.

wild rocket

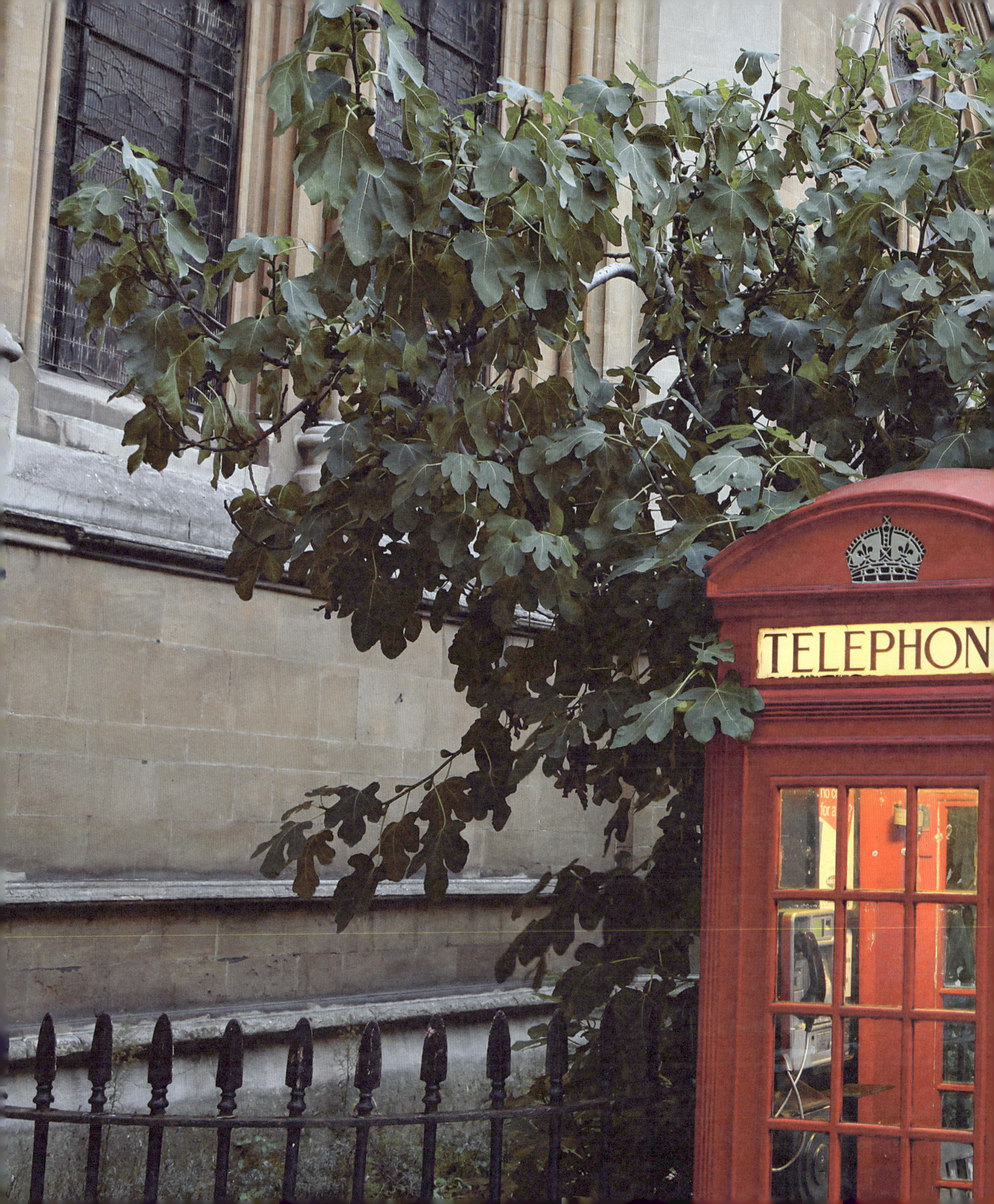
TELEPHON

fig

## FICUS CARICA
### Fig
Early autumn fruit

*I love unexpected finds, like a fig on the corner of Bloomsbury Square, its feet firmly in the church ground, probably supping up the buried and fruiting in great plenty. Even though figs hail from Mediterranean climes, they do very well in cooler parts, particularly in cities where the ambient temperature is high, so good for germination and growth. Once you start looking, you'll see lovely great big figs popping up all over the place. They do best with restricted roots, they like the restrictive corners and cramped spaces that cities tend to offer. The fruit ripens in late summer.*

**How to recognise** Figs are deciduous trees, often multi-branched with a spreading head and rounded 3–5 lobed grey-green leaves, up to 10–25cm long, with a heart-shaped base. Fruit are up to 10cm long, green when young and maturing to dark brown, purple or green, depending on the variety.

**What to eat** Fresh is best, heaven indeed, but fig preserve is quite a heady thing. Figs are high in pectin and natural sugars, so add lemon if you need a hint of acid in all that sweetness.

**Note** The sap from the tree can be an eye irritant.

## FOENICULUM VULGARE
### Herb fennel
Early spring to early summer leaves, early to mid autumn seeds

*Fennel adorns the banks of motorways, turns up on canal sides and in disused and forgotten spaces. Native to the Mediterranean, it's a garden escapee that is as happy along coastal clifftops as in inner city plots. It likes to bake in the sun and does very well in poor soils.*

**How to recognise** Its blue-green stem and feathery leaves have a very distinct aniseed smell and its umbels of bright yellow flowers are very popular with bees, followed by distinctly ridged ovate-oblong seeds, 4–6mm long. This short-lived perennial is not the same as the bulb fennel you buy in shops, it's a tall herb up to 180cm high with erect striated stems that are hollow when old.

**What to eat** The young foliage can be used in salads, sauces or as a garnish. Whole stems can be used when cooking fish, particularly oily fish, such as salmon or mackerel. Lay the stems under the fish and wrap in tinfoil – the whole fish will be imbued with a gentle anise flavour. Seeds can be used in making bread, for flavouring liqueurs, cakes and savoury dishes. Rub pork skin with a lot of fennel seed, salt and a little lemon and roast slowly for an exceptional dish. Gather the brownish seeds in autumn on a dry day, and continue to dry them completely indoors.

**How to grow** Fennel will self-seed merrily, so one source is to ask someone with plants. Otherwise, sow the seed in spring in pots or in good, fertile soil. Fennel loves the sun and needs to bake to be happy. The variety 'Purpureum' has bronze-purple foliage that goes grey with age.

herb fennel

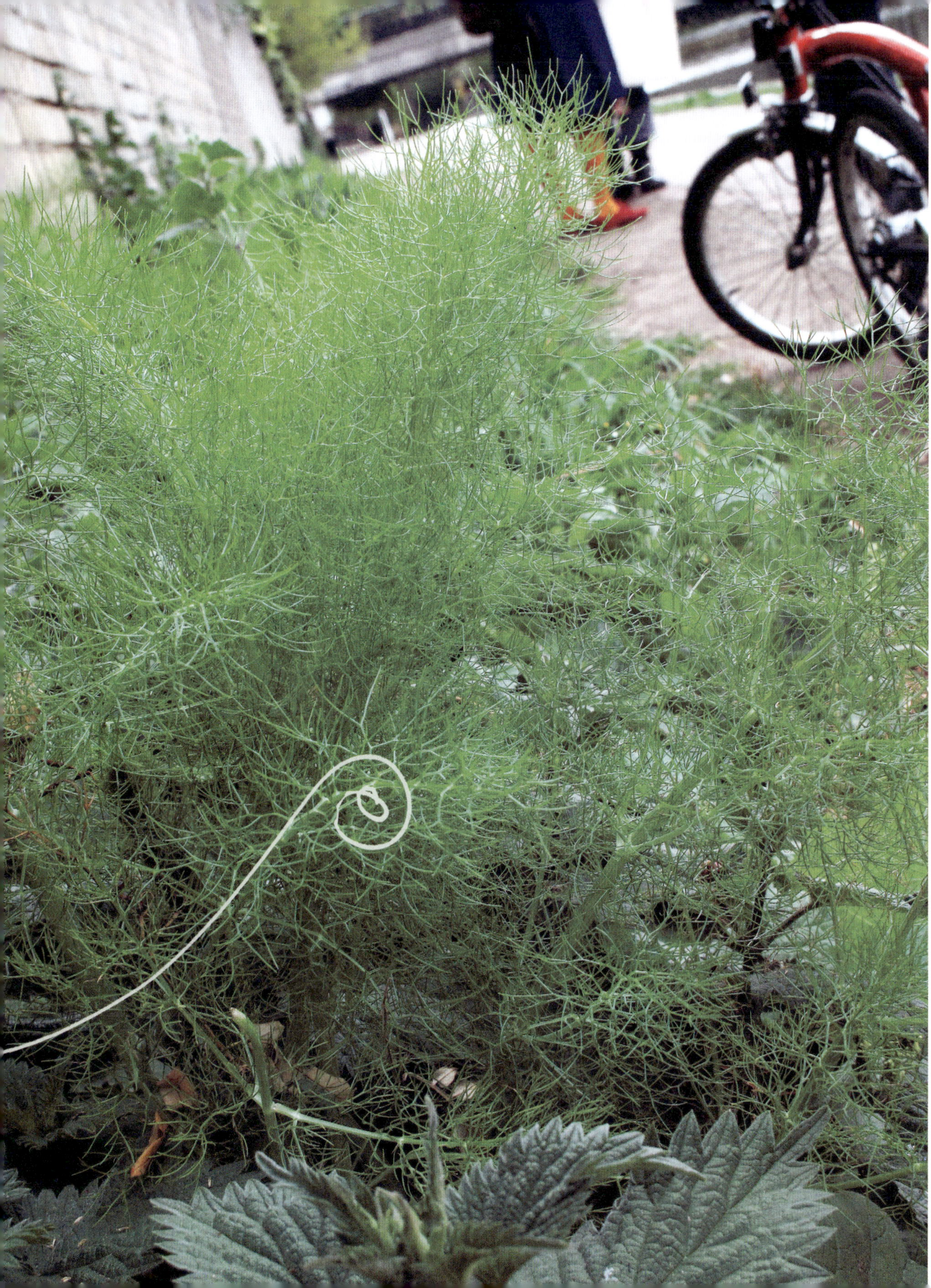

## FRAGARIA VESCA
### Alpine strawberry

Early to mid spring leaves, late spring to early summer fruit

*The charm of this tiny berry is both its fragrance (hence its Latin name) and its intense strawberry flavour. You can cultivate wild strawberries in the garden, they make a good ground cover for shadier areas under trees, but fruit best in the sun. There are several cultivated forms with slightly larger berries or without runners – a happy wild strawberry will quickly take over bare ground. I have wild strawberries growing in my local park, but the best I found were growing in very thin soil over rocks in Norway. The berries were quite dry, but the flavour was extraordinary.*

**How to recognise** The wild strawberry looks like a skinnier version of its cultivated counterpart. It's perennial and, with age, the roots and stem can become woody. It produces large numbers of stolons (runners) on very thin arching stems. The leaves are a distinctive trifoliate shape (three leaflets up to 6.5cm long) with toothed margins, forming a basal rosette. The flower stems are upright, up to 30cm tall, and reach just above the leaves. Flowers are open-faced, sometimes with the sepals pointing backwards, with white petals up to 1.8cm across. The fruit is bright red, 1–2cm long.

You'll find wild strawberries in woodlands, grasslands, hedge banks and scrub, mostly on dry ground. Make a note early in the season when you find a colony, as they can become swamped by larger plants and hard to see.

**What to eat** The fruit is clearly the best bit of this plant, but the young leaves are said to be fairly high in Vitamin C and can be eaten raw or used in tea; one recommendation is to spice the tea; with dried lemon rind and honey. The leaves are an important source of food for certain butterflies, so do not over pick.

FUCHSIA SPECIES
## Fuchsia
Early to late summer flowers, early to mid autumn fruits

*Fuchsias are my 'on the way to the shops' snack. There are so many in front gardens around here that, come autumn, there's always a small bounty to be collected. The fruits taste rather odd, a little like watery honey with a peppery twist. I find them rather moreish, though the pepper taste gets you if you eat too many. Many fuchsia fruit well, but the largest berries are from* Fuchsia magellanica *which are often used as bedding plants in municipal plantings.*

**How to recognise** Fuchsias are a deciduous shrub, growing up to 3m tall; in warmer areas it often keeps its foliage through winter. It has ovate, scalloped to toothed leaves, 1–6cm long, that are often tinged red on their undersides. The bright pink and red tubular pendant flowers are easy to recognise, loved by bees and produced all summer long.

**What to eat** The obvious flowers are edible but not particularly tasty. The oblong fruit is a little more hidden and the berries are best when they darken to a purplish red. Unripe berries are tasteless, so wait until they are ripe and a little squishy. I've never found enough berries to process, so just snack on them or use them as a garnish for puddings (delicious with good vanilla ice cream). You can use them in fruit leathers and fuchsia is supposed to make a very good jam.

**How to grow** They grow pretty much anywhere in surprisingly poor soils and aren't bothered whether they are in full sun or partial shade. They are not completely hardy (though my front-garden specimen survived a very white winter) and it's best to plant a fuchsia so that the base of the stem is below the soil and mulch well in winter. If the frost does take the plant out, the base will resprout and the dead stems will act as a little extra frost protection. Overgrown specimens can be hacked and will merrily resprout. It's pretty hard to kill this plant, so just prune it to keep it a shape you like.

The Plant Directory

goosegrass

## GALIUM APARINE
### Goosegrass, sticky willie, cleavers, scratch tongue
Mid to late spring stems

*Goosegrass is that sticky plant that you use to chuck at your friend's back as a kid to watch it stick – apparently Velcro was based on it. The plant has tiny hooked hairs that allow it to stick to animals' coats so that the stems and seeds travel to new ground and goosegrass can take over new territory. It's also a wonderful spring vegetable and is found in grassy places, roadsides, margins and growing along fences.*

**How to recognise** Its scrambling stems are set with distinct, recurved prickles along the angled stem. The leaves are narrow, linear and set around the stem, which easily breaks into segments. The flowers are nondescript, followed by greenish or purplish round seeds, up to 6mm wide with white hooked prickles.

**What to eat** You need to eat the stems very young before the plant sets seed and becomes tough. Pick shoots up to 10cm long and steam or wilt them in butter and add a little grated nutmeg or pepper. I love to mix them with nettles. They work well in omelettes and are a good ingredient for stone soup (*see page 82*).

## GEUM URBANUM
### Herb Bennet, wood avens, clove-root
Early to late spring and early autumn leaves,
late spring to early winter roots

*Herb Bennet is a common wildflower of woodlands and damp, shady places and, as its Latin name suggests, it's equally happy in the city. Although its leaves are edible, its main use is for its roots – when you cook them they impart a wonderful clove flavour. I'd go as far as to say that they are better than cloves, the flavour is more subtle and permeates the food better, particularly with apples.*

**How to recognise** Herb Bennet is a perennial that can grow 30–60cm, but is often much smaller. The stems are wiry, slightly branching and erect, covered with small hairs. The basal leaves grow on longer stalks and are interruptedly pinnate, meaning that there are irregular spaces between the leaflets. The terminal leaflet is large and club-shaped, the smaller leaflets are rounder and not uniform in size. The flowers look rather like nondescript buttercups, the fruit is round and bristly and looks like a dark red burr. Like goosegrass, it gets caught in clothes and animal fur. Herb Bennet flowers and fruits all summer long, making it a useful nectar source for pollinators.

**What to eat** The young leaves can be used as steamed or boiled greens, they tend to be a little hairy in a salad. I use it for its roots – they can be used wherever a recipe calls for cloves. They are rather small and wiry and right at the base of the plant is a small tuber, but even a little handful will give a good clove flavour to dishes. The fresh roots smell faintly of clover, the smell intensifies with drying. It is said that dried roots were placed amongst clothes to keep moths away.

You will need five or six large plants to gather a handful of roots to tie together and add to the cooking pot. First, they must be cleaned. Young plants will give you a number of white roots, the ones from older plants turn brown and you may have to scrape them before using them. Remove the bundle of roots once the dish is cooked, or once you get to them in a pie.

Herb Bennet

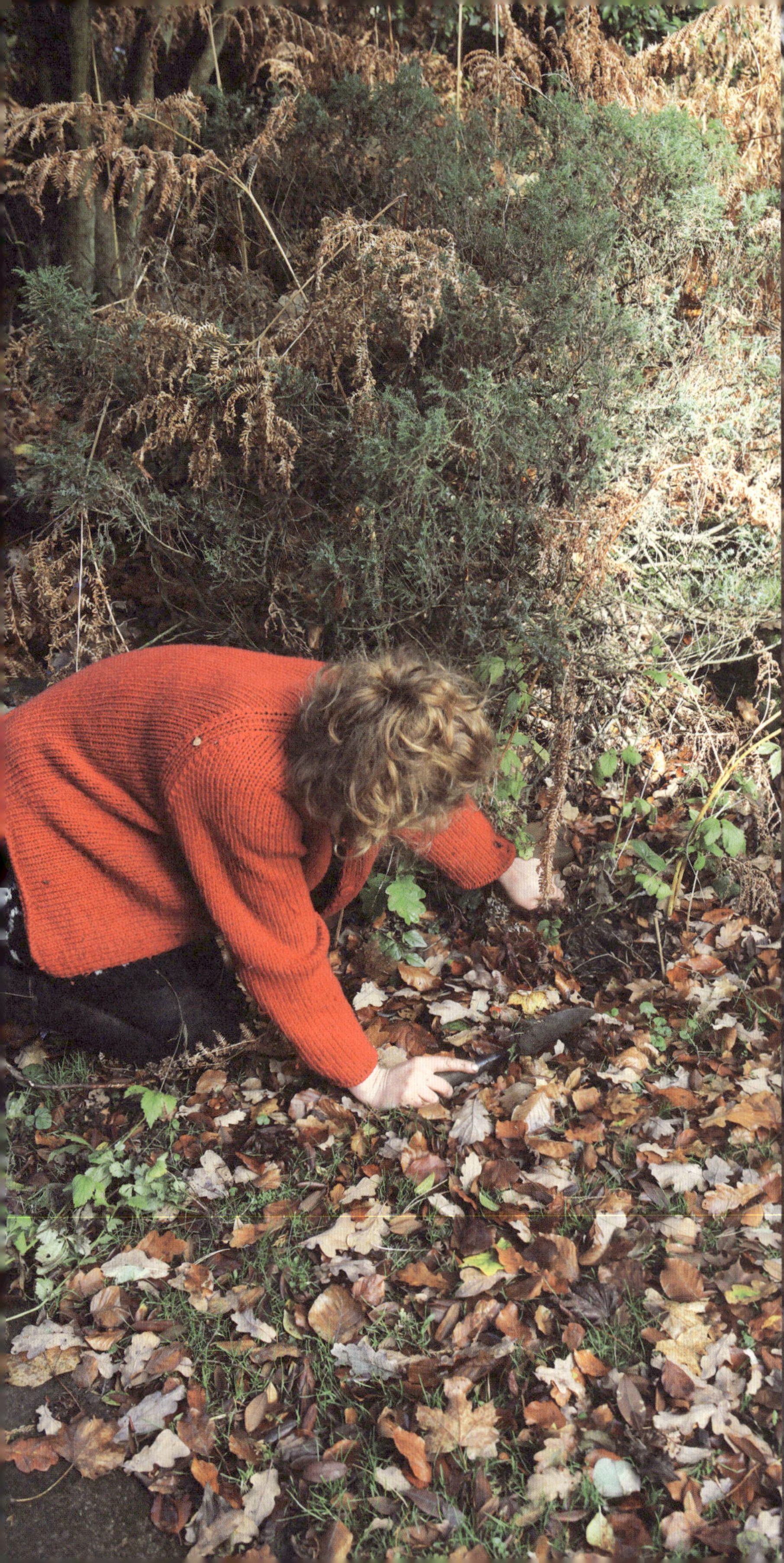
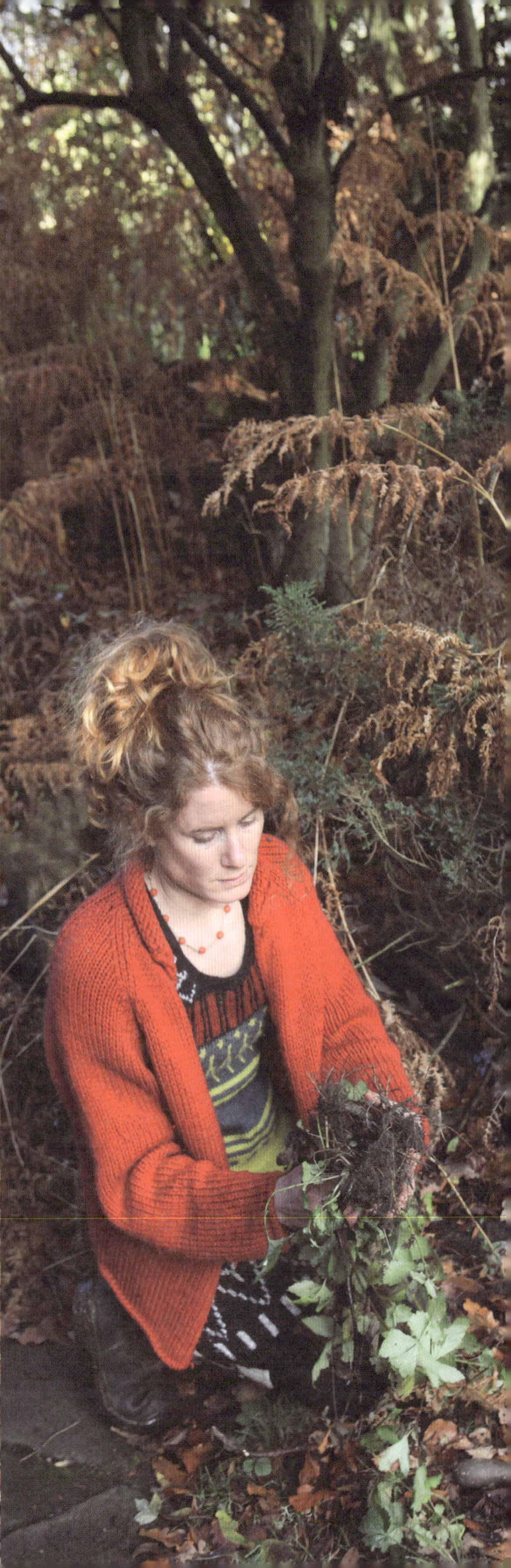

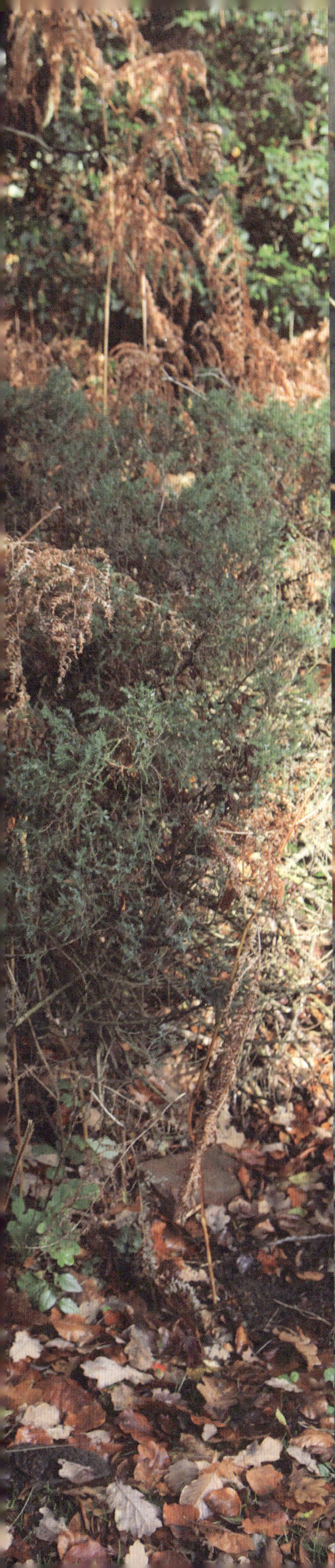

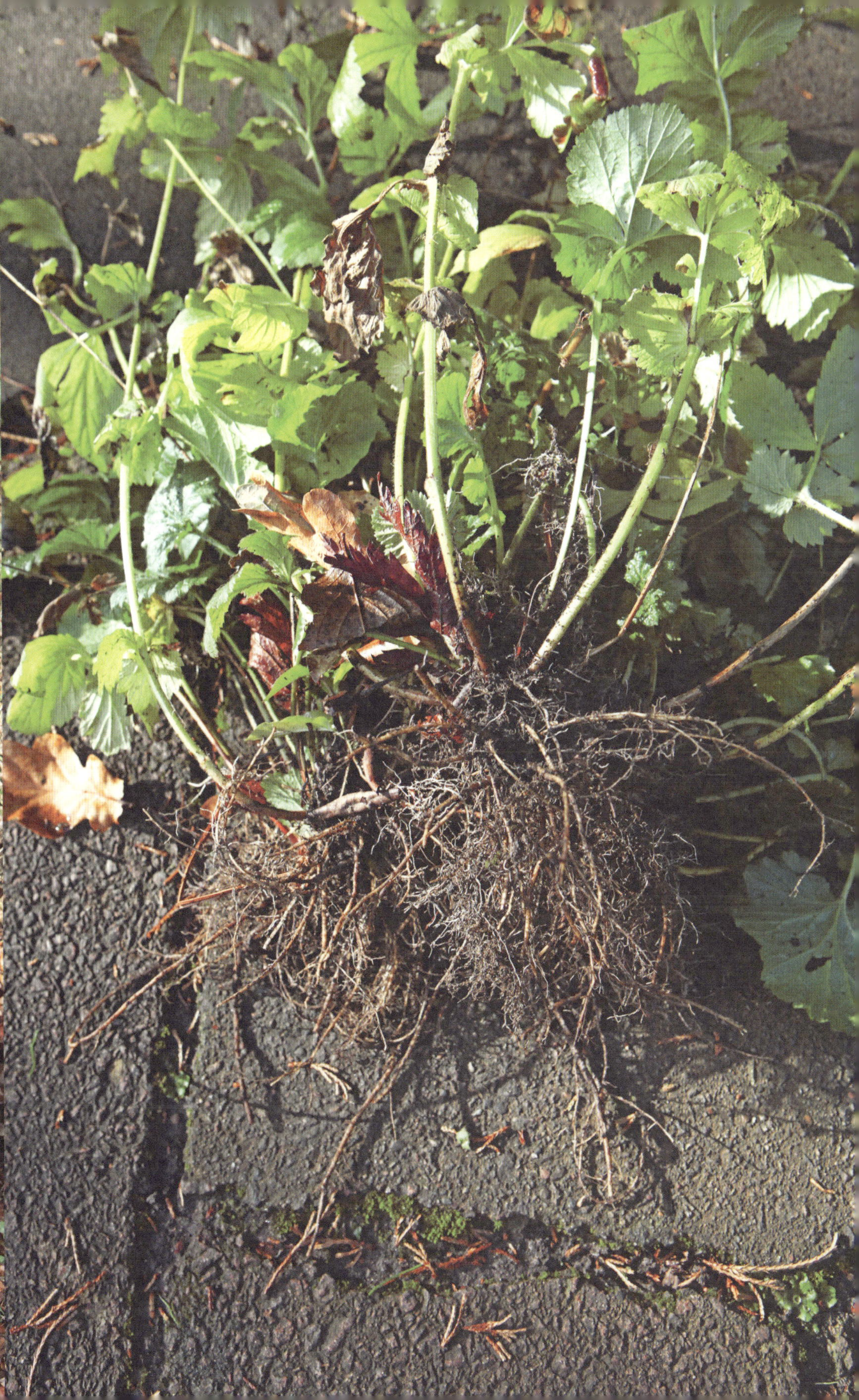

## GINKGO BILOBA
### Maidenhair tree
Early to mid autumn fruit

*The maidenhair tree is extinct in the wild. It is also a living fossil, meaning that those ginkgos you find in fossil form are identical to the living species, as it hasn't evolved over thousands of years. Remarkably, it's very good at surviving atmospheric pollution, so it is often planted as a street tree. The female plant produces nuts that are delicious, but have a fleshy outer coating that smells just like baby puke or worse. Every once in a while you'll find a street with a female tree close enough to a male to be pollinated, and the pavement will be littered with yellow plum-like fruits, stinking to high heaven. Be wise, get gloves and get collecting.*

**How to recognise** This is a tall, deciduous upright tree with furrowed, dull grey bark; trees often reach 20–35m. The leaves are very distinct, they are flat, fan-shaped, yellowish green, turning a wonderful butter yellow in autumn. They are up to 12cm across, lobed at the tip, and taper into a stalk with prominent ribs. The fruit is yellowish green and plum-like with a pale nut inside.

**What to eat** Roast the pale nut in a little olive oil and peel it to reveal a yellow fleshy inside that tastes both nutty and cheese-like – a little like cooked Swiss cheese, and very moreish. But first you must clean them. This requires rubber gloves, a bucket and holding your breath! The fleshy outer coating can be sluiced off in hot water and then you will need numerous washings to get rid of any further flesh and a good scrub to remove the smell. Eventually, you will be left with a smooth, pale nut, about 1cm long. The shell of the nut is very thin.

## HEMEROCALLIS SPECIES
### Daylily
Early to late summer flowers

*Daylilies are so called because their flowers last a single day before withering. There are literally hundreds of cultivars and the jury is out as to whether all daylilies are edible, so go easy and don't eat them everyday. The flowers and unopened buds are much prized in Chinese cuisine where the double orange-yellow* Hemerocallis fulva 'Flore Pleno' *is used widely. I prefer the yellow and orange varieties to reds.* Hemerocallis *are found in gardens and often used as low-maintenance plants for bedding schemes in parks and other municipal areas, but make sure that they haven't been sprayed before picking. Clearly it's not very sociable to go and remove a load of flowers from a park's display and, in this situation I pick the dried, spent flowers so I get something for my pot and the park gets some free deadheading.*

**How to recognise** Daylilies are clump-forming perennials with long, arching strap-like leaves, 70–100cm long, though there are also dwarf varieties less than half that size. The flowers start trumpet-shaped with six petals on erect, sometimes branching stalks and they appear from late spring to late summer, depending on the variety.

**What to eat** Unopened flowerbuds can be steamed or stir-fried and used much like green beans in salads or as a side dish. The open flowers can be used in salads and the dried flowers, called 'golden needles' in Chinese, can be used to thicken soups. The best way to eat the flowers is to pick off the spent flowers from the plant and dry them rather than trying with fresh. You can dry unopened flowers buds to store, but they will need to be soaked for a while before cooking. There is a pest called the Hemerocallis gall midge that lays its eggs inside the unopened flowerbuds and these hatch into tiny maggots, but you can usually tell if there's a problem because the buds are slightly swollen and, when you open them up, they are mushy inside.

maidenhair tree

### IMPATIENS GLANDULIFERA
# Himalayan balsam

Late summer to early autumn flowers and seeds

*This is an invasive weed introduced as a garden plant from the Himalayas in the mid-nineteenth century. A pretty one, but a menace, particularly along waterways where it will quickly colonise banks and muscle out other plants. The pink flowers resemble orchids and plants reach 2m in one season, but it's not just the rapid growth that makes it so successful, it is the plant's amazing seed distribution mechanism. The seed pods literally explode, flinging the seeds up to 7m away. It is found in damp places, wasteground, woodland and along riverbanks.*

**How to recognise** It's a tall, upright annual with reddish stems and red lanceolate toothed leaves, 5–23cm long, in whorls of three. The leaves smell musty when crushed. The flowers are 3–4cm long, pink to purplish pink, speckled with a distinct hood to the back of the flowers. The seed pod is 2–3cm long and inflated – when ripe, it explodes open and showers grey to brown seeds far and wide.

**What to eat** The whole pod can be eaten before they explode, but I eat the ripe seeds that taste both peppery and nutty. The seeds can be added to breads or toasted, but make sure they're completely dry before you store them. I've found the easiest way to collect large amounts is to place a plastic bag over the entire head of flowers and then shake the plant so the ripe seed pods explode.

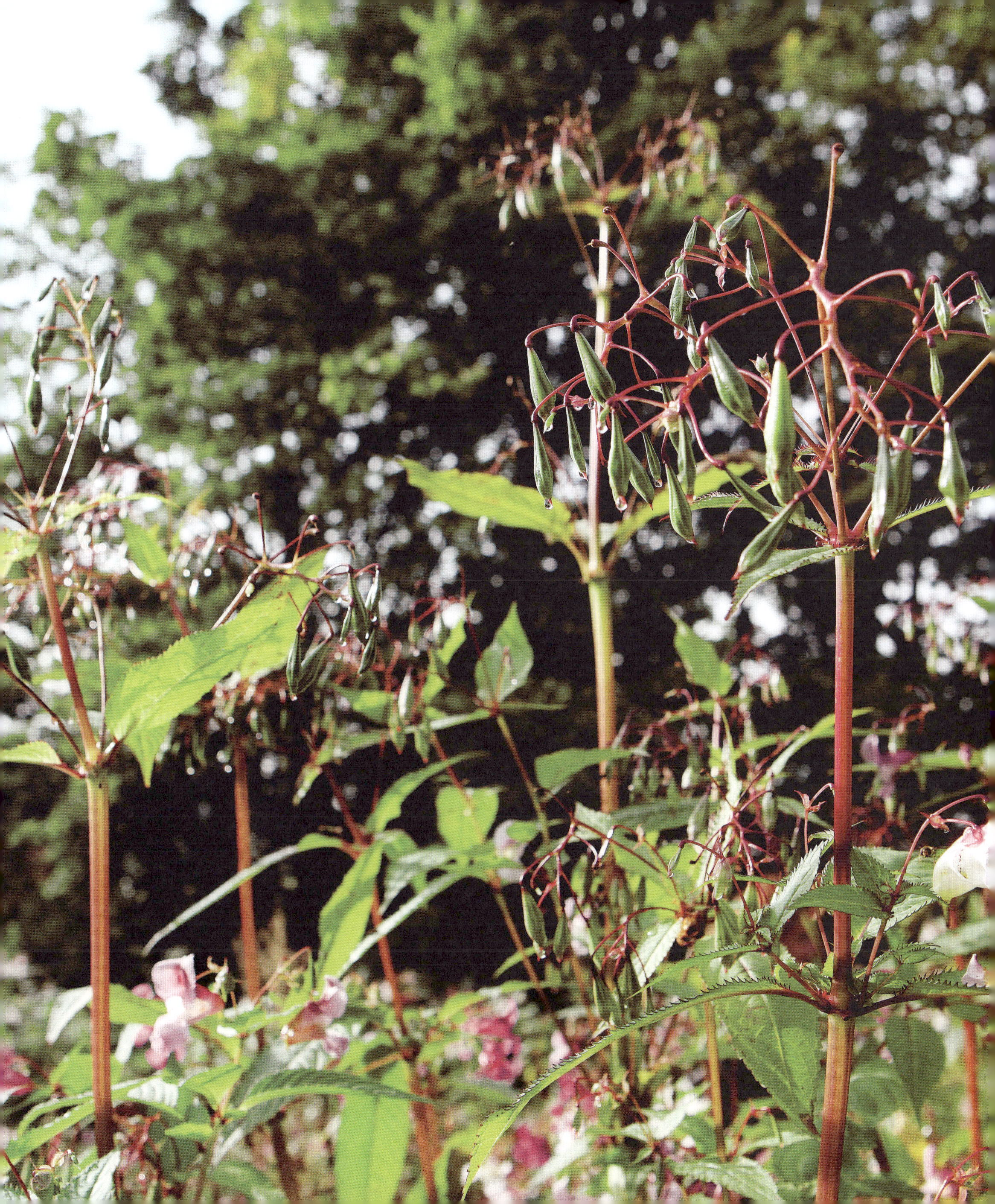

## JUGLANS REGIA
# Walnut
Early summer and early autumn fruit

*These walnuts (in the main photo) are growing around a housing estate in town. The estate has its fair share of problems, around the tree were dirty nappies, needles, various bits of junk and hundreds of walnuts. Picking the walnuts (staying clear of those on the ground) was made possible by someone who had prised apart the bars of the railings, I still can't quite imagine how someone had the strength to do that. I'm also bemused by why there are so many walnuts around this estate. Walnuts are not a typical municipal plant, as the trees have an allelopathic effect on other plants, which means that their rotting leaves and their roots produce a chemical known as juglone that retards the growth of other plants. That's why walnuts have little or nothing growing under them. Was this some altruistic planting in the late eighties by some landscape architect? I suppose it might have been an enlightened attempt at cutting down weeding, or perhaps they were planted by someone living there.*

*Originally from Southern Europe, walnuts are widely planted around Britain, seedlings sometimes appear in unlikely places, thanks to squirrels burying the nuts.*

**How to recognise** It's a large tree, up to 30m tall, with grey, distinctly furrowed bark. Large pinnate leaves, up to 30cm long, have 5–9 elliptic, glossy leaflets with prominent midribs and veins. The leaflets are a glossy bronze when young. The leaves are highly aromatic when crushed. But mostly you know when you're near a walnut because you start to see discarded nut cases on the ground. The nuts are contained in a fleshy outer husk, which is bright green and blends in rather well with the leaves.

**What to eat** The nuts are hidden inside a fleshy green case that smells bitter. This outer husk turns everything, including your fingers, a dark blackish brown. It's not surprising then, that the husks are the source of a rich brown natural dye, so rich in tannins that you don't need to add anything else to fix the colour. I leave the fruit outside and the weather tends to rot the cases off (but watch out for squirrels getting hold of your bounty). Walnuts are a natural source of manganese, which is important in maintaining healthy cells, strong bones and keeping your blood sugar levels normal.

Squirrels are your biggest enemy with walnuts. They'll start picking them in mid summer and, by early autumn, there won't be a single one left. That's why truly urban trees are best, as the squirrels are more interested in skip-diving than collecting nuts. Once the nuts are completely dry, they'll store for several months, but they must be really dry or they'll go mouldy. The nuts are much smaller than commercial ones, but taste delicious milky and flavoursome. I like to use mine in granola, salads and my mother's walnut cake. You can pickle green walnuts too, but you have to pick them in early summer before the nuts begin to harden, I've never managed to pick them early enough.

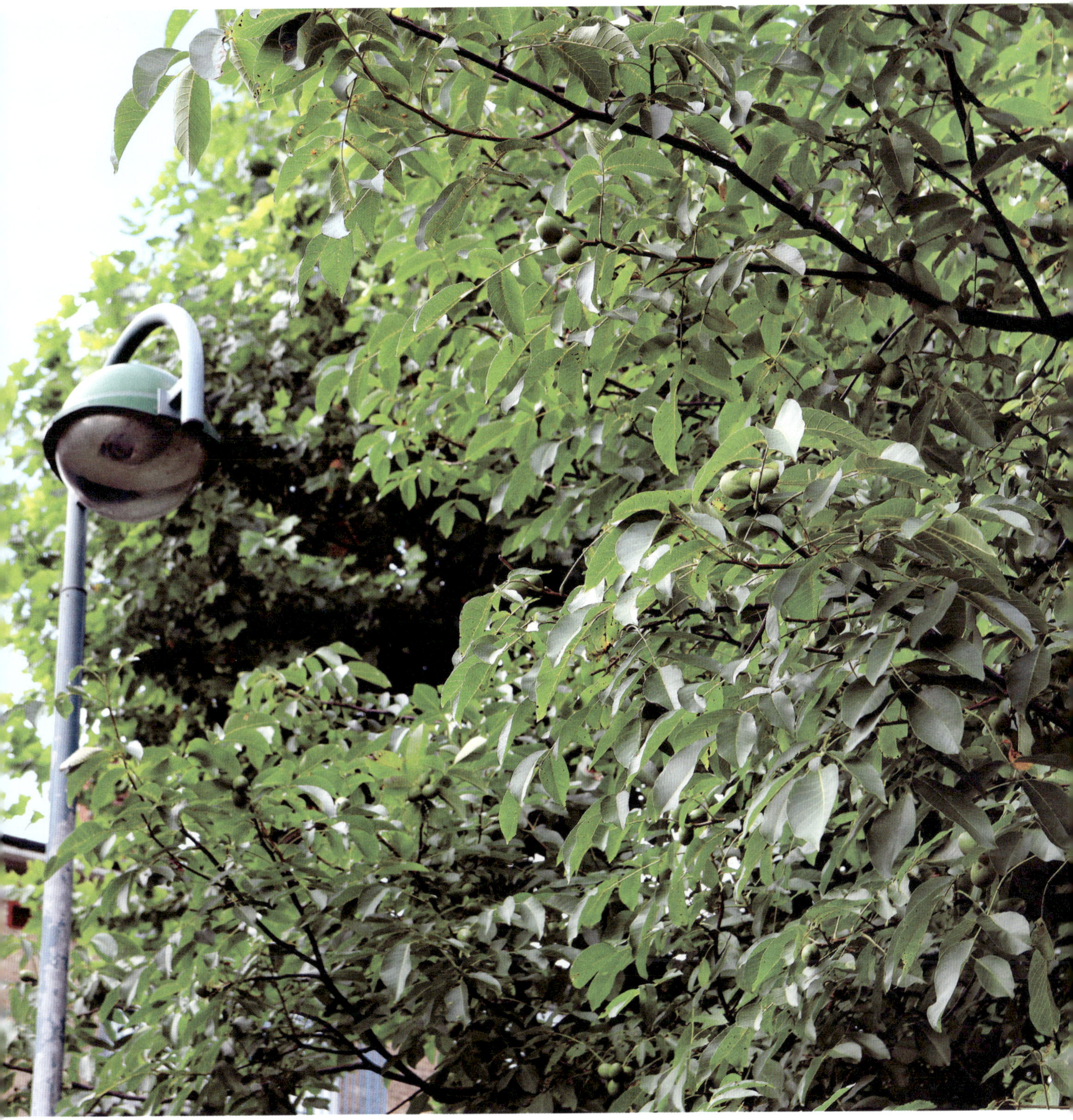

## LAMIUM SPECIES
### Archangel, deadnettle
Late spring to early summer, late summer to early autumn leaves

*At first glance, deadnettles look remarkably similar to stinging nettles, but they don't sting and, once you recognise the flower, it's very easy to tell the two apart. Deadnettles are found growing alongside nettles, cow parsley and garlic mustard. They are at home in hedge banks, verges and slopes, on the edges of woods, waste places, roadsides and gardens.*

**How to recognise** The flowers are two-lipped and hooded and arranged in a whorl around the stem. The stems are also distinctly square-shaped (an identifying characteristic for the mint family). White deadnettle, *Lamium album*, is a hairy perennial that creeps along the ground rooting wherever the stems touch soil. The stems are upright, 15–65cm tall. The leaves are opposite, ovate, with a heart-shaped base and a toothed margin. They look like nettles but are paler. Flowers are white, the upper lip is hood-like, and the lower lip has one large and two smaller lobes. Red deadnettle, *Lamium purpureum*, is a small annual, no more than 25cm high with upright stems that branch outward. The leaves are coarsely toothed and flowers are pinkish-purple.

Henbit, *Lamium amplexicaule*, is another small annual, up to 25cm high, with rounder leaves than red deadnettle but similar pinkish-purple flowers. The leaf margin is bluntly toothed.

Yellow archangel, *Lamium galeobdolon*, looks very like white deadnettle but with yellow flowers – although equally edible, its leaves have a distinctly unpleasant smell when you crush them.

**What to eat** All four species should be picked young, before flowering, when no more than about 10cm tall. These greens are mild, tender and juicy and can be used raw in salads (though some people aren't keen on the slightly furry texture of the leaves) or cooked as greens. Some chopped chives or spring onions make a lovely addition to serve as a side dish, or use these greens to bulk out supplies with other wild greens. They're excellent in stone soup, or as mild greens for salsa verde and green sauce.

## LEUCANTHEMUM VULGARE
### Marguerite, ox-eye daisy

Early to mid spring leaves and young shoots, early to mid summer flowers

*The large daisy flowers of the ox-eye daisy flood motorway banks in mid summer; you find them in pastures and meadows and they are a main species in many wildflower mixes. The flowers are edible, but don't really taste of anything much, however the young leaves pack a punch with a strong perfumed flavour.*

**How to recognise** This perennial grows 60–100cm tall in full sun – its creeping rhizomes sit just under the soil. The basal leaves are ovate to paddle-shaped with loosely toothed margins, while stem leaves are longer and thinner. You'll probably know the flowers, they're 2.5–5.5cm wide with a bright orange centre and white ray florets (petals).

**What to eat** The middle of the flower is hard and bitter, so I only use the white petals to decorate salads or soups. The flowers can be used to brew some sort of country wine, a bit like dandelion wine, but I've never tried. You can eat the young leaves raw, but the flavour is a bit overpowering, so use sparingly. I think it's best to use the young shoots and leaves much like you might use chrysanthemum greens in Chinese cooking – boil them for around 10 minutes and then stir into soups, stews or stir-fries. They are also good dressed with strong vinaigrette, using red wine or lemon juice to counteract the perfumed flavour.

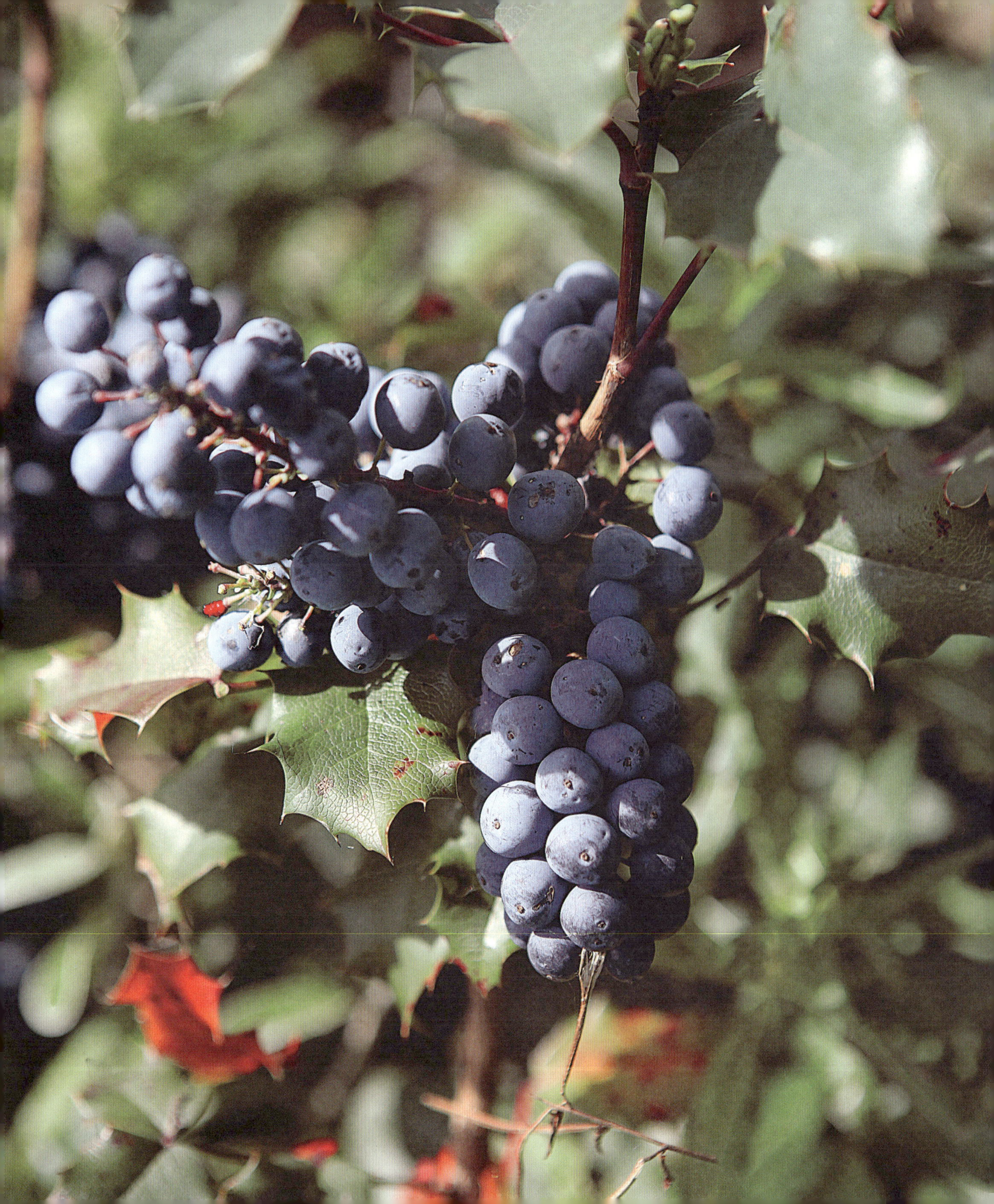

## MAHONIA SPECIES
Early to late winter flowers, mid to late summer fruit

*All Mahonia species are edible, long-used for jams and juices in their native homes. They are evergreen woodland plants with yellow winter flowers – often highly scented – followed by dusky purple fruit with intense dark juices.* Mahonia x media *and* Mahonia japonica *tend to get planted in parks, car parks and around offices.* Mahonia aquifolium *is popular in council schemes, as its suckering habit means that it quickly forms a tall ground covering. Sometimes, you'll find* Mahonia nervosa, *the Oregon grape, with the roundest grape-like berries. It looks very like* Mahonia aquifolium *but usually fruits later, around early autumn.*

### MAHONIA AQUIFOLIUM
**Oregon hollygrape, Holly barberry**

*Oregon hollygrape jelly is the jam of my husband's home. It's an intense, deeply dark jelly, both tart and sweet and so good in peanut butter jelly sandwiches. You have to be quick to beat the birds to the berries.*

**How to recognise** This is a hardy, evergreen shrub with an open, suckering habit. It is most identifiable by its large spiny, pinnate, bright green leaves, up to 30cm long, that may turn a wonderful reddish-purple in winter. In earliest spring the pale, lemon-yellow flowers appear in clusters and smell wonderful. From mid summer the berries appear, long clusters of grape-shaped, dark blue-black berries that burst bright red flesh when you squeeze them.

**What to eat** Even when they're fully ripe, the acidic berries are too bitter to eat raw – they should be cooked into pies, jellies and jams. The flowers are edible, but bitter. The fruit needs to be picked and processed into jam or jelly very quickly, and it stains everything. It's very low in pectin so either add crab apples or add liquid pectin, following the usual jam making rules. You can also make an Oregon grape cordial, which tastes a bit like blackcurrant cordial. Because of the low sugar content, it will need to be frozen if you want to store it – it's a very sharp cordial, I use 350–400g (just under 1lb) of granulated sugar to 600ml (1 pint) of fruit. If that's still too sharp, try mixing it with concentrated apple juice to sweeten it.

The Plant Directory

MALUS SPECIES
# Apple, crab apple
Late summer to early winter fruit

*Cultivated apples are everywhere, on street corners, along the edges of motorways, along railway lines, in parks and hedges. Wherever someone has thrown an apple core, an apple will spring, given half a chance. Many suburbs are built on old orchard sites, and you can often find the remains to pick, one tree from one garden, another from another.*

*The crab apple,* Malus sylvestris, *is the wild counterpart to the domestic apple. They may have thorny branches and vary in size, but they are always smaller than cultivated apples. One of the largest, and fairly commonly planted, is the* 'Wisley Crab', *its fruit the size of small apples and brilliantly red with red flesh. These red crabs make excellent jellies and fruit leathers. Crab apples are ideal for small gardens. Purple-leaved forms must be grown in full sun, but others don't mind a bit of shade.*

**How to recognise** When you cut a crab apple across its circumference, it will have a star shape with pips in the star – if you cut a similar looking fruit and it has a stone-like seed, it's not a crab but a haw. Crab apples are very common, as birds and mammals distribute their seeds; they appear in most ancient woodlands, in old hedgerows and along roads. Many are planted for their ornamental value, for their lovely blossom and pretty fruit. 'Profusion' has dark red flowers and red crabs, 'John Downie' has orange-yellow fruit, and the golden yellow fruits of 'Golden Hornet' stay on the tree for months. 'Red Siberian' and 'Yellow Siberian' crab apples are particularly good eaters.

Flowers are sometimes scented and appear either singly or in groups. The flowers are shallowly cupped with five petals, though some cultivars are double. The leaves are alternate, oval to ovate with toothed margins.

**What to eat** Crab apples are naturally high in pectin, so if you are making jam with a fruit that is low in pectin, a few crab apples will sort that out and save you buying liquid pectin. But crab apples are so much more than practical pectin providers – they are wonderful baked with lots of sugar, and make fine jellies and cheeses in their own right. I like to make spicy crab apple jelly and fruit cheese by adding fresh cayenne peppers, which are wonderful with strong cheeses or meats. I make a fine winter tipple by flavouring vodka with a spiced crab apple mix, adding cinnamon, cloves, vanilla, ginger and sugar. And I use them to bulk out fruit leathers.

## SPICY SIBERIAN CRAB APPLE JELLY

2kg (about 4lb) crab apples (red or golden-yellow for the best colour)
1 heaped teaspoon of grated ginger
Granulated sugar
3 fresh cayenne peppers (or more, depending on their heat), deseeded and cut into strips

Wash and cut the apples in half and put into a heavy-based pan with just enough water to cover them. Add the grated ginger and simmer gently until the apples are tender. I tend to use a potato masher to mash up the apples at this point.

Remove from the heat and strain through a jelly bag (or clean pillowcase) overnight as for standard jelly-making. It's really important not to squeeze the pulp or you'll get a cloudy jelly and, although it will taste lovely, half the joy of this one is its jewel-like colour when you hold it up to the light.

In the morning, measure the liquid and use 450g (1lb) of sugar for every 600ml (1 pint) of juice. Return to the heat with the peppers and add the sugar, stirring constantly until the sugar is dissolved. Boil rapidly until it's set. Take it off the heat and allow to cool slightly to stop the peppers floating to the top before pouring it into clean jars and covering as usual.

INDOOR KARTING

WHARFSIDE DINER
CAFE
THAI SPICE

THE STUDIO

### MELISSA OFFICINALIS
# Lemon balm
Early spring to mid autumn leaves

*This is a garden escapee, one that has been around since Elizabethan times. It's an adaptable plant that is as happy in the shade as full sun – in a sheltered spot it will stay green all year round. The slightly furry leaves have a hint of lemon; some swear by it as a salad ingredient, but I use mine mostly for tea. Bees love it.*

**How to recognise** A 25–65cm tall perennial with scented, pale, yellow-green leaves, it's upright, branched and the stem is square. Leaves are opposite and 3–7cm long, rounded at the base and crenate, which means the leaf has rounded projections, as though it had been gathered up with a needle and thread. Unspectacular flowers are small and in whorls around the stem, mostly white or flushed pink.

**What to eat** The young leaves can be added to salads, custards and sandwiches; they are good in Pimms or added to dry white wine with mineral water. But I think they're best as tea. They make a mild, sweet flavoured brew, particularly lovely if you add lemon verbena or mint leaves. The tea is particularly calming, and great if you have an upset stomach or headache.

If you need to unwind, pop a handful of leaves into your bathwater, perhaps along with a bit of lavender, and you have the perfect bath to relax in.

**How to grow** Lemon balm is very adaptable and a great plant for shady, dry corners. If it likes you, it tends to seed itself around a bit – cut the flowers off before they set seed to stop it taking over. This will also give you a flush of new leaves for picking. Sow seed in spring or autumn in seed trays and keep in a cold frame. Prick out plants into individual pots when large enough and plant them out when they reach about 15cm. I tend to cut mine back after flowering in mid summer so it doesn't spread and gives me a new flush of leaves for early autumn.

You can divide mature plants in autumn or spring, or you can take stem tip cuttings in mid summer, but it's likely someone will have a spare plant if you ask around. *Melissa officinalis* 'Aurea' has lovely green and gold splashed leaves but reverts to green if grown in full sun.

---

### MENTHA SPECIES Wild mints

*There are many different species of mint and their rampant nature means they often naturalise and cross-breed with other mints. You'll find them in old plots, as garden escapees and any places where humans have lived. All mints are edible, but some are much more pleasing than others.*

---

### MENTHA AQUATICA
# Water mint
Late spring to mid autumn leaves, early to late summer flowers

*Our commonest wild mint is water mint, which you'll find growing in swamps, fens, marshes, damp woods and near streams, rivers and ponds. It has to have wet feet to be happy and you will smell it before you see it.*

**How to recognise** Strongly scented and perennial, if it likes its spot then there'll be great strands of the stuff, about 65cm tall. It has ovate leaves, bluntly toothed, 3–9cm long. Pale pink to lilac-coloured flowers are arranged in 2–3 dense whorls up the stem and form a large round cluster at the stem tip. When young, both stems and leaves are often blushed reddish.

**What to eat** Leaves and flowers taste mildly of peppermint. Use in salads, with peas, in sauces and sweet dishes. The clean flavour makes it perfect for cocktails, great in Mojitos and Mint Juleps. Strawberries and watermint are a good combination.

water mint

## MESPILUS GERMANICA
# Medlar
Mid to late autumn fruits

*The medlar is one of the last fruits of the foraging year, as it usually ripens in mid autumn and hangs on into early winter. You either love this fruit or loathe it, mostly because you have to eat the fruit rotten and slightly fermented and this pushes some people over the edge. Personally, I think medlars are as good as it gets, so I don't want to persuade too many people to fall in love with them – then there are more for me! They are lovely specimen trees with colourful autumn foliage and beautiful late spring blossom. You're most likely to find them in parks, large gardens and arboretums.*

*Medlars are an ancient British fruit – before we imported oranges and lemons they were an essential source of Vitamin C and were often eaten alongside rich meats and port (a quick way to get gout if ever there was one). It's jokingly known as cat's arse fruit or arse fruit as the fruit does bear an uncanny resemblance.*

**How to recognise** A spreading deciduous tree, this eventually grows to 6m tall and 8m wide with alternate, lance-shaped to oblong leaves up to 15cm long that turn a wonderful yellow-brown in autumn. The bark is greyish and the branches often criss-cross and grow gnarled, giving the tree a wonderful architectural look. The flowers are white, sometimes pink-tinged, bowl-shaped and up to 5cm across. The round, fleshy fruits have russet-brown skin and a distinct crown-shaped base and a star-crossed bottom.

**What to eat** The fruit is eaten bletted, a polite term for semi-rotten. You can either wait for the first frost to do this, so that the fruit ripens on the tree or collect unripe windfalls and bring them indoors to ripen. Once the fruit has turned dark brown and is soft and squishy, they are ready to eat and should be eaten quickly as they don't store. The taste is somewhere between dates, apples and apricots, sometimes slightly lemony. I like to eat them raw, spitting out the many stones, but they make excellent preserves and jellies (they are low in pectin so add crab apples for a firm set) and are good for fruit leathers.

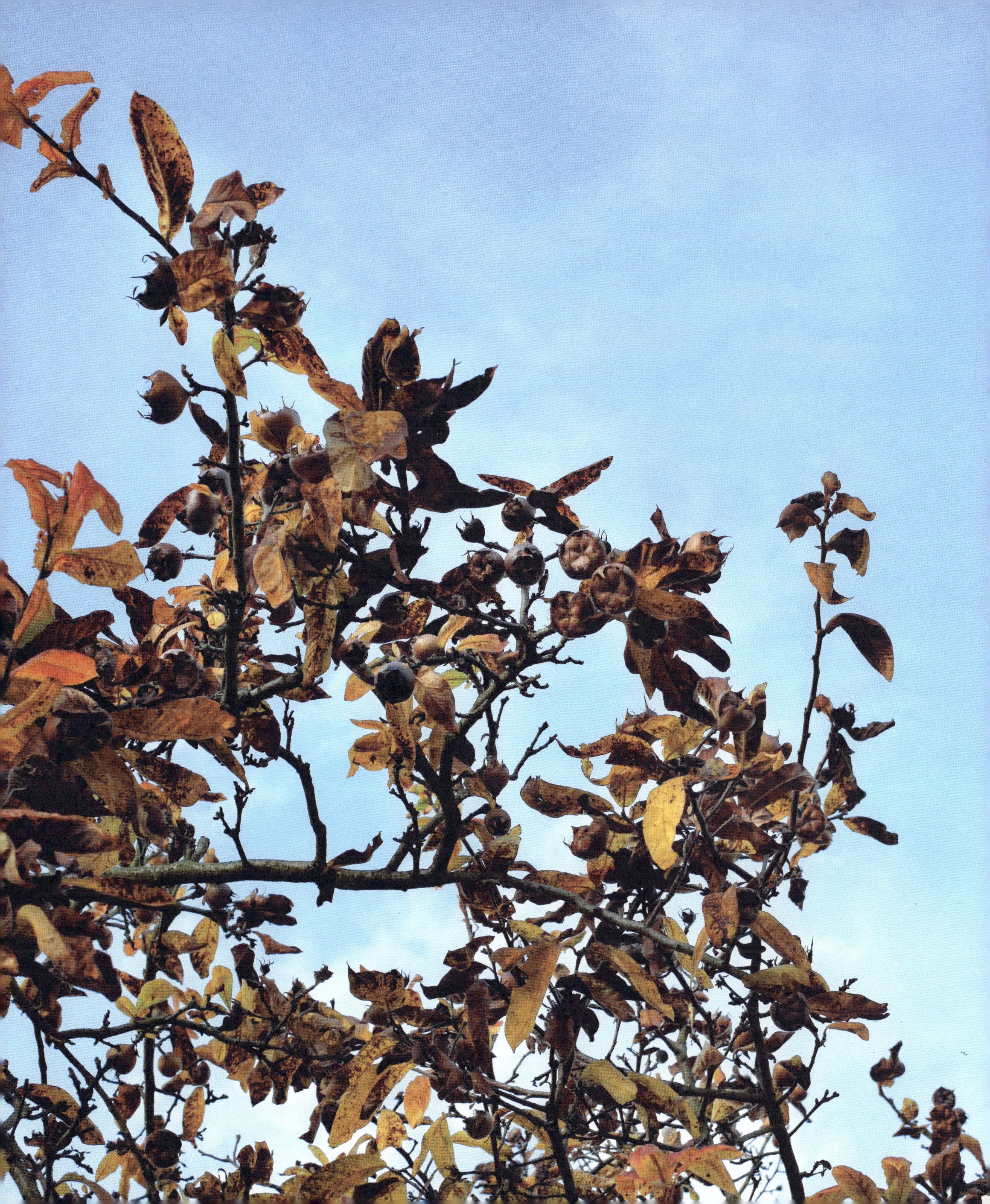

MORUS NIGRA
## Black mulberry
Late summer fruits

*I grew up in a garden with a huge old mulberry that lay almost prostrate across the bottom of the garden. She was like a graceful old grandmother with many walking sticks to keep her upright. You could run up her trunk to reach the sweetest, largest mulberries. And there I would sit and gorge myself until my fingers and arms were stained pink. Later, as a teenager, I would spend my summer in Toronto. Here, black mulberries are common street trees, the sidewalks below stained dark blood red from years of falling fruit. After a typical teenage row with my cousin I ran under one such tree and consoled myself by munching on mulberries. My history with this tree means I can spot one a mile off. I remember exactly when I found this one (pictured) in my local park. I stalked the tree, waiting patiently for its bounty. I heard on the grapevine that there was a Polish couple who picked the tree dry every year – but I can't imagine anyone could eat that many mulberries. A large mulberry is a giving tree and there's always plenty for anyone who stops by.*

**How to recognise** Two types of mulberries are fairly commonly planted: the white mulberry, *Morus alba*, (the most popular variety *M. alba* 'Pendula' is often planted in gardens), and the sweeter tasting, and, happily, most common, black mulberry *Morus nigra*. This is the best species for edible fruit. A rarer, third edible species, the red mulberry, *M. rubra*, has more rounded fruit. *M. nigra* was introduced to England in the seventeenth century as a potential source of food for silk worms but, in fact, they only actually eat white mulberries.

*M. nigra* is a round-headed tree with ovate to heart-shaped leaves, up to 15cm long, with toothed margins. There are separate male and female flowers on the same plant. The male flowers are pale green catkins. Avoid green fruit (actually the female flower cluster that develops into fruit) appear in spring. These turn red and eventually ripen to dark purple in late summer. They look a little like a larger, longer raspberry. The tree grows up to 15m high and 12m wide, and older specimens often have branches sweeping down to the ground.

**What to eat** The delicious fruit can be slightly acidic, but the deeper purple they are the sweeter they taste. You can put a sheet below the tree and shake the branches so that the ripe fruit falls to the ground, but this might look rather greedy in a public place! The fruit freezes well and can be used to make smoothies, ice cream, fruit leathers and preserves (add liquid pectin or crab apples for a firm set). Or bake it in muffins, cakes and clafoutis. Or just eat handfuls of them fresh. In my local Afghani corner store, they sell white, red and black mulberries dried to use for jam and sherbets.

The Thrifty Forager

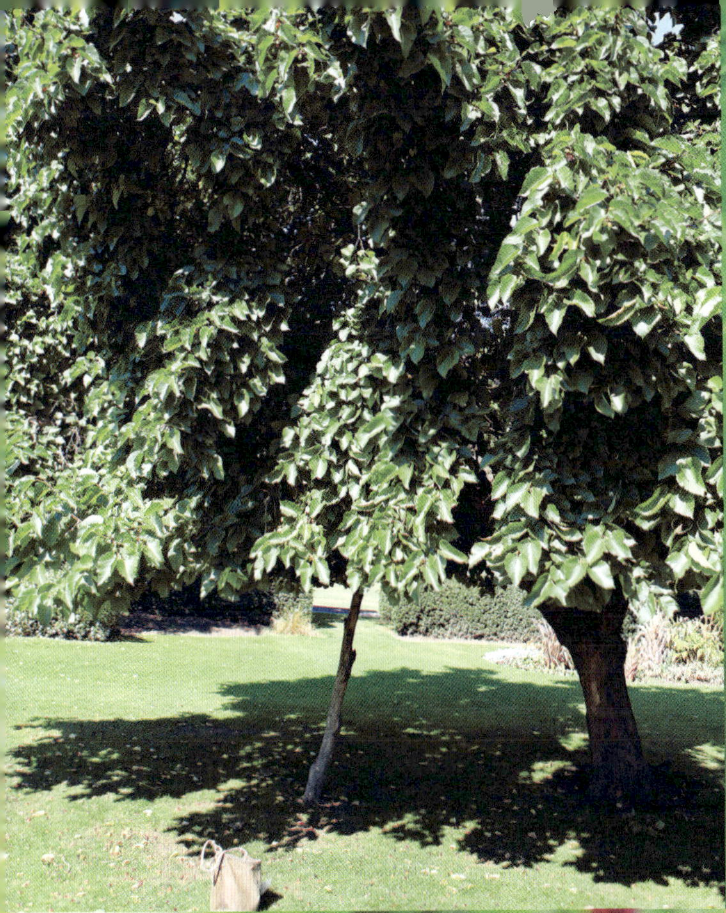
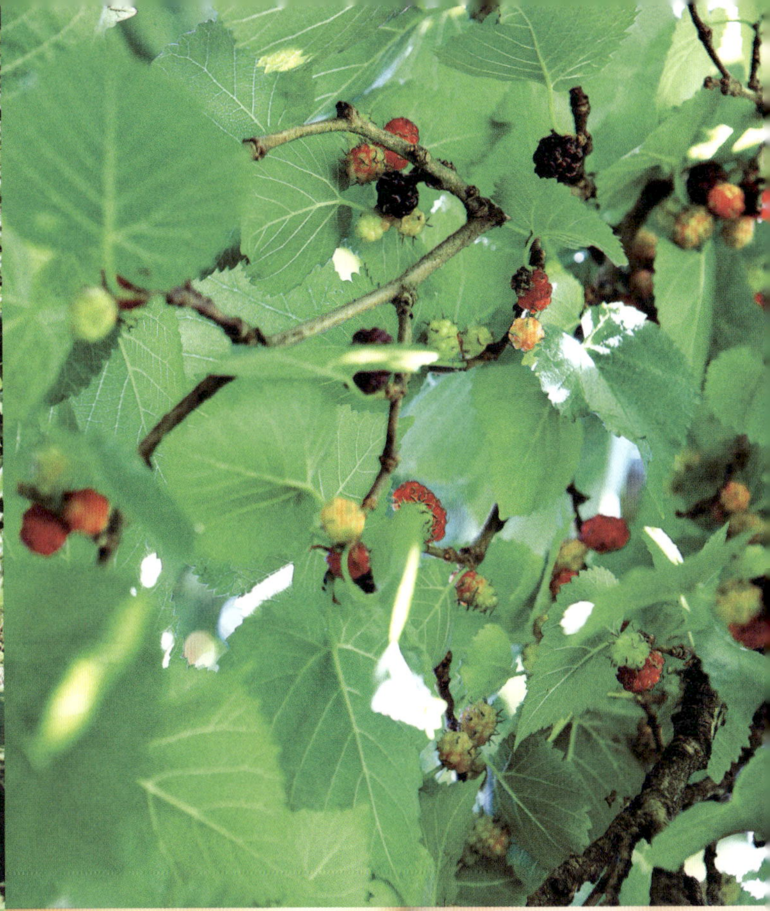
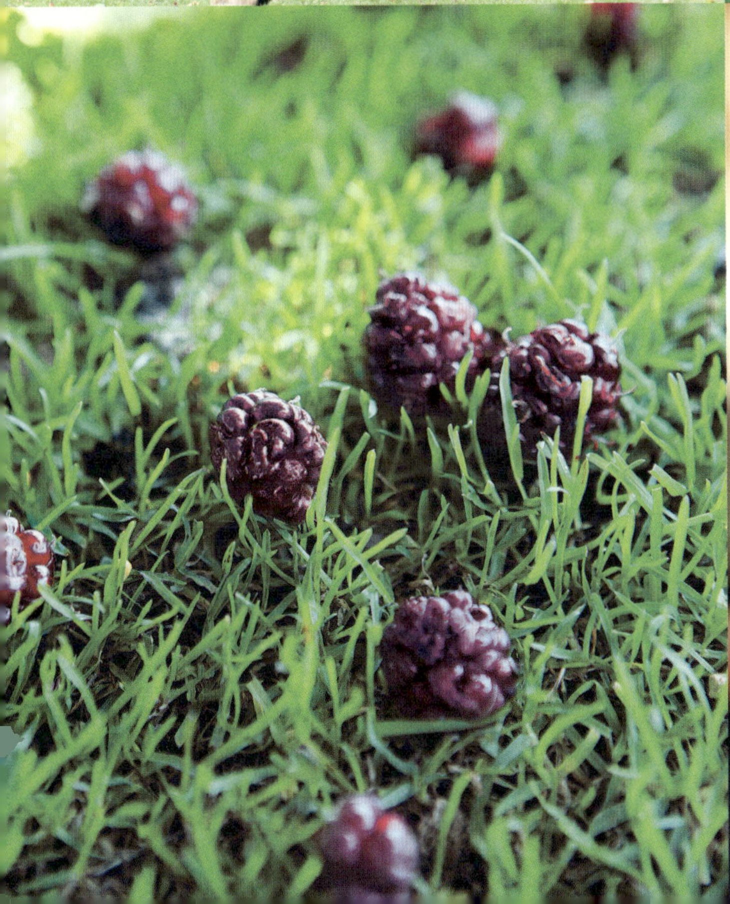
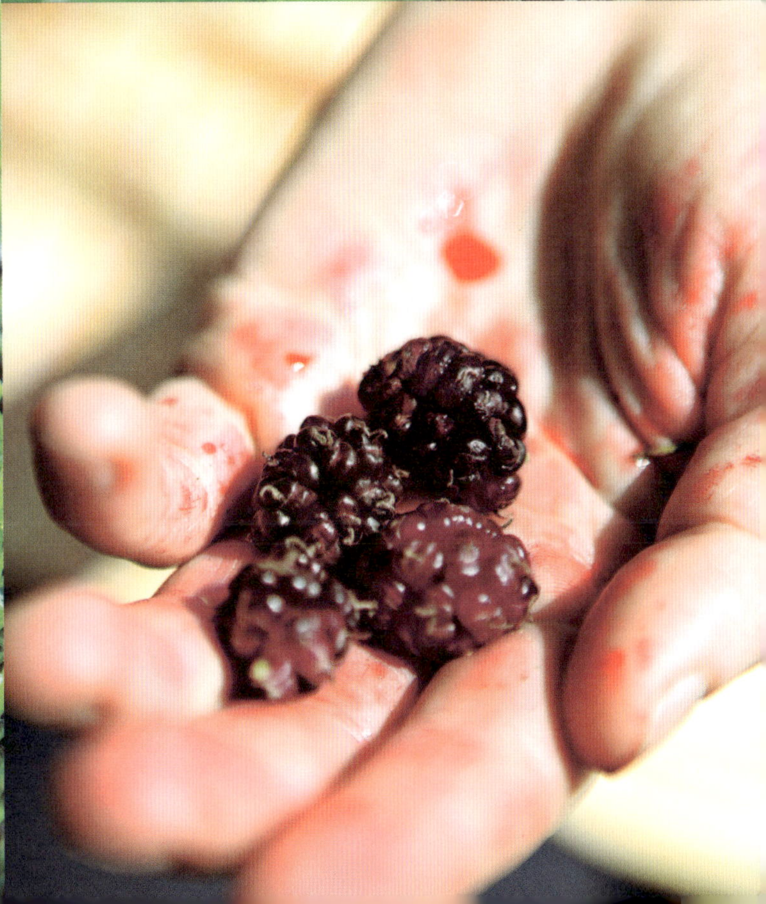

## MYRRHIS ODORATA
### Sweet cicely

Year round leaves and roots, late summer to mid autumn seeds

*Sweet cicely is wonderful and I eat huge amounts all year round in salads. To the uninitiated, it could be confused with hemlock, which would kill you if you ate enough – you'd do a lot of vomiting first – so you need to get this one right. Both are found growing in similar spots: in hedgerows, banks, verges and grassy places, though sweet cicely tends to be found only near human habitation. There are key differences: hemlock smells very unpleasant when crushed, very musty and a bit like urine; sweet cicely smells like aniseed. Hemlock grows to 2.5m tall and has a hairless stem and leaves, the stem is hollow, smooth and shiny with purple blotches; sweet cicely can grow to 1.25m, but is usually 10–60cm high, it has erect hollow stems, but they are distinctly grooved. Hemlock seeds are round; sweet cicely seeds are pointed and grooved.*

**How to recognise** This is a sweet aniseed-smelling perennial, usually up to 60cm tall, with erect hollow, grooved stems. The leaves are 2–3 times pinnate, 10–30cm long and slightly fuzzy to touch; they're pale green beneath, darker above and older leaves have white splodges. Flowers are white open umbels, much like cow parsley. Seeds are 1.5–2.5cm long, sharply ridged and slender with a prominent point. They start off green and eventually turn a dark brownish black.

**What to eat** All parts are edible. The roots can be boiled and taste a little like sweet parsnips that have been cooked with star anise. Leaves can be eaten raw or used in cooking as a natural sweetener; I cook them with rhubarb, apples and berberis fruits. Young green seeds taste like aniseed balls – truly one of nature's own sweets.

**How to grow** It is very easy to please and will happily grow in partial shade in good soil. It grows fast, so keep it in check by eating the roots. It is semi-evergreen and in all but the coldest weather you can harvest leaves. It can be tricky to germinate from seed, as it needs to go through a cold period to break its dormancy and takes around five months from fresh seed. It's easier to buy a young plant and it will quickly bulk up.

## ORIGANUM VULGARE
### Oregano, pot marjoram

All year leaves, early to late summer flowers

*Wild oregano is much stronger than cultivated forms and is incredibly widespread, particularly on chalk soils. Try and pick from plants growing in full sun, as these will have the best flavour. It grows in great swathes where my mother lives, so I dug a bit up for my allotment where the bees love it as its stays in flower for months. I went botanising on the chalk soils of the Chilterns and walked over a carpet of the stuff – the smell was wonderful.*

**How to recognise** Until it flowers, it's a low-growing, slightly hairy perennial with a woody base, but its flower stems can reach 60cm. The stems are erect and branched above. The leaves are 1–5cm long, opposite, entire, dark green and slightly hairy on both sides. The rose-purple flowers are arranged in dense clusters with a terminal panicle.

**What to eat** The leaves can be used to flavour pizza, pastas and anything tomato-based, in stews, sauces, breads and herb vinegars. The young flowers can also be used to flavour vinegars or scattered through salads.

Sweet cicely

Oregano

OXALIS ACETOSELLA
## Wood sorrel
Mid to late spring flowers, early spring to mid autumn leaves

*We went walking this spring in one of my favourite woodlands. It was early in the year when little was showing, but here and there were carpets of lime-green leaves and dainty white flowers. The wood sorrel had awoken. It is found growing in woodlands, damp places around the base of trees and in shady scrub. It has a very long history as a salad ingredient – it was used in the fourteenth century in Britain and, when I lived in New York, I was introduced to it as a native American edible. The tiny heart-shaped leaves taste like lemon juice, so sour that you only need a scant handful in a large salad to make an impact.*

**How to recognise** Look for low-growing mats of pale green or light yellow with clover-like leaves. The leaflets of this little perennial are 0.9–2cm long, each one a perfect folded heart. The flowers are solitary, five-petalled, with each petal overlapping like tiles. They are usually white, veined in lilac, though sometimes all lilac or light purple. The seeds are held in a capsule that explodes when ripe.

**What to eat** The young leaves are delicious in spring. The plant is shallow-rooted and if you tug too hard you'll uproot the entire plant. If this happens, dig a shallow hole nearby and start a new colony. It's best to take a pair of scissors with you to snip off the leaves. The lemon flavour comes from high levels of vitamin C and oxalic acid. Because of the concentration of oxalic acid you shouldn't eat too much too often but, as it's so sharp, you'll never want more than a quarter of a cup in a good salad for four people.

*wood sorrel*

OXALIS CORNICULATA
## Procumbent yellow sorrel
Early summer to early autumn flowers

**How to recognise** This is a fairly common garden weed. It's annual, sometimes biennial, with long trailing stems that root at the nodules. The leaves are heart-shaped and clover-like but a little smaller than wood sorrel. Flowers are bright yellow. Several larger-flowered cultivated varieties are grown in rock gardens, such as *Oxalis depressa*, *O. oregana* and *O. lobata*. All are edible.

**What to eat** Use the young leaves in spring, like wood sorrel.

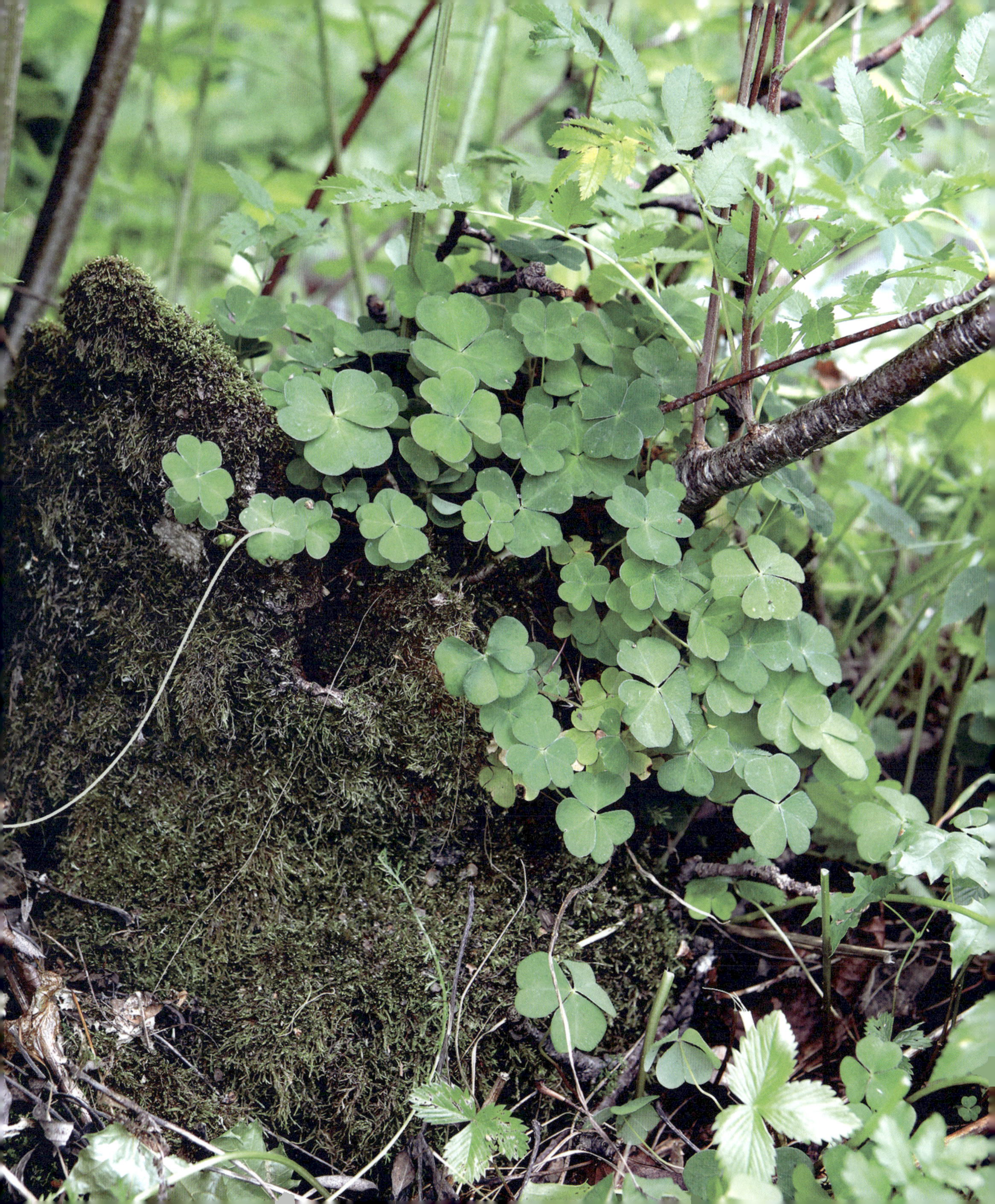

PAPAVER RHOEAS
## Field or common poppy

Early to late spring leaves, early to late summer flowers, early to mid autumn seeds

*On mainland Europe, young poppy leaves are regularly gathered and braised as young greens, used in mixed salads or folded into breads. Sam and Sam Clarke, from the restaurant Moro, have a wonderful recipe for gozleme, a Turkish flat, stuffed griddle bread that uses mallow leaves and poppies. I do most of my harvesting from my own allotment; I scatter the seed between crops and harvest some for leaves and the rest for seed. The flowers bring in the pollinators and help to confuse pests. Poppies were once common weeds of arable land, but modern farming practices have put an end to that. They grow in very free-draining, poor, often recently disturbed soil, as the seed needs light to germinate.*

**How to recognise** It is a delicate annual with a slender taproot. The stems are erect, sometimes branched, with stiff prominent hairs. The basal leaves are serrated, toothed, hairy and lobed, up to 15cm long. Solitary flowers have paper-thin red or, sometimes, pink petals with a blackish blotch at the base.

**What to eat** Young leaves can be cooked or eaten raw, though they are quite hairy, but that's less noticeable mixed with other salad leaves. Once the flower bud has formed, do not eat the leaves. **A note of caution**: Poppy leaves can be toxic to mammals; although this is a very low toxicity, it is wise not to eat too many leaves too often.

The petals can be added to salads, seeds used in bread and cakes. It is easiest to collect the seed in a bag or jam jar then just tip the ripe brown seedheads over to release the seed. The seeds are not toxic.

## PRUNUS SPECIES
## Cherries, plums, bullaces, damsons and sloes
Late summer to mid autumn fruit

PRUNUS AVIUM
### Wild cherry
Early to mid summer fruit

*Wild cherries are fairly common woodland trees and in many hedgerows, but the real bounty of foraged cherries comes from all those that were planted throughout the 1970s as cheap trees for housing estates, partly because they don't seem to mind pollution. This rather inconspicuous tree sits outside apartment blocks, high-rise towers and in numerous shopping centres. The cherries are often a little hidden by the leaves, so it's best to stand under the tree and spot the darkest ones. The quirk of this tree is that some trees will have sweet fruit and others sour, you just have to go and taste them. The fruit tends to ripen over a period of weeks, so keep coming back to see what you can harvest. I have a rule only to pick cherries from the tree – rats love the sweet fruit so those on the ground are a little dubious.*

**How to recognise** Deciduous trees, up to 25m high, they have a spreading habit and distinct red-banded, shiny bark and ovate, dark green leaves up to 15cm long. The young leaves are often bronze-coloured and turn red and yellow in autumn. White spring flowers are bowl-shaped, in 5–10cm clusters. The fruits are heart-shaped and range in colour from red to black.

**What to eat** If you find a sweet tree, then eat them as they come – I've gorged on them this way. You can bake with them, make wonderful chutney or a very runny jam, or make wild cherry brandy – fill a bottle with cherries, add sugar so that it fills up to half the bottle, top up with brandy. The cherries quickly leach out their colour so the brandy turns blood red. Add cola to it and you have a devilish cocktail that is far too easy to drink. My friend Birgit has used rum and says it's just as good. I can't say I really enjoy drinking the stuff, but it's just so good for soaking the Christmas cake!

**Similar species** *Prunus padus*, the bird cherry, is a wilder looking tree, often multi-stemmed. It has much smaller, darker cherries that are always very bitter, but they can be cooked into something sweet.

PRUNUS CERASIFERA AND SELECTED FORMS
# Cherry plum or Myrobalan

Early autumn fruit

*This tree is native to the Balkans where it is cultivated for its fruit, and is the first to flower in early spring. In cold winters, the flowers are often caught by frost, so it fruits erratically. They're widely used in amenity plantings and can be found in hedgerows, by motorways, on street corners and in parks. The fruit varies from yellow to red and the plums can be quite sour, especially if the trees grow in shade.*

**How to recognise** Deciduous trees reaching 9m tall, they have a rounded shape and may be multi-stemmed. The leaves are ovate with a pointed tip, deep, glossy green above and paler beneath with a toothed margin. The flowers are up to 2cm across, palest pink to white. Fruit is spherical, plum-like, 2.5cm across, sometimes much larger, ripening yellow to red in late summer.

**What to eat** The fruit can be very sharp so you need to add plenty of sugar when you cook with them. I successfully dried a bunch and use them in my homemade granola where their sourness is surprisingly pleasing amongst the sweet oats.

The plums in the tarte pictured opposite come from the photographer Simon's garden. He said that they were too tart for him to do anything with them. When a French friend, Perrine Puyberthier, came to stay, the first thing she did was choose these plums for a tarte – I don't think they'll go wasted next year. This is her recipe.

# PERRINE PUYBERTHIER'S PLUM TARTE

**FOR THE PASTRY**
300g (10½oz) flour
150g (5oz) butter
50g (2oz) caster sugar
2 egg yolks
1 glass of milk

Mix the flour with the butter and sugar until it becomes sandy textured.

Add the egg yolks and milk and mix together into a ball.

Cover with clingfilm and put in the fridge to stand for 1 hour.

After 1 hour, roll out the pastry to fit a 23cm (9in) tart case.

Line the pastry with baking paper and baking beans or dried pulses and bake blind at 180°C/gas mark 4 until it turns pale brown.

Let it cool (obviously get rid of the paper and beans!).

Meanwhile prepare the **crème pâtissière**:

500ml (18fl oz) milk
1 vanilla pod
100g (3½oz) caster sugar
2 egg yolks
50g (2oz) cornflour

Heat the milk in a saucepan with the vanilla pod. Do not let it boil.

In a bowl, mix the sugar with the two yolks until it becomes smooth and shiny – or sparkling in Perrine's delightful French-English!

Add the cornflour and stir well.

Take the hot milk off the stove and remove the vanilla pod.

Put it back on a low heat and add the sugary egg mixture, stirring constantly. It usually takes about 15 minutes for the crème to cook. It should become stiff and come away from the sides of the pan, but it can take a little longer.

Let it cool in the saucepan off the heat. It's important that the crème pâtissière doesn't form a crust by drying out, so cover the pan with clingfilm to stop this happening.

**THE PLUM FILLING**
1kg (approx. 2lb) plums

Wash the plums, halve them and take out the stones.

Spread the crème pâtissière on the pastry and cover neatly with the plums. You can spread a layer of plum jam between the crème and the plums to add a touch of sweetness but Simon (who's pretty picky about these things) said the greatest joy of this tarte was its delicious tartness.

Bake the tart at 180°C/gas mark 4 for 15–20 minutes – the plums will become soft and slightly caramelised.

PRUNUS DOMESTICA SUBSP. INSITITIA
# Damson
Early to mid autumn fruit

*Damsons are an early autumn delight. The larger forms are often sweet enough to eat straight from the tree. The smaller the fruit (there's a great deal of variety), the more sour. In a good year, a tree will be absolutely laden, allowing plenty for experimenting with. The damson is derived from the bullace, which is native to Britain. It is thought that damsons originally come from Damascus, where it was widely grown (hence the name) and introduced to England by the Romans. Bullaces are larger and rounder than damsons and often sweeter.*

**How to identify** A deciduous shrub or small tree, up to 5m tall, with a mass of crossing branches, damson trees look very like sloes, except they are thornless and flower in mid spring after the leaves open. The fruit is oval in shape, usually tapering at the stalk end, and it has a larger stone than a bullace.

**What to eat** Damsons sweeten as they age, so allow them to fully ripen. They can be used in jams, fruit cheeses, to make damson vodka (like sloe gin, but with less sugar as the damsons are sweeter). Also use them in tarts, sponges or stewed, but they may need plenty of sugar.

**How to grow** There are several selected forms, the most famous is 'Merryweather' which is self-fertile and has the largest fruit. Damsons are very successful in harsh conditions and make an excellent addition to native hedges.

## DAMSON, CARDAMOM AND VANILLA JAM

2.5kg (approx. 5lb) damsons
6 green cardamom pods
1 vanilla pod
Granulated sugar

Place the damsons in a heavy-based pan with the cardamom and vanilla pod. Add a cup of water and bring slowly to the boil, then allow to simmer until the fruit is soft. You will need to strain the pulp to remove the stones. Fish out the vanilla pod and any cardamom pods you can find to return to the pan.

Measure the pulp and, for every 600ml (1 pint) of pulp, you'll need 450g (1lb) of sugar. Add the sugar and stir until it is dissolved and then bring to a rapid boil until setting point is reached. Bottle into clean, sterilised jars and cover as usual.

I have made this jam using honey instead of sugar. It was quite exceptional, though rather expensive. You don't need to boil the honey (and can get away with less than the pound for pint rule) as this jam will not set in a traditional way. Heat the pulp and add the honey, mix well and then heat gently to reduce the mixture into a thick syrup. Bottle as usual.

### PRUNUS SPINOSA
## Sloe or blackthorn

Early to late spring flowers, mid to late autumn fruit

*Sloes are the smallest and tartest of all the plum fruits. The most common way to use them is soaked in gin and sugar (though sloe vodka is equally as good). Sloes are a widespread native hedgerow shrub and are often found in the wilder bits of parks, along motorway plantings and in neglected spots.*

**How to recognise** A dense, multi-branched deciduous shrub with prominent spines, sloes often form a dense thicket up to 4m tall. The leaves are simple, up to 4cm long, ovate with a wedge-shaped base and a toothed margin. The flowers are white and simple, 8mm long, and appear before the leaves, often solitary but sometimes in pairs. The round fruit is up to 1.5cm long, dark blue with a purplish bloom and green flesh.

**What to eat** Sloes are too tart to eat raw or in pies, but they are so good in gin. Sloe gin is a fine, strong, tasty, very sweet liqueur. Fill a large jar or bottle with sloes, add granulated sugar up to half the bottle (it does need to be sweet) and then top up with gin. Traditionally, you wait until the first frost to pick sloes (this softens the fruit), but if you wait this long it becomes a competition between you and the birds. The easier alternative is to pick the sloes early on and put them in the freezer before using them. Shake the bottle regularly in order to dissolve the sugar, at least once a week for the first month or so. The gin is ready after a couple of months but it is best after a year. If you want to keep it longer, take the sloes out or they'll start to disintegrate. Don't throw these away but use them to make fantastic chocolate brittle. Melt dark chocolate in a bain-marie, pour it over the sloes and put into the freezer for a couple of hours. Break into chunks and serve immediately, but for your teeth's sake, remember the stones.

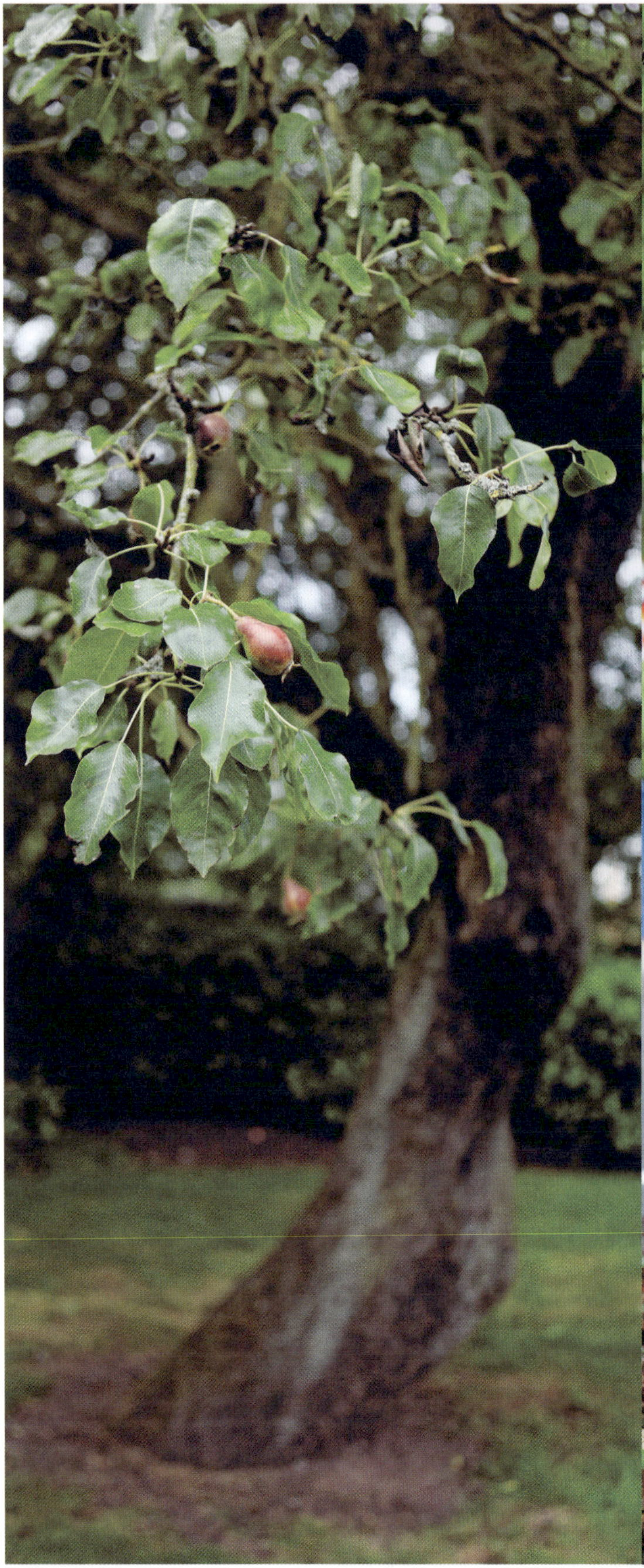

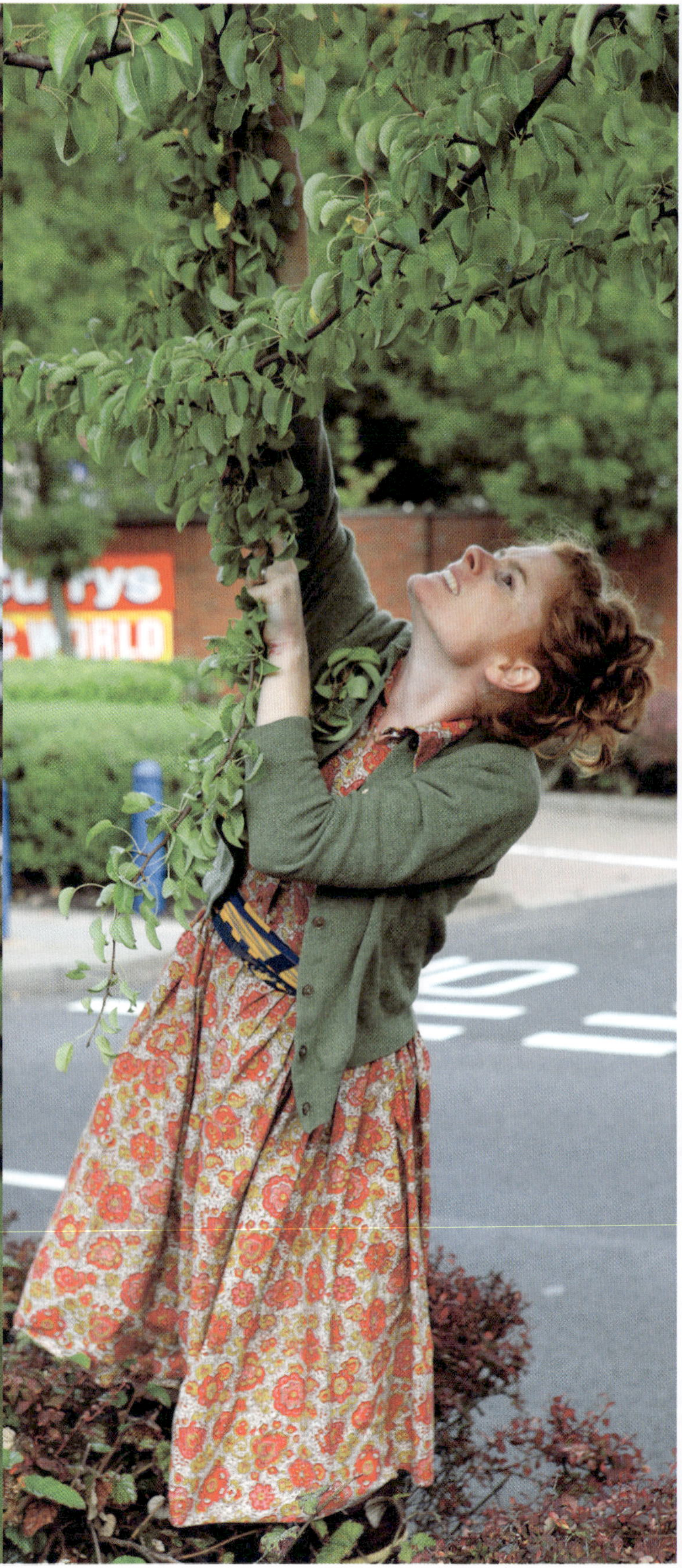

PYRUS COMMUNIS
## Common pear
Early to mid autumn fruit

*Much like apples, feral pears often appear where people have tossed a core, turning up in hedgerows and along roadsides. The front garden of an apartment block near me hosts a wonderful collection of large pears, which, I assume, are remnants of some long-forgotten orchard. The problem with pears is that they usually ripen all at once and then drop to the floor and mush. A Perry pear is a tiny, hard fruit that's hardly edible until you brew it into pear cider, known as Perry. These trees are most often found in cider country, such as Herefordshire.*

*Old pear trees are often huge, so picking the fruit is complicated. If you're dedicated, the answer is to get a fruit picker, a sort of basket on the end of a long pole. If the pears are not too mushy on the ground, but slightly past the stage of eating them straight, try drying them in thick slices on the lowest setting in your oven or in a dehydrator. Dried pears are a revelation, chewy and sweet, and they store for ages. Otherwise use the pears in tarts, upside-down cakes, fruit butters or to bulk out fruit leathers.*

**How to recognise** Pears are deciduous, upright trees, generally larger than apples and sometimes thorny. The leaves are alternate, entire, ovate to elliptical, glossy dark green with fine, forward-pointing toothed margins. The flowers are saucer-shaped, white, often tinged pink, in clusters of 5–9 and appear in mid-spring, followed by pear-shaped yellow or green fruits, usually around 10cm long.

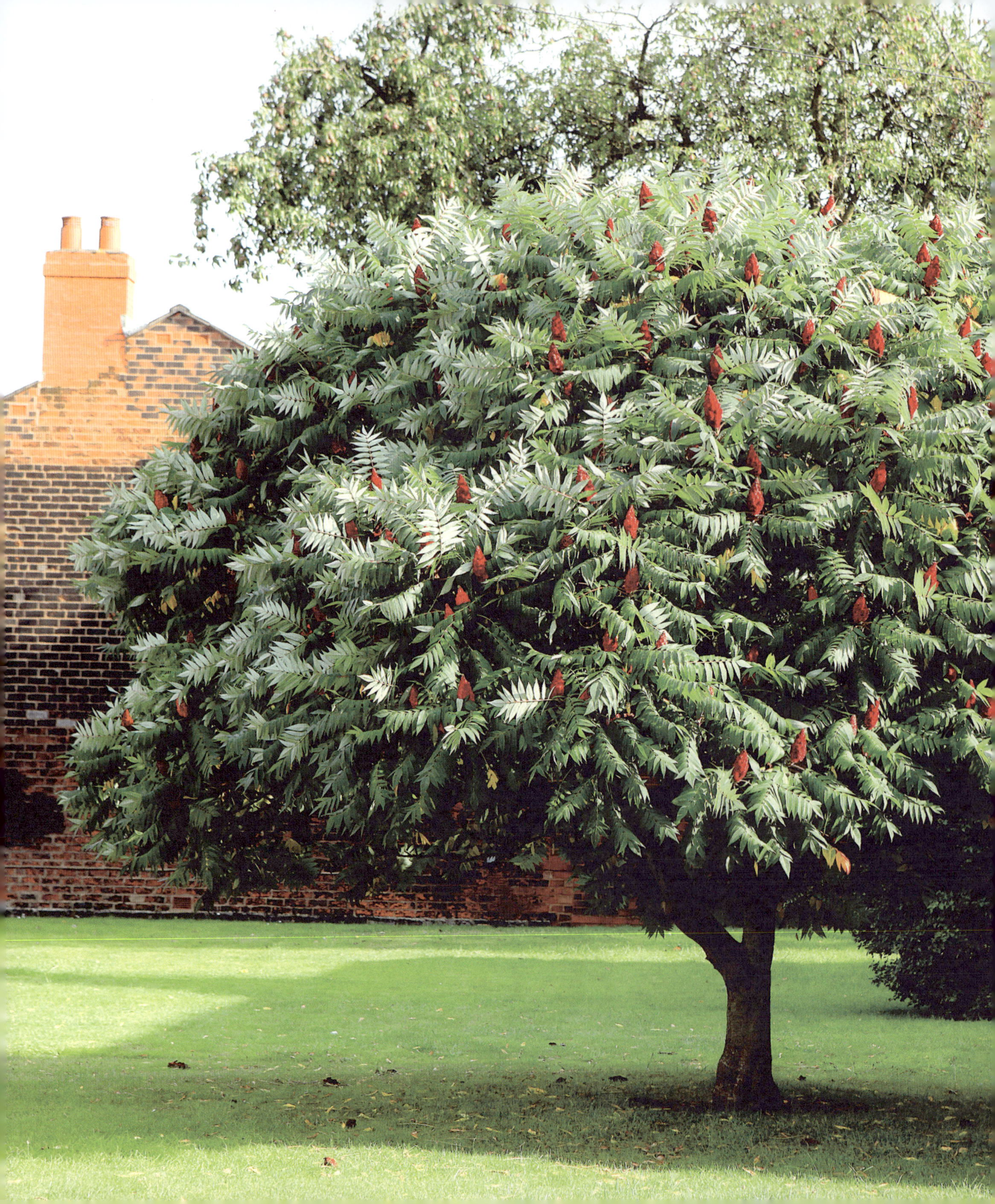

RHUS TYPHINA
# Stag's horn sumach, velvet sumach

Early to mid autumn fruit

*Stag's horn sumach is another garden escapee that comes from North America. Traditionally, the native peoples of North America make a kind of lemonade by soaking the fruit in water for several hours. The fruit has fine red hairs that can be dried and rubbed off. From the fruits is formed a red powder called sumac which is used in Lebanese and Turkish cuisine. You usually find stag's horn sumach growing on roadsides, railway embankments and in poor, free-draining soils. It is quite a common front-garden specimen. You need to gather the fruits at the beginning of autumn, as winter rains will wash away the flavour.*

**How to recognise** The sumach is an upright, suckering deciduous shrub that stands up to 3m tall and wide. It has velvety red branches that resemble stags' horns against a winter sky. Large, pinnate leaves, up to 60cm long, have 11–31 lance-shaped dark green leaflets that turn bright orange and red in autumn. The yellow-green flowers are produced on upright, conical shoots, up to 20cm, long in mid summer. These are followed on the female plants by dense clusters of spherical, hairy, deep crimson fruit on the tips of the branches.

**Note of caution** Beware of *Rhus verniciflua,* which is known as the varnish tree because of its glossy leaves. It is very toxic and will cause painful blisters and aggravate skin allergies. It has yellow fruit.

**What to eat** The red fruits taste like lemon juice. Soak them in water for several hours with a little honey or sugar to produce a lemonade-style drink. Dried berries can also be used as a lemonade substitute.

I break up the fruiting head into berries and dry them. Theoretically, these should then be rubbed through a nylon sieve to remove the red hairs, but it takes a lot of berries to get just a little powder, so I usually keep the berries whole. They become the sumac used in cooking, good on rice, excellent rubbed into the skin of a roasting chicken or used in marinades. I also use whole dried berries in jam to give a lemon flavour, though you need to sieve the berries out before bottling the jam.

RIBES ODORATUM
## Buffalo currant
Mid spring flowers,
late summer to early autumn fruit

*The buffalo currant is native to North America and is often used as a shade-tolerant shrub in municipal planting and parks. I've found quite a few recently in churchyards. The flowers have a wonderful clove smell, they taste sweet and can be used in spring salads though, clearly, if you eat all the flowers you won't get any fruit.*

**How to recognise** It is a spineless, erect deciduous shrub with hairy young shoots. The leaves are bright green, broadly ovate with 3–5 prominent lobes. They have a very distinct currant smell and turn red to purple in autumn. Bright yellow flowers, up to 5cm wide, appear from mid to late spring. The fruit is dark bluish black, sometimes yellow, dark red or brownish, but most often dark blue with a bloom. They look like tiny gooseberries.

**What to eat** The flavour of each plant varies widely, so you have to sample around. The sweetest are always quite large. The fruit ripen over a long period and I find they are best towards the end of the season. You can use them for pies, cakes, jams and fruit leathers or just eat them straight off the bush. The fruit can be dried for winter use.

**How to grow** The species is very hardy and quite rampant – it will happily grow to 2–3m tall and wide and will sucker if left unpruned. Yet it's a useful ornamental for shady areas and tolerates a wide range of soils, though it prefers moist, rich conditions.

**Similar species** Occasionally, you'll find escapees from this family such as blackcurrants, *R. nigrum*, redcurrants, *R. rubrum*, and gooseberries, *R. uva-crispa*. They all have very similar leaves. Blackcurrants and redcurrants have leaves with 3–5 prominent lobes and heart-shaped bases – blackcurrants have brown glands on the base of the leaves, redcurrant leaves are slightly rounder without glands, and gooseberries have very prominent thorns usually up a single-trunked multi-stemmed bush. All three are most likely to be found in damp woodlands or hedgerows.

ROSA SPECIES
## Rose

Early summer to early autumn flowers,
mid autumn to early winter fruit

*You wouldn't imagine that a wild rose would offer so many possibilities for foraging. The common dog rose,* Rosa canina, *is found everywhere from the wildest countryside to urban wasteland; its simple, charming pink flowers welcome our summers and its bright red hips brighten dull winters. The apple or Japanese rose,* Rosa rugosa, *offers deep pink petals for wonderful jams and jellies, and hips so sweet and soft you can eat them raw from the plant. The burnet rose,* Rosa pimpinellifolia, *has dark black hips, which make for smoky-looking rosehip syrup. All rose petals are edible, though many cultivated forms don't have hips. Don't collect from plants that have been sprayed with pesticides or fungicides. When harvesting wild roses for their petals only, take the petals and not the whole flower so that the hips can still form.*

**How to recognise** The dog rose is a large shrub, up to 3m tall, deciduous, with erect or arching stems with stout, curved or hooked prickles. The leaves are pinnate, with 2–3 pairs of leaflets with toothed margins and sometimes with slender prickles along the midrib. The flowers are solitary, pink (the white-flowered ones are usually the field rose, *Rosa arvensis*) with prominent sepals that turn black when fruiting. The hips are bright scarlet, 1–2cm long, shiny and smooth.

The burnet rose is a short shrub, around 1m high, with straight prickles and bristles. The little 0.5–2cm long leaves are pinnate with up to seven individual leaflets, each rounded with toothed margins – they look much like salad burnet leaves, hence the name.

The apple or Japanese rose forms a dense shrub, up to 1–2m tall, with very prickly stems and small, fern-like, leathery dark green leaves, with 7–9 leaflets, 0.5–2cm long. The flowers are cup-shaped, single and very fragrant, violet-carmine coloured in small clusters and flower from summer to autumn. These are followed by large, tomato-shaped red hips, around 2.5cm wide.

The Plant Directory | 163

## CRYSTALLISED ROSE PETALS (AND OTHER FLOWERS)

You can crystallise any edible flowers with egg white, a little water and caster sugar, but as the process involves raw eggs it's not for everyone. It's pretty hard to crystallise a whole rosebud or flower, so use individual petals and make sure that they are free from pesticides. Mix egg white with a little water to make the mixture a little more fluid. Using a pair of tweezers, dip the petal in the mixture so that either side is coated and then dip or sprinkle sugar over the egg white and place on baking parchment on a tray to dry somewhere cool, dry and out of direct sunlight. These will take about 8 hours to dry properly. You can move the petals about from time to time to make sure they don't stick to the parchment. In humid conditions the petals will melt!

## CHOCOLATE ROSE LEAVES FOR DECORATING A CAKE

These are a childhood favourite, and along with a few crystallised petals, transform a cake into something really special. Melt 4 or 5 squares of a bar of dark chocolate in a bain-marie. You don't need much chocolate, so just melt a little at a time rather than having lots of melted chocolate around (though it does make for a lovely hot chocolate!). Using a small paintbrush, paint the chocolate onto the underside of a firm rose leaf (you can use other leaves but they need a prominent midrib and need to be soft enough to peel the chocolate away, for instance you could use young holly leaves), leaving the stalk attached and unpainted. Put the leaves in the fridge for several hours and, once the chocolate is fully set, just peel off the leaves and decorate your cake.

## ROSE PETAL VINEGAR

Fill a bottle or jar with rose petals, then add very good-quality white vine vinegar and seal with a cork. If you use deep pink petals, the vinegar will go a lovely colour. Keep out of direct sunlight and the vinegar will be ready after two months.

## ROSE PETAL JAM

- 250g (9oz) rose petals (that's roughly a quarter of a standard carrier bag of petals). I mix pink dog rose with a creamy yellow, highly scented rose from my garden
- 1.1 litres (2 pints) water
- Juice of 2 lemons
- 450g (1lb) granulated sugar

The petals may have a few bugs on them, so gently shake them free of any intruders, place in a bowl, add half the sugar and leave for several hours or overnight. This infuses the rose flavour into the sugar and darkens the petals.

In a heavy-based pan, add the water, lemon juice and remaining sugar, then gently heat until all the sugar has dissolved. Stir in the rose petals and simmer for 20 minutes or until the rose petals look as if they are melting and have softened – pull a few out and chew if necessary, they should melt in your mouth but have a slight bite. Turn the heat up and bring to a rapid boil for 5 minutes or until setting point is reached. Remove any scum that may have risen to the top and allow to cool slightly, stirring gently so that the petals are evenly distributed. Cover and bottle as usual.

## ROSEHIP AND GINGER SYRUP

*This recipe will take an afternoon to make and is best with a spare pair of hands to help. You can use any hips, but I like to use a mixture of the intense flavours of dog roses and apple roses.*

- 1kg (approx. 2lbs) rosehips, washed
- 1kg (approx. 2lbs) granulated sugar
- 3 litres (5 pints) water
- A large piece of fresh ginger, say 3cm long, grated
- A little lemon zest

Place 2 litres (3½ pints) water with the rosehips in a pan and bring slowly to the boil so that the rosehips soften.

Take them off the heat and blitz with a blender (if you don't have a blender, chop the rosehips up first). Dog rosehips are very hard, so either put them in the freezer first or wait until they have softened after a frost, otherwise you'll bust your blender.

Strain the juice through a jelly bag.

Add the ginger and lemon zest to the strained juice, then set aside. Return the pulp to the pan, add one more litre of water and bring back to the boil and cook briefly – another 10 minutes max. You want the water to turn a lovely pink colour.

Remove from the heat and strain through the jelly bag.

Clean your pan and add both lots of juice, together with the sugar, and bring to the boil. You need to boil the juice until the volume has reduced by half. Do not do as my friends Beth and Syd did and drink a bottle of wine, fall asleep and awake to rosehip toffee. Although tasty, it stuck terribly to our teeth and took us all winter to eat!

Use clean, sterilised bottles or small jam jars. Old-fashioned glass tomato ketchup bottles are great, but you shouldn't use bottles with plastic tops, as these won't be sterile. Once the jars are opened, the syrup will only store for a week or so in the fridge, so you want small amounts that you can use up quickly.

I like it as a drink, diluting the syrup with freshly squeezed lemon and fizzy water. And I like pouring the syrup neat on porridge, ice cream or over baked apples, but my favourite way of using rosehip syrup is to mix it with Kefir (a fermented milk drink).

The Plant Directory

RUBUS FRUTICOSUS
## Blackberry, bramble
Early to late spring leaves, early autumn fruit

*'The blackberry vines grew all around and climbed like green dragon tails up the sides of some old abandoned warehouse in the industrial area that had seen its day. The vines were so huge that people laid planks across them like bridges to get at the good berries in the centre of them… This is not a place you went casually to gather a few berries for a pie or to eat with some milk and sugar on them. You went there because you were getting blackberries for the winter's jam or to sell them because you needed more money than the price of a movie. There were so many blackberries back in there that it was hard to believe. They were huge like black diamonds.'*

FROM 'THE BLACKBERRY MOTORIST, REVENGE OF THE LAWN', STORIES 1962-1970 BY RICHARD BRAUTIGAN.

**What to eat** Glossy, very young blackberry leaves taste just like the fruit and are delicious in salads. By mid-season they are too tough to eat like this, but make a lovely tea, rich in vitamin C and, supposedly, very good for indigestion. Choose bright green, younger leaves, if possible. Traditionally, the leaves are 'fermented' before drying for tea, as this improves the flavour. It is not a true fermentation, but the process of allowing the leaves to oxidise so the chlorophyll is broken down, the tannins are released and the leaves darken. Pick young leaves and allow them to wilt in the sun (or at least somewhere warm) for several hours, then crush them lightly with a rolling pin. This quickens the process of oxidation and releases some of the juices, improving the flavour. Wrap the leaves in a damp cloth and hang them somewhere warm and airy. After 2–3 days, they should be 'fermented' and smell slightly of roses. Take them out of the cloth and allow to dry naturally before storing them in an airtight container.

Do I need to tell you how to eat blackberries? Try making vinegar or syllabub, perhaps tarts or pies, jellies (rather than jam which has too many pips), ice cream, cream and sugar, a wild walk snack, cheesecake, a mousse, in leathers, wines or champagnes.

## RUBUS IDAEUS
# Wild raspberry
Early summer to early autumn fruit

*Wild raspberries are truly at home on hillsides, woods and scrubs, in wild places to match their wild taste, but every now and then they stumble into urban areas. They run along the banks of the river Rea here in Birmingham and sprout around the fences of the parks. Their fruit is tiny but the taste is so wonderful; it's pure essence of raspberries with a little sherbet, bursting from a tiny, fragile fruit. I dare you to try and get some home, I doubt you'll make it – they are definitely for eating straight off the bush.*

**How to recognise** It is a deciduous shrub that suckers by buds from the roots, so you'll often find it in strands. The stems are up to 1.5m tall, a ghostly grey after a year of growing, but pale green when young. They are armed with numerous straight prickles. The leaves are pinnate, the leaflets up to 7cm long, ovate with an irregular heart-shaped base and dense white below, bright green above. The margins are toothed and they have prominent midribs and veins. The white flowers are about 1cm in diameter with long green sepals, arranged in a terminal cluster. The fruit is just like a small cultivated raspberry, usually red but sometimes an opaque yellow.

**What to eat** The young leaves in spring make a good tea, deliciously mild and full of vitamin C if you use them fresh. If you can collect enough fruit I recommend raspberry syrup, or amazing raspberry vodka that will rival or surpass any commercial one.

## RASPBERRY VODKA
A bottle of vodka
As many raspberries as you can pick
A tablespoon of sugar (white or light brown so as not to colour the vodka)

Drink a little neat vodka so that there is space in the bottle to fill with wild raspberries. Add the sugar, but do not shake, as this will destroy all the raspberries. Instead, keep the bottle on its side or at an angle and turn every few days till the sugar is dissolved. After a couple of months, strain the contents and store in suitable bottles. This is a subtle flavour with none of the chemical taste of commercial raspberry vodkas and needs to be treated accordingly in cocktails. It is particularly good with soda water and lime.

## RUBUS TRICOLOR
### Chinese bramble

Early to mid summer flowers,
late summer to early autumn fruit

*The Chinese bramble is a brilliant ground cover under trees, its glossy leaves reflecting light into dark corners and its rampant nature keeping weeds down, which is why it is favoured in parks and municipal plantings. You'll find it in car parks, on university campuses and all those other difficult-to-maintain places and I guarantee, unless I happen to be there, that these jewel-like fruits will be all yours.*

**How to recognise** An evergreen, low-growing shrub, this has creeping shoots and very obvious red bristles that are soft to touch. The leaves are ovate, entire, glossy dark green, up to 10cm long, with a heart-shaped base, white and hairy beneath. Flowers are saucer-shaped, white, up to 2.5cm long and tend to be on their own but sometimes show in pairs. The fruit is raspberry-like but bright orange-red.

**What to eat** Eat the berries straight off the bush. They are very sweet and tend to fall apart in your fingers. The fruit hangs down and is often hidden by the leaves, so get down on your hands and knees, if necessary.

**How to grow** This is a bit of a beast for most small gardens, but can be semi-tamed into a dishevelled hedge. The only pruning it will need will be keeping it at bay. It prefers moderately fertile soil in sun or partial shade – the deeper the shade, the less fruit you'll get. A similar, but slightly less rampant species for smaller gardens is *Rubus nepalensis* that has similar fruit and is equally happy in shadier spots.

## RUMEX ACETOSA
### Common sorrel

Mid summer to early autumn flowers,
spring to early summer and again from autumn onwards leaves

*The sour flavour of sorrel means that it acts as a perfect lemon substitute. The leaves are tart, fresh and crisp – mouth-wateringly so. I like to mix sorrel with more bland leaves in salads and just dress with olive oil (the sour tang acting as the acid in a vingarette). Finely chopped leaves can be used as a garnish and you can cook with the leaves, though they do turn an unappetising brown and disintegrate rather. I like them in omelettes and they are good with oily fish. There is a garden variety* (subsp. ambiguus) *that has large leaves and is less tangy. Once a plant flowers, the leaves become small and tough and are little use to the forager. It is, however, a good time to spot a large clump for future pickings. It grows in grassy places, on banks, verges, parks and open spaces, occasionally in clearings in woods.*

*As sorrel is high in oxalic acid you should not eat too much (once a week is fine, I probably consume far more). Anyone with kidney stones should stay well away.*

**How to recognise** It is a perennial with stems up to 20–70cm high. The leaves are alternate, 3–10cm long, pointed, with two distinct lobes pointing downwards on the base of the leaf and a long green stalk. Once the plant produces a flower stalk, these basal leaves all but disappear and you are left with much smaller stem leaves with almost no stalk that somewhat clasp the stem. The flower stem is pinkish and the pink, heart-shaped flowers are arranged in clusters up the branching stem.

**What to eat** The young leaves are best and most bountiful in spring, though it is possible to pick small amounts pretty much all year round. Once the plants flower, there is little to pick, the stem's leaves often being tough, but the unopened flower buds, individual flowers and fresh seed can be used as a garnish and sprinkled across dishes to add a little lemon sparkle to the flavours.

**Similar species** *Rumex acetosella,* sheep's sorrel, has smaller leaves, 10mm, rounder and the lobes are more prominent often pointing outwards more. It tends to be found in more acidic conditions.

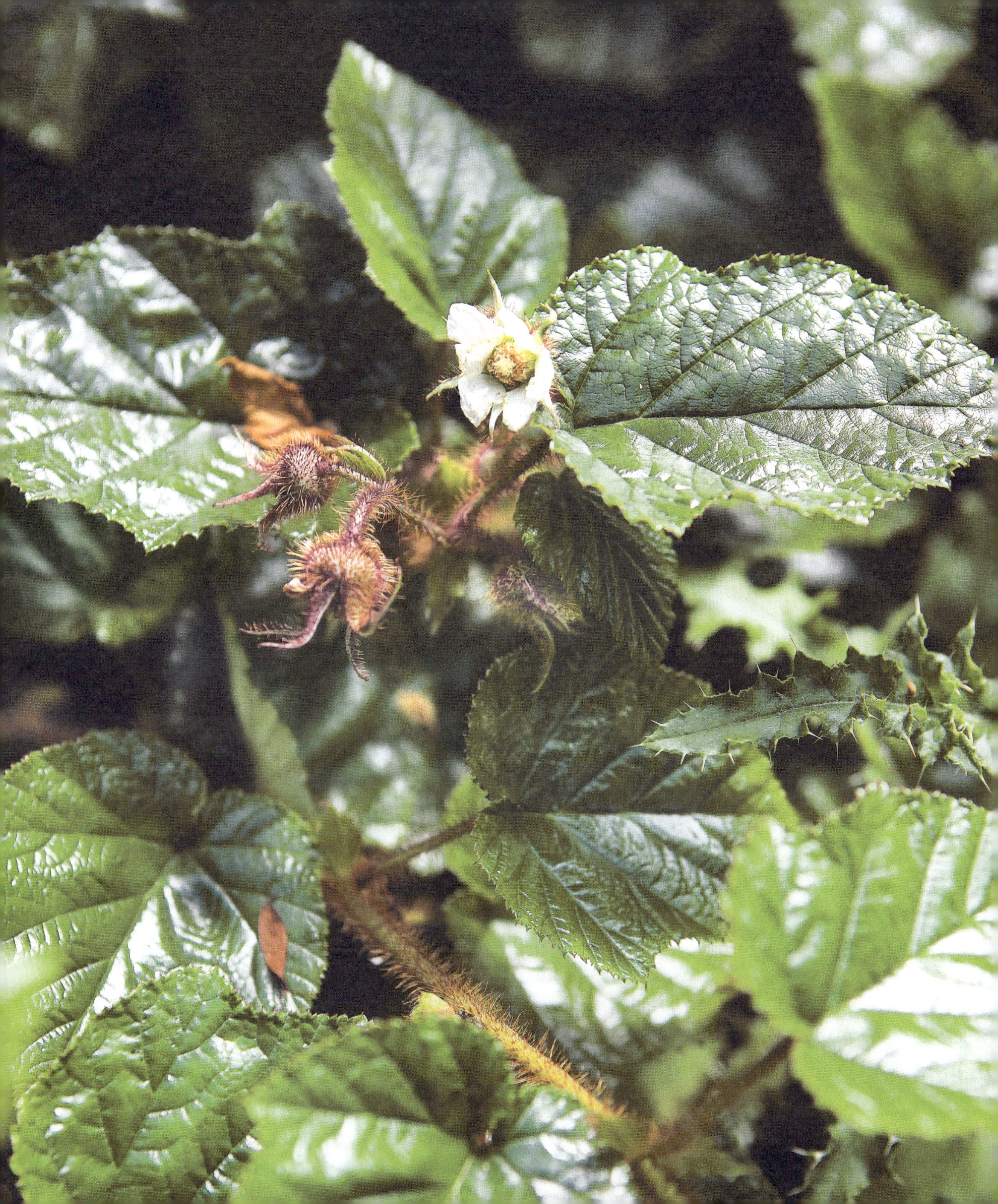

## SAMBUCUS NIGRA
### Elder
Early to mid summer flowers, early to mid autumn fruit

*The elder is a reminder that, however much concrete we pour into our cities, nature will still find a way to make herself at home. Its rampant weedy nature and the rank smell of its broken branches offends many, but then it blooms. Those frothy heady panicles herald British summer and promise fritters and cordials. Two summers ago, we made a batch of elderflower champagne so good that we had to keep celebrating just to drink it up. You can also make a dry elderberry wine. But don't assume you can eat all parts, the leaves will make you very sick.*

**How to recognise** Deciduous shrubs up to 10m tall, elders have arching branches and rather corky grey-brown bark. The youngest branches have conspicuous black or brown pores (known as lenticels) up the stem. The leaves are pinnate with 3–9 leaflets per leaf. Leaflets are ovate with a toothed margin and prominent midribs. Flowers are creamy white, sometimes pink, regular and arranged in large flat panicles. They smell of bananas in the morning and cat's piss by night. Berries are round, fleshy and black, 6–8mm diameter, growing in dense bunches.

**What to eat** All green parts of the plant are poisonous. The flowers are delicious made into fritters in a sweet pancake batter or used in cordials. Fresh flowers can be added to all sorts of summer jams; they lend something quite extraordinary to strawberry or rhubarb jam and the marriage of gooseberries and elderflowers is sublime. You can use fresh or dried flowers to infuse vinegars. The berries can be used to make wine and some people like to use them in jams, chutneys and pies, but I find that they have a slightly rank taste so it's always the last jam in our house to get eaten. Drying the berries first and then rehydrating them to use in cakes and muffins seems to improve their flavour and then they make an acceptable substitute for blueberries or barberries. I recently used elderberries in a Moroccan rice dish as a substitute for raisins and was so impressed that I felt quite bereft that I hadn't collected and dried more.

**What to grow** *Sambucus nigra* 'Black Lace' has dark, finely cut leaves and pink flowers which make a lovely coloured cordial. The simple cut-leaved form *S. nigra* f. *laciniata* has a slightly wilder look for more naturalistic gardens. 'Aurea' is a golden-leaved form that is useful in the shade. In a garden, elder needs to be regularly pruned to keep a tree in check. Prune in winter, remove any suckers, cut half the stems to the ground and shorten the remainder by half. The following year you shorten the year-old wood by half and cut the older stems to the ground. You can prune overgrown specimens back hard, but they tend not to flower the following year.

## MY MOTHER'S ELDERFLOWER AND GRAPEFRUIT CORDIAL

25 elderflower heads or as many as you can pick
1.8 litres (3 pints) water
1.35kg (3lb) granulated sugar
4 oranges or 2 grapefruit, sliced
1 lemon, sliced
50g (2oz) citric acid

Elderflowers are often home to lots of little insects, so shake them gently to dislodge any creatures before you start.

## ELDERFLOWER CHAMPAGNE

*Elderflower champagne is a wonderful drink – so easy, cheap and delicious.*

4.5 litres (8 pints) water
650g (1¼lb) white sugar
6–8 elderflower heads fully open (the largest you can find)
2 unwaxed lemons
2 tablespoons white wine vinegar
a packet of champagne yeast or a dessertspoon of dried yeast (not always necessary)
You also need a scrupulously clean 15-litre (2-gallon) bucket with a lid

Boil roughly half the water and add the sugar, stirring until it is completely dissolved. Allow this to cool.

Next add the elderflowers (give them a good shake first to dislodge any insects or debris), squeeze in the lemon juice and chuck in the lemon rind for good measure. Add the vinegar and the cooled water and cover with a lid.

You need to leave this for 4 days to ferment, then you should start to see bubbles and foam appearing. The process is temperature-dependent and sometimes takes longer – if it's a little chilly, move it somewhere warmer.

If you don't see any fermentation after 4–5 days, add the yeast (the benefit of using champagne yeast is that it ensures no rogue yeasts get in which can cause the 'homebrew' hangover). If you've added yeast, leave for another 4 days, by which time it really should bubble!

Next you need to strain out the flowerheads and lemon rind, and bottle.

It is safe to say that elderflower champagne really fizzes and if you use glass bottles they will need to have swing tops (the type some continental beers come in), but be warned these can sometimes explode. I buy the cheapest supermarket value water in 2-litre plastic bottles, use this in the recipe and bottle in these – rather than worrying about the nice looking bottle, I'd rather actually have the champagne! You can tell if the champagne is fizzing too much as the plastic bottle will become rigid and sound hollow when tapped with a finger. Release a little of the gas by unscrewing the top just a little.

After 10 days, your champagne should be ready to drink. It doesn't store for long, about 6 weeks, but it's so good to drink I doubt that you'll have any left.

## ELDERFLOWER VINEGAR

Take a large wide-mouthed jar and fill with 10–15 flower heads, packing them in well, and cover with 600ml (1 pint) of white wine vinegar (some prefer cider vinegar). Leave this somewhere warm but out of direct sunlight for a minimum of 2 weeks, 3 is better. Decant into clean bottles and store out of direct light. It makes for a summery vinaigrette.

The Plant Directory

S

## SISYMBRIUM OFFICINALE
## Hedge mustard

Early spring to late summer leaves, early to mid summer flowers

*This thin-looking thing always makes me think of asphalt; it may have started out in life as a hedge plant, but it's happy in the concrete playground now. The thinner the soil and the more tenuous the situation, the stronger the mustard flavour.*

**How to recognise** It looks like slightly starved rocket with a thin stem, thin leaves and small, bright yellow flowers.

It is annual and not frost-hardy, but will appear fairly early on in the year and seed itself about. It can grow up to 90cm, the basal leaves are arranged in rosettes, each with 3–5 lateral lobes and one rounder terminal one. The stem leaves have 1–3 lobes and a spear-shaped terminal lobe. Flowers are 2–3mm and have four yellow petals. Stiff seed pods are 1–6cm long, inside are orange-brown seeds. When you crush the leaves, they have a strong mustard smell.

**What to eat** A few shredded leaves are good in winter and spring salads for a bit of a kick. When cooked, the leaves have a cabbage flavour. They can be used in soups, omelettes and sauces and the seed can be ground up and used as a mustard substitute.

## SORBUS AUCUPARIA
## Rowan, Mountain ash

Late spring to early summer flowers, early to mid autumn fruit

*A friend of mine was genuinely surprised to find that I made rowan jelly. She said it was a common belief that the berries are poisonous. Well, they're not and my beautiful rowan jelly is proof of that. They are, however, terribly bitter but, as a Scottish friend once pointed out, they're our version of cranberry jelly, perfect for roasted meats. The rowan is a very common tree in hedgerows, woods, mountains, along roads and even growing out of old buildings and walls.*

**How to recognise** It is a deciduous tree, up to 8m tall, with a very distinct, smooth grey bark and pinnate leaves to 30cm long, with up to 12 pairs of oblong lance-shaped, sharply toothed leaflets. In late spring, it has white flowers and in late summer clusters of round, orange-red berries, each up to 8mm across. There are numerous cultivars, all of which are edible, some fruit very profusely.

**Similar species** There are several other species of *Sorbus* with edible fruits. The Devon sorb apple, *Sorbus devoniensis*, has large, apple-like russet green fruit. The service tree, *Sorbus domestica*, has pear-shaped or round yellow-green fruit, flushed red, that are best cooked or you can eat them bletted (allowed to soften) like medlars. The wild service tree, *Sorbus torminalis*, has russet yellow-brown fruit that can be cooked or added to fruit leathers.

**What to eat** The berries are incredibly tart and rather low in pectin, so you'll need to add crab apples. The trick is to bring the berries to the boil and then pour away the water to remove some of the astringency. You can then make the most beautiful jewel-toned jelly for meat, gravies or, my new favourite, as a coating for granola. I melt the jelly with a little water or apple juice until I have a suitably viscous syrup with which to coat my oats, nuts and seeds, you can add some maple syrup or honey if you like your granola sweet. There's something very good about the natural sweetness of roasted oats and the tarter coating.

### ROWAN JELLY
**Rowanberries**
**A handful of crab apples, halved**
**Granulated sugar**

Put the berries and apples into a heavy-based pan with enough water to just cover the fruit. Simmer gently until tender, then let the fruit cool and put it through a potato masher, mouli or blender to pulp it. Remove from the heat and strain the juice overnight as for any jelly. Then use the pound to pint rule (600ml of liquid to 450g of sugar), return to the heat to dissolve the sugar and bring to a rapid boil, until setting point is reached. Bottle as usual.

## SONCHUS SPECIES
# Sowthistle

All year round leaves and young shoots, except mid summer

Sowthistles look much like thistles but they are less prickly and have a dandelion-like yellow flower. There are three main edible species: the perennial field sowthistle, *S. arvensis, the prickly sowthistle, S. asper and the smooth or milk sowthistle, S. oleraceus*. They are arable weeds that occur across the world and are common foraged foods in many communities. The Romans used sowthistle as a salad herb and vegetable. Today it is widely used by Maoris in New Zealand and pops up in all sorts of Mediterranean recipes, mostly cooked like spinach. Sowthistles are opportunists, particularly in bare ground. You'll find them on allotments, in gardens, parks, pavements, roadsides and around the bases of street trees – where there's a crack in the concrete the sowthistle will makes itself at home.

**How to recognise**  The field sowthistle is a perennial with creeping rhizomes for roots. The hollow stems are up to 50–150cm, furrowed and with sticky yellow hairs (generally more to the top of the plant). The basal leaves are pinnate and roughly oblong shaped. The margins are spiny and fringed with spiny hairs. The stem leaves are less pinnate, clasped around the stem with a heart-shaped base. Flowers are branched, 3–5cm wide and golden yellow. This plant likes wet ground and can tolerate some degree of salt.

The milk sowthistle can be distinguished by its pointed lobes at the base of the leaf that wrap around the stem. The leaves are often a dull greyish green without prickles but still with a serrated leaf margin. The flowers are smaller than those of the field sowthistle, 10mm wide and paler yellow.

**What to eat**  I like to peel the stems of the milk sowthistle and munch on them raw – they have a slightly nutty, bitter flavour, but cooking reduces the bitterness. Steam or lightly boil the stems and leaves until they go a brilliant bright green, rinse and serve with butter and seasoning. Alternatively, they work well with feta cheese and make a good addition to pasta. I adapted an Italian recipe for mustard greens, using half a cup of breadcrumbs, a few crushed cloves of garlic and a few chilli flakes fried together in olive oil and then added to boiled sowthistles (rinsed and chopped) over spaghetti – their bitterness is tempered by the breadcrumbs and olive oil. Generally, the basal rosettes of leaves are less bitter than the upper leaves. Conversely, the basal rosettes will have more prickles, so slice these off, if necessary. Prickly sowthistle, *Sonchus asper*, needs to be eaten young.

STELLARIA MEDIA
# Chickweed
Late winter to early spring leaves

*This is a wonderful green that comes into its own in winter when little else is about. Come summer, it becomes tough and there are better, more seasonal, things to eat, but in the depths of winter I love this plant. It's predominantly a garden weed and can make a huge mat of fleshy leaves if left to its own devices. It has a long history as a cooked vegetable and was once sold in England at markets. It is widely eaten in Japan and is part of the rice porridge dish at their springtime Festival of Seven Herbs – Nanakusa no sekku.*

**How to recognise** Annual or biennial, chickweed forms a loose mat with many stems. It is found growing everywhere, between cracks in the pavement, in gardens, on wasteland, in arable fields. The leaves are small (less than 2.5cm long), bright green, soft and rounded at the base, pointed at the top. Flowers are star-shaped, white with five deeply divided petals. It is identifiable by a single line of hair that alternates up the sides of the stem.

**What to eat** Eat the soft, young green leaves in late winter and early spring, shred them off the stem and use them in salad. If the plants have become too tough, then steam or cook the leaves in a knob of butter. They work well with fried onions or slightly spiced with chilli – lovely with butter.

SILENE VULGARIS,
(SOMETIMES SOLD AS
SILENE INFLATA)
## Bladder campion
Late spring to early summer leaves and young shoots

*This is a common wildflower along roadsides in summer. Only the leaves and young shoots are edible and they are said to rival spinach when puréed. I grow mine from seed in the garden, rather than forage for them, as it's easier to get supper this way. I've seen quite a few references to this plant in Italian cookbooks and it has been traditionally used in Spanish, French, Greek, Turkish and Lebanese cuisine.*

**How to recognise**  It's a perennial, which has tough woody roots by year three. Bluish green leaves are about 4cm long, opposite and stalkless so wrapped around the stem. The branching flower spikes are 60–90cm tall and flowers are white with a distinct bladder behind them, which will eventually hold the seeds.

**What to eat**  Eat the young leaves and shoots before the flowers appear in early summer. The shoots are best in late spring.

**How to grow**  Sow the seed in early spring in a cold frame. Do not cover the seeds. Prick out into individual pots when large enough to handle and plant out in summer. Young plants do best with a little shade. You can treat this as an annual if you have enough seed. Large established plants can be divided in spring.

TILIA CORDATA,
TILIA PLATYPHYLLOS,
TILIA X EUROPAEA
## Small-leaf lime or linden, large-leaf lime, common lime
Mid spring to early summer leaves, late spring and early summer flowers

*You'll find limes in parks, woods, coppices and anywhere with limestone soils. You can use their leaves or dry their delicious delicately-scented blossom.*

**How to recognise**  Small-leaf lime is a large tree, over 25m tall, with smooth, dark grey bark and hairy young twigs. The leaves have a heart-shaped base and are broadly ovate with a pointed tip. They have dull green uppers, hairy and pale green beneath. The flowers are yellow, usually in clusters of three, and smell divine. The stamens stick outside the petals and the fruit is nut-like, hairy and round, up to 1cm.

Large-leaf lime is a taller tree, up to 40m high. It has large leaves, up to 15cm wide, with short hairs on the upper side of the leaf and tufts of hairs below on mature leaves. But, essentially, it looks much the same with the distinct heart-shaped base and ovate leaf. *Tilia* x *europaea* is a cross between the two, often found in parks and gardens. The leaves are smooth on top and hairy below.

**How to use**  Pick young lime leaves in spring; they are mild and delicious and taste slightly of cabbage. They can be substituted for lettuce and are a great way to bulk up salads. Look for young, pale, slightly glossy leaves as these taste best. The glossiness is often because of honeydew from aphids, which gives the leaves a sweet flavour. You might find that deeply revolting, but it does taste good. You can also blanch slightly older leaves and use them for salsa verdes or similar sauces.

The blossom should be dried for tea – gather it as soon as the flowers open and dry them indoors out of direct sunlight. The tea tastes of vanilla and is deeply satisfying. This is the tea that gives rise to Proust's most famous evocative memory, those madeleines dipped into his aunt's linden tea. More prosaically, it is said to be a good decongestant.

bladder campion

## TARAXACUM OFFICINALE
# Dandelion

Early to mid spring leaves,
early to late spring young unopened flower buds,
late summer to mid autumn crowns,
early to late autumn roots

This spring, when the roadsides and playing fields were covered in dandelions, I felt with each bud that I might cry, that I had never seen anything quite so beautiful. A strange thing to admit, I know, but there was a time when all I could have said about it was that it was a weed and that its seed head was a rather inefficient method by which to tell the time. A weed that you shouldn't put on the compost as it would only come back.

How did we ever get to the point of thinking that one of the most delicious, beneficial, healthful foods was nothing more than something we should try to eliminate? You can't really blame it for being so successful (it can reproduce asexually by seed, a far more efficient way to exploit new territory). The plant is rich in vitamins A, C and potassium. It has appreciable amounts of protein, carbohydrates and fibre, as well as calcium, iron and manganese (a lot more than spinach). And it tastes really very good.

You're most likely to find dandelions in grass, roadsides, banks, waste places, between pavements and in the garden. Dandelions growing in long grass that hasn't been mown will give you the largest roots. Multi-headed specimens will have thin roots. The better the soil, the bigger the roots.

**How to recognise** Dandelions can be quite variable, but are robust perennials with a white latex sap in both the leaves and roots. A dandelion has a fleshy, long, simple or branched taproot. The leaves are spirally arranged in a rosette (it may be very flat in mown grass and often deeply pinnately lobed with the terminal lobe the largest). Flower heads are solitary, 2–6cm wide, bright yellow and flat. The stem is hollow and exudes a lot of sap. The seed head is spherical and made up of numerous seeds, each on its own helicopter to take it off in the wind.

**What to eat** You'll need to wear gloves if you are going to pick a lot, because the white latex will stain your hands brown. All parts of the dandelion, except the seeds, are edible – the unopened buds, the young flowers, the leaves and roots, even the crown of new leaves. Mostly people know to eat the leaves which are incredibly bitter and really only palatable when young in spring or after a very hard frost, which sweetens them a bit. You can do a lot to alleviate the bitterness by blanching them (excluding the light). Otherwise, soak the leaves for several hours in cold water, wringing them out and changing the water, if necessary.

The crown is the cluster of naturally blanched leaves that are hidden just below the surface of the soil. These tender white stems can be eaten raw or cooked. Wash them thoroughly and soak in salt water until you are ready to cook them. They are good fried with onions or cooked for about 5 minutes in boiling water. Then drain and coat in butter and season. Young unopened flower heads can be treated in the same way, though you only need to cook them briefly, for no more than 3 minutes, drain, season and serve with lots of butter – it's fiddly to get many, but the flavour is worth it.

**Note** It has been noted that if the flowers are too old they may cause 'narcotic intoxication', though I've never found this.

TRIFOLIUM PRATENSE
## Red clover
Late spring to early autumn flowers

*Clover is at home in grass: if you keep it mown, it will stay low and small; when allowed to grow amongst long, lush grass you'll be rewarded with lovely pink flowers. At the base of each flower is an appreciable amount of nectar, making the flowers a sweet addition to salads. I have childhood memories of lying in long grass sucking each floret for that tiny hit of something sweet.*

**How to recognise** Red clover is a perennial, growing anywhere from 5cm tall in mown grass to 60cm in long. The leaves are ternate and distinctly clover-shaped with a whiteish chevron on each leaflet. The flowers are arranged in dense terminal heads up to 3cm wide with purplish pink, sometimes dull, whitish pink flowers.

**What to eat** For salads, the flowers should be broken apart and the middle discarded. They can also be dried for tea with honey, a deliciously mild drink that is supposed to be good for coughs. The young leaves can be used as greens or in salads, but before the plant flowers or the leaves become tough.

The Plant Directory

## URTICA DIOICA
### Stinging nettle

Mid to late spring and early to mid autumn leaves

*The stinging nettle, with its jagged heart-shaped leaves, is pretty easy to recognise – you'll get stung if you touch it. However, the sting is fragile and if you just roll the plant or put it under one burst of hot water, the sting will be destroyed making it safe to eat. Stinging nettles are associated with places of human habitation, hedge banks, woodlands, along fences, waysides and grassy places. They're often found in nitrogen-rich soil.*

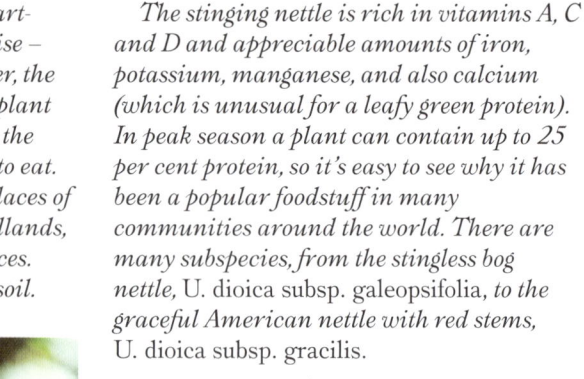

The stinging nettle is rich in vitamins A, C and D and appreciable amounts of iron, potassium, manganese, and also calcium (which is unusual for a leafy green protein). In peak season a plant can contain up to 25 per cent protein, so it's easy to see why it has been a popular foodstuff in many communities around the world. There are many subspecies, from the stingless bog nettle, U. dioica subsp. galeopsifolia, *to the graceful American nettle with red stems,* U. dioica subsp. gracilis.

**How to recognise** It's a perennial herb that grows 25–150cm high. The entire above-ground plant is covered in stinging hairs. The roots are creeping, sending up new shoots from nodes. The leaves are opposite, 3–8cm long, ovate with a heart-shaped base and deeply toothed. Unisex flowers are green, small and arranged below the leaves in dense thin clusters. The small annual, *Urtica urens*, is up to 65cm tall with smaller leaves. Whereas *U. dioica* tends to have fewer stinging hairs on the underside of the leaf, *U. urens* has more.

Not only good food for humans, nettles can also be used to make a nitrogen-rich feed for plants. Rot down a large quantity of leaves in some water and, once it smells revolting, it's ready to use on any vegetables or plants that need a pick-me-up.

**What to eat** The young tender tips are the best to eat, the top five or so leaves. By mid-season, from early to late summer, the leaves start to accumulate gritty particles, which are bad for the kidneys and urinary tract. The leaves also become too tough to eat. Nettles have two growth periods, in spring and a second flush again in early autumn. The spring leaves taste best; use the autumn leaves to bulk up foraged green recipes rather than on their own. You can eat a nettle raw by rolling it up between your fingers vigorously and then chewing thoroughly – all the stings will be destroyed and little children will be very impressed.

## NETTLE POTATO CAKE

*This is adapted from Paula Wolfert's Mediterranean Grains and Greens. The original recipe calls for cavolo nero, which is fantastic, but my chickens got out one day and stripped my kale bare, leaving rather a lot of nettles and other greens. So I adapted and it has become one of those very useful dishes that will take any number of greens.*

- 450g (1lb) nettles or mixed greens (that's about 9 cups of chopped greens)
- 1 garlic clove, chopped
- 450g (1lb) potatoes – I like to use Pink Fir Apple or something similarly waxy
- 1 tablespoon olive oil
- 140g (5oz) sliced semi-soft cheese, such as Taleggio, Fontina or Raclette, or if you want something pungent try Stinking Bishop

Wash the greens in plenty of water, soaking any bitter ones for half an hour or so and discarding this water. Remove any tough stems or damaged bits and cook in plenty of boiling salted water until tender – this may be a couple of minutes for very fresh nettles. When cool, coarsely chop and season and mix with the garlic.

Peel and shred the potatoes. I use a cheese grater. You need to wash the potatoes several times to remove the starch – keep washing until the water runs clear.

Heat the oil in a large frying pan with a lid. Spread half the potatoes and then half the greens, leaving an inch or so around the margins. Then add the sliced cheese, more greens and the rest of the potatoes and pat down to form a flat cake. Cover with the lid and cook for 5 minutes over a medium heat. Shake often to stop the potatoes from sticking (a non-stick pan helps here). Lots of steam might collect under the lid and, rather than allowing this to dribble back into the food, take a tea cloth and soak up the excess.

When 5 minutes is up, you need to flip the cake. This is the tricky bit but, if all has gone well, the bottom will be nicely brown and stuck together so you can flip the cake onto the lid and slip it back into the pan. Cook for another 10–15 minutes over a low heat with the lid on until it looks golden brown and the edges are nicely crispy. Serve cut into wedges with nothing more than salt and pepper.

## NETTLE RISOTTO

Add nettles at the end of cooking a basic white risotto. Nettles need to be cooked very briefly to ensure that the brilliant green colour is kept, along with all the vitamins. Wash the leaves thoroughly in several changes of water and add to boiling, salted water (sometimes I use a little stock in the water to add flavour) and cook for no more than 5 minutes. Drain, wring dry and finely chop. If you don't want flecks, you can purée the nettles with a little cooking water and swirl this into the risotto at the last minute. Or, alternatively, wash and steam them directly on top of the risotto. Season to taste and serve with Parmesan.

The Plant Directory | 181

# V

## VACCINIUM MYRTILLUS
### Bilberry, whinberrry, whortleberry, huckleberry
Late summer to early autumn fruit

*I live very close to Bilberry Hill and the local park, Lickey Hills, is covered in bilberries. They shouldn't be here within the city limits as their true home is on moors, peat bogs and upland heaths; basically, wherever there are dry acid soils you'll find bilberries. Like many of the smaller fruits, they've been neglected in recent years in favour of imported blueberries and other exotics but, in the past, they were often harvested and sold at market. They are an important source of Vitamins B and C.*

**How to recognise** A deciduous shrub that looks much like a blueberry, this is anywhere from 20–60cm tall with creeping rhizomes. Stems are upright, green and square with alternate leaves, 0.8–3.5cm long, finely toothed, light green and ovate. The bell-shaped flowers are greenish-pink or pink and look similar to blueberry flowers. The berry is dark bluish black with a violet bloom, similar, but darker and smaller than a blueberry.

**What to eat** The fruits can be eaten raw or cooked. They are best straight from the bush but, if you can bear to pick them and not eat them immediately, they have masses of uses. Pop them in pies, sponges, cakes, muffins, pancakes, fruit leathers, preserves, wines and jam. I made a very good bilberry-infused vodka from just bilberries and vodka, no sugar, which has a very intense blue colour that makes for some astonishing looking cocktails.

## VACCINIUM VITIS-IDAEA
### Cowberry, red whortleberry
Early autumn fruit

*I admit, I actually discovered this one in Norway and I think, on the whole, it's pretty hard to find unless you're on some peat bogs in the Peak District. Miles Irving gives quite an extensive map in the Foragers' Handbook but I've yet to find them. The ones in Norway weren't ripe so I can't tell you what they taste like but Stephen didn't seem to think too much of them. They are typically cooked with sugar and served with heavy meats, such as moose or beef. Irving notes that they have their own preservatives so, once harvested, they will last forever, which I guess means, if you only find them once, you can at least be assured they'll last a long time.*

**How to recognise** It looks like a bilberry, but it doesn't grow as tall and, more importantly, is evergreen. The leaves are leathery, flowers are white tinged with pink, the bright red fruits are 0.8–1.1mm across.

**What to eat** The berries can be cooked with sugar to make syrups, jam or jelly, but they are very bitter and it takes quite a lot of sugar to make them palatable.

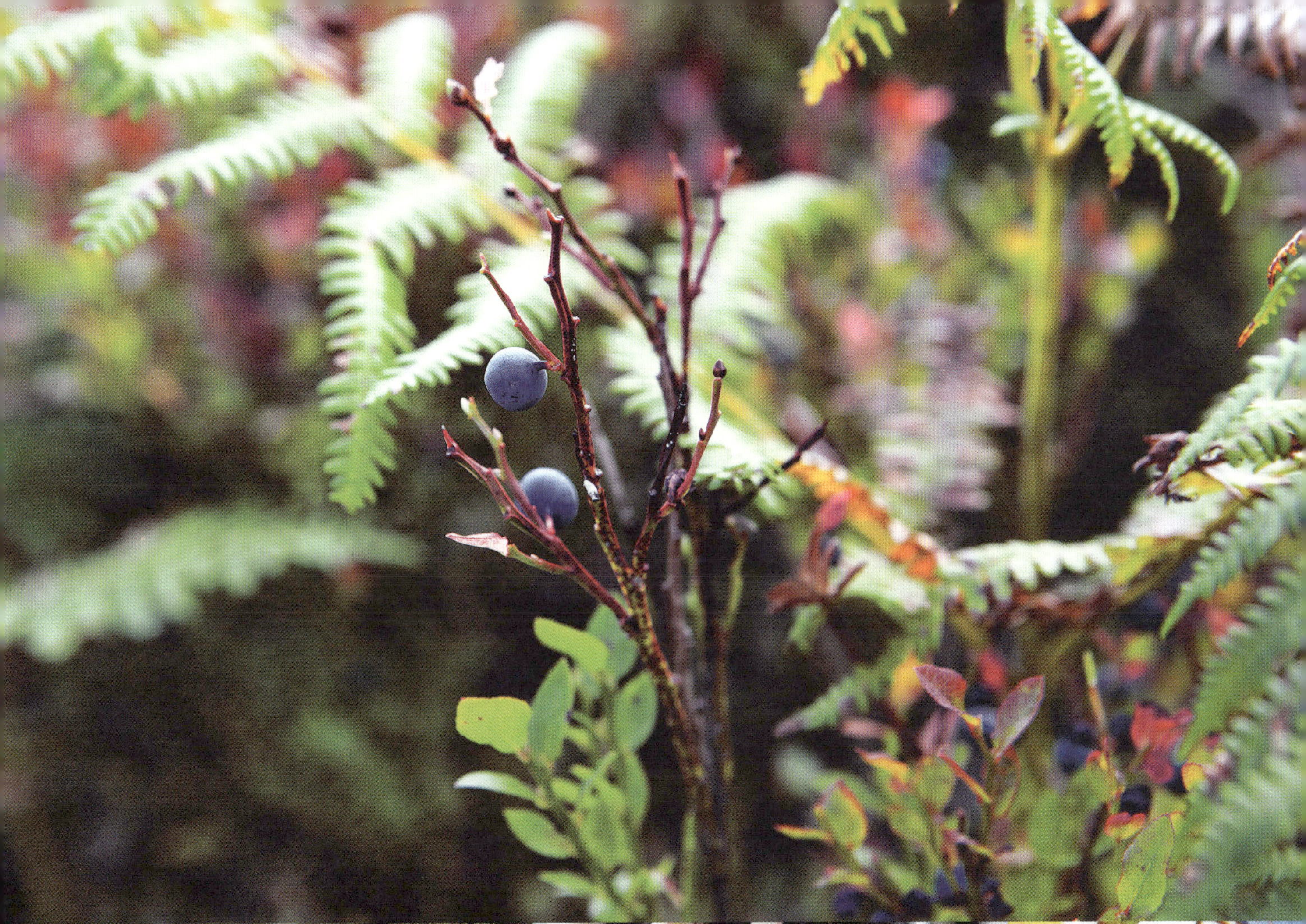
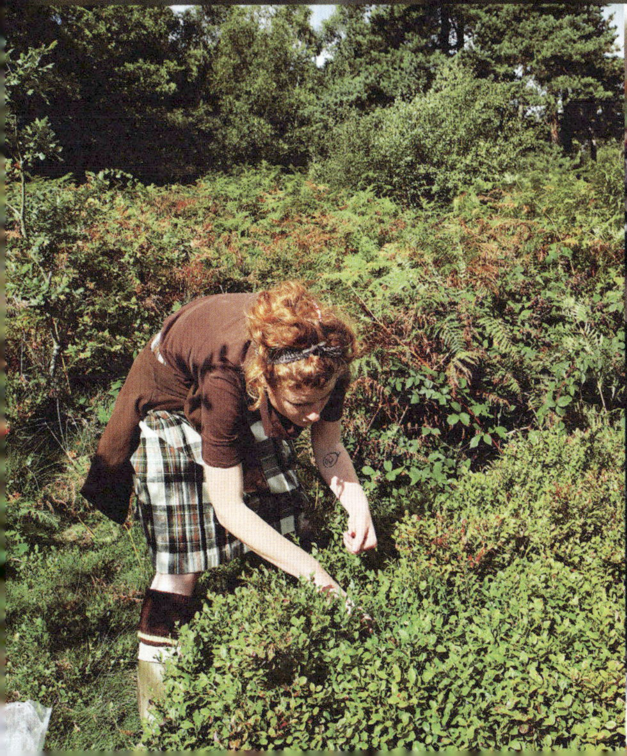
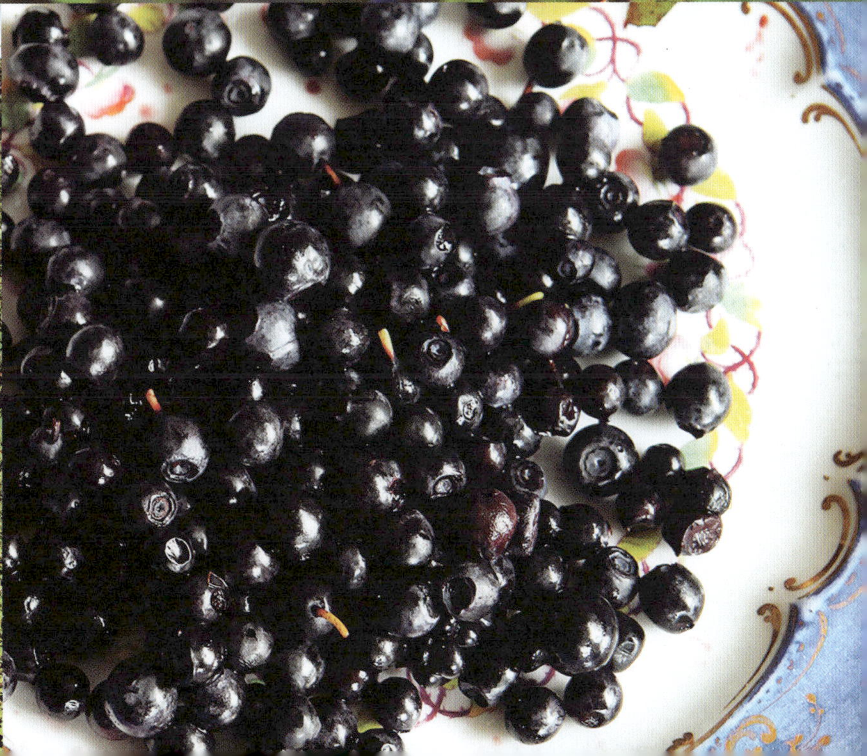

## VIOLA SPECIES
### Violets
Mid spring to mid autumn flowers

*All violet flowers are edible, from the giant pansies in park bedding schemes to the pretty little sweet violets of Parma violet fame. Some clearly are more rewarding to eat than others. Violets are the first flowers I think to pick when I want to decorate my dinner. They don't have much nutritional value, but the sight of them warms the heart and that is sometimes enough. Wild violets,* Viola odorata, *are found growing in woodland edges, along the base of hedges and in damp grass.*

**How to recognise** All have distinctive 'violet-like' flowers with equal slightly spreading petals – two above, two below and one basal petal. The flowering stem comes straight out of the rootstock and the leaves are alternate, rounded to kidney-shaped, often with a deeply heart-shaped base. Some species are fragrant including sweet violet, *Viola odorata*, white violet, *V. alba*, pansy *Viola* x *wittrockiana*, the Canada violet, *V. canadensis*, and Johnny jump-ups or heartsease, *V. tricolor*. The fen violet, *V. persicifolia*, is protected by law under the Wildlife and Countryside Act and should never be harvested, due to its scarcity.

**What to eat** The flowers can be eaten raw in salads or used to decorate cakes, muffins and other sweet or savoury dishes. They are good crystallised or candied. They can be used for vinegars, jellies, marmalades and syrups, work well in salad dressings and can be used to make a tea. The leaves of *Viola odorata*, *Viola* x *wittrockiana* and *V. canadensis* can be used in salads or dipped in batter and fried.

**What to grow** *Viola odorata* is a perfect species for shadier areas under deciduous trees or just allowed to self-seed around the place. *V. canadensis* is a perennial North American species suitable for woodland areas. Pansies are great for containers and pots, but it's advisable to remove all the flowers and wait for a second flush before eating shop-bought varieties, as they may have been sprayed with chemicals.

## VITIS COIGNETIAE
### Crimson glory vine
Late spring to early summer leaves, early to mid autumn fruit

*The crimson glory vine is often used in public places to rapidly cover a surface, such as a fence or wall. It has small blue-black grapes that are only passably edible, but could, I suppose, be thrown into a medley of fruit for fruit leathers. The large heart-shaped leaves are edible but you need to pick them before the felt on the back of the leaf gets too thick.*

**How to recognise** This is a vigorous, woody climber with large, heart-shaped leaves up to 30cm long, coarsely toothed and with deeply impressed veins above and a thick brown felt below. The leaves turn bright red and purplish red in autumn. Bluish black fruits appear mid autumn, that are only about 1cm in diameter.

**What to eat** The leaves should be used when young and are good wrapped around food and baked or used in stuffed vine leaf recipes. Lightly boil them first. Any vine leaf will keep cucumbers and other pickles perfectly crisp; just place a single vine leaf at the bottom of your jar, add pickles and vinegar and seal.

*violets*

crimson glory vine

# RESOURCES

## LOOKING FOR LAND?

**British Trust for Conservation Volunteers** is a wonderful resource for community groups. It offers all sorts of advice from how to set up a community group, cost-saving services, technical and expert advice.
www2.btcv.org.uk/display/community

**Common Ground** is a charity that looks at linking people and nature together by 'encouraging new ways of looking at the world to excite people into remembering the richness of the common place and the every day'. It is home to Apple Day, Tree Dressing Day and community orchards.
www.commonground.org.uk

There are also leases created by the **Development Trust Association.** This allows community gardening groups a chance to use a space for an agreed amount of time while the owner is waiting for the right economic climate to start work again. These spaces tend to be old building sites and such. This is perhaps less useful for anyone wanting to create a long-term project, such as an orchard, but it doesn't rule out possibilities of shared land partnership and, what you don't ask for, you don't get.

**The Federation of City Farms and Community Gardens** supports local projects for food growing and is setting up a Community Land Bank, which would support access to unused land for either temporary or long-term use. In essence, it would act just like a bank or trusted broker, loaning out land and looking after the legal and technical issues of such loans. It is still in progress but watch this space.
http://farmgarden.org.uk/home

**Garden Organic** is the home of UK organic gardening and offers advice to members on organic practices.
www.gardenorganic.org.uk

**Gardenshare** is a wider term where people share their garden spaces with those who are without space. There are several versions; many run in conjunction with the Transition Towns' Movement.
www.transitionnetwork.org

**Groundwork Trust** can provide professional and technical assistance.
www.groundwork.org.uk

**Guerilla gardening** is rapidly moving from the floral to the edible. Find some fellow gardeners and tackle that space:
www.guerrillagardening.org

**National Rail, British Waterways and the National Health Services** are all working with communities to offer access to land that they own.

**Incredible Edible Todmorden**
www.incredible-edible-todmorden.co.uk

**Landshare** is an internet-based system that puts individual growers in touch with land and garden owners. You can post to request or offer land.
www.landshare.net

**The Royal Horticultural Society** offer advice to members on all horticultural matters, as well as a service identifying unknown apples.
www.rhs.org.uk

**Wildlife Trust** is dedicated to maintaining and increasing wildlife habitats in the UK. It can advise on habitat maintenance and all aspects of wildlife.
www.wildlifetrusts.org

## HOW TO GUIDES

Martin Crawford
**Creating A Forest Garden Working with Nature to grow Edible Crops**
GREEN BOOKS, 2009
This book changed growing for me. A fantastic guide to growing all sorts of unusual foods.

Richard Mabey
**Food For Free**
COLLINS, 1972
This may be 40 years old but it's still a wonderful book to refer to. There is a newer version with colour photographs and a Collins Gem pocket guide, which is handy for longer forays.

Miles Irving
**The Forager's Handbook**
*A guide to the edible plants of Great Britain*, EBURY PRESS, 2009.
This is one of the best and most extensive guides to foraging. Unfortunately, all the pictures are black and white photography, so it may be necessary to use in conjunction with a colour guide.

Edmund Launett
**The Hamlyn Guide to Edible and Medicinal Plants of Britain and Northern Europe**
HAMLYN, 1981.
It's out of print now, though there are enough second-hand copies floating around to purchase one. A wonderful guide with good descriptions, medicinal and edible uses, slightly out-of-date on some edibles, so cross-reference.

Roger Philips
**Wild Flowers of Britain**
MACMILLAN, 1977
A very good colour identification book for cross-referencing. The plants are ordered by flowering times, so even if you have no idea what it is, as long as you have a flower, you'll find it.

Roger Philips
**Wild Foods**
PAN MACMILLAN, 2007
Another old, but good text with hilarious staged pictures in the countryside – great for inspiration and odd recipes. I grew up on this one.

186 | The Thrifty Forager

## COMMUNITY ORCHARD BOOKS

Harry Baker,
**The Fruit Garden Displayed**
THE ROYAL HORTICULTURAL SOCIETY, 1991

Richard Abernethy
**Fruits from the Forest**
*The first steps in developing community orchards and edible landscapes*
RED ROSE FOREST COMMUNITY FOREST CENTRE, MANCHESTER
Out of print, but a charming guide to how to set up a community orchard.

**The Common Ground Book of Orchards**
*Conservation, culture and community*
COMMON GROUND, 2000
The definitive guide to starting a community orchard.

Jane McMorland Hunter
**For the Love of an Orchard:**
*Everybody's guide to growing and cooking orchard fruit*
PAVILLION, 2010

## LIBRARY

Wendell Berry
**The Art of the Commonplace:**
*The agrarian Essays of Wendell Berry*
SHOEMAKER AND HOARD, 2003

Stephen Facciola
**Cornucopia II**
KAMPONG PUBLICATIONS, 1998
(OUT OF PRINT)

Audrey Wynne Hatfield
**How to Enjoy Your Weeds**
FREDERICK MULLER, 1976

Paula Wolfert
**Mediterranean Grains and Greens**
KYLE CATHIE, 1999
A wealth of recipes for 'greens' and some specific foraged food ones, everything I've ever made out of this book tastes divine.

A.P. Simopoulos
**Omega-3 Fatty Acids and Antioxidants in Edible Wild Plants**
BIOLOGICAL RESEARCH 37: 263-277, 2004

Joy Larkcom
**Oriental Vegetables**
KODANSHA INTERNATIONAL, 2008

S.Schaffer, G.P. Eckert, S. Schmitt-Schillig, W.E. Müller
**Plant Foods and Brain Aging: A Critical Appraisal**
FORUM. NUTR. BASEL KARGER, 2006, VOL 59: 86-115

Susan Allport
**The Primal Feast:** *Food, Sex, Foraging, and Love.*
HARMONY BOOKS, 2001

Susan Allport
**The Queen of Fats**
*Why Omega-3s Were Removed from the Western Diet and What We Can Do to Replace Them*
UNIVERSITY OF CALIFORNIA PRESS, 2006

## FORAGING AND THE LAW

I am very grateful to Jennifer Lee from the University of Liverpool for her correspondence on the tricky subject of law and foraging. She has written an excellent article that informs much of my take on the subject:
www.plant-talk.org/uk-where-hunter-gatherers-gone.htm

## ONLINE RESOURCES

### FRUIT TREE HARVEST

**Abundance**, by Grow Sheffield, is an exceptionally well-written guide to harvesting urban fruit and setting up community fruit tree projects. As my uncle would say: a jolly good read.
www.growsheffield.com

**Fruit city** is a growing map of fruit trees across London:
www.fruitcity.co.uk

**Solid Ground** has written a brilliant guide to community harvesting called Gather IT – How to Organise an Urban Fruit Harvest: www.solid-ground.org/Programs/Nutrition/FruitTree/Pages/default.aspx

USA

**City Fruit** is a community-based fruit project mapping existing trees, teaching maintenance, pest and diseases control and pruning for urban fruit trees.
www.cityfruit.org

**Forage Oakland** Advocating the exchange of neighbourhood fruit, the meeting of neighbours and the redistribution of excess resources with a rather lovely manifesto!
http://forageoakland.blogspot.com

**Not far from the tree** This Toronto-based project involves picking fruit and distributing it around Toronto on a bike. Lovely blog to boot.
www.notfarfromthetree.org

### COMMUNITY ORCHARDS

A resource on Community Orchards:
www.england-in-particular.info/orchards/o-comm1.html

The **Capital Growth campaign** will offer practical support to communities around London, helping people get access to land and create successful food growing spaces: www.capitalgrowth.org

**The London Orchard Project** aims to develop a skilled community of Londoners to plant, care and harvest fruit trees across the capital:
thelondonorchardproject.org

**Permaculture course**
The Permaculture Association has details on numerous courses on permaculture, forest gardening and design. They often offer fruit tree pruning and community orchard courses at various locations:
www.permaculture.org.uk/education/course-listing

# INDEX

## A
abandoned ground 18, 19
*Aegopodium podagraria* 19, 64, 86
*Agastache foeniculum* 32
*Alliaria petiolata* 19, 64, 93
*Allium* 36–8
   *A. ampeloprasum* var. *babingtonii* 64, 88
   *A. cepa proliferum* Group 38
   *A. cernuum* 36
   *A. moly* 38
   *A. sphaerocephalon* 92
   *A. triquetrum* 64, 88
   *A. ursinum* 92
   *A. victorialis* 36
allotments 18, 19
alpha-linolenic acid 12
Alpine leek 36
Alpine strawberry 64, 124
*Amelanchier lamarckii* 19, 64, 94
anise hyssop 32
antioxidants 12
apple rose 163
apples 11, 19, 65, 140
   *see also* crab apples
archangel 65, 136
Arctic raspberry 39
*Armoracia rusticana* 64, 86
*Atriplex hastata* 64, 97
   *A. hortensis* 64, 97
   *A. patula* 64
avens, wood 64, 127

## B
Babington's leek 64, 88
balsam, Himalayan 64, 132
barberries 19
   Darwin's 19, 25, 64, 99
   holly 65, 139
Barstow, Stephen 26–41
bee balm 32
bellflowers 64, 103
   Dalmatian 64, 103
   nettle-leaved 64, 103
*Bellis perennis* 64, 98
*Berberis* 19
   *B. darwinii* 19, 64, 99
bergamot 32
berries 11
   *see also* bilberries, raspberries *etc*
bilberries 8, 65, 182
bird cherry 153
Birgit's stone soup 82
bittercress 19, 64, 104
   hairy 106
   wavy 104
blackberries 11, 19, 65, 166
blackcurrants 162
blackthorn 65, 157
bladder campion 65, 176
borage 16, 64, 100
*Borago officinalis* 64, 100
Botanical Society of Great Britain 21, 22
brambles 58, 65, 166
   Chinese 19, 65, 168
brassicas 11
Brautigan, Richard 166
breeding plants 25
broad-leaved willowherb 19, 64, 118
buffalo currant 65, 162
bullaces 65, 153, 156
burnet rose 163
Burns, David 44–6
byelaws 22

## C
cake
   castagnaccio 108
calendar 64–5
*Campanula* 64, 103
   *C. cochlearifolia* 103
   *C. lactiflora* 103
   *C. persicifolia* 103
   *C. portenschlagiana* 64, 103
   *C. poscharskyana* 103
   *C. rapunculus* 64
   *C. trachelium* 64, 103
campion, bladder 65, 176
Canada violet 184
canals 18
*Capsella bursa-pastoris* 64, 104
car parks 18, 19
caraway 39
*Cardamine* 19, 64, 104
   *C. flexuosa* 104
   *C. hirsuta* 106
   *C. pratensis* 64, 106
cardamom pods
   damson, cardamom and vanilla jam 156
*Carum carvi* 39
castagnaccio 108
*Castanea sativa* 64, 108
Caucasian spinach 35
*Cerastium vulgare* 19
*Chaenomeles* 19, 64, 110
*Chamaemelum nobile* 19
chamomile 19
champagne, elderflower 171
cheese
   nettle potato cake 181
*Chenopodium album* 64, 115
   *C. bonus-henricus* 64, 116
cherries 19, 65, 153
   bird 153
   wild 65, 153
cherry plum 19, 154
chestnut, sweet 64, 108
   castagnaccio 108
chickweed 19, 65, 175
chicory 19
Chinese bramble 19, 65, 168
chocolate rose leaves 164
churchyards 18
chutney 79
*Cichorium intybus* 19
*Cirsium vulgare* 19
cities
   Fallen Fruit 44–6
   land use 21
   Portland Fruit Tree project 48
cleavers 64, 127
clove-root 64, 127
clover, red 65, 179
cobnuts 19, 64, 116
code of conduct 22, 24
community orchards 57–61
   conservation legislation 22
cordials 78
   my mother's elderflower and grapefruit cordial 171
   Oregon grape cordial 139
*Corylus avellana* 19, 64, 116
   *C. maxima* 64, 116
Countryside Rights of Way Act (2000) 21
cowberries 65, 182
crab apples 19, 65, 140
   rowan jelly 173
   spicy Siberian crab apple jelly 140
*Crataegus* 19, 64, 114
   *C. arnoldiana* 114
   *C. ellwangeriana* 114
   *C. laciniata* 114
   *C. missouriensis* 114
   *C. monogyna* 114
   *C. tanacetifolia* 114
Crawford, Martin 110
Crete 12
crimson glory vine 65, 184
crystallised rose petals 164
cuckoo flower 106
currant, buffalo 65, 162
*Cydonia oblonga* 64, 113

## D
daisy 64, 98
   ox-eye 65, 137
Dalmatian bellflower 64, 103
damsons 65, 153, 156

damson, cardamom and vanilla jam 156
dandelion 19, 65, 178
Darwin's barberry 19, 25, 64, 99
daylilies 19, 64, 130
deadnettle 65, 136
　red 136
　white 136
decorations
　chocolate rose leaves 164
design, community orchards 60
Devon sorb apple 172
*Diplotaxis tenuifolia* 64, 118
dog rose 163
drinks
　elderflower champagne 171
　my mother's elderflower and grapefruit cordial 171
　Oregon grape cordial 139
　raspberry vodka 167
　sloe gin 157

E
Egyptian walking onion 38
elderberries 65, 170
elderflowers 65, 170–1
　elderflower champagne 171
　elderflower vinegar 171
　my mother's elderflower and grapefruit cordial 171
environmental searches 21
*Epilobium montanum* 19, 64, 118
equipment 15
essential fatty acids 12

F
Fallen Fruit, Los Angeles 44–6
fat hen 11, 16, 64, 115
fen violet 184
*Ficus carica* 19, 64, 122
field poppy 19, 65, 152
figs 19, 64, 122
filberts 64, 116
flavonoids 12

flowers, crystallised 164
*Foeniculum vulgare* 64, 122
foraging
　calendar 64–5
　code of conduct 22, 24
　equipment 15
　Fallen Fruit, Los Angeles 44–6
　identifying plants 16
　Incredible Edible Todmorden (IET) 50–5
　laws 21–2
　safety 11, 16
　where to go 18–19
*Fragaria vesca* 64, 124
fruit 11
　community orchards 57–61
　Fallen Fruit, Los Angeles 44–6
　fruit cheeses 79
　fruit leathers 80–1
　jams 77–8
　jellies 79
　juices 78
　pollination 60
　Portland Fruit Tree project 48
　preserving 77–81
　seeds 25
　*see also* individual types of fruit
*Fuchsia* 64, 125
　*F. magellanica* 125

G
*Galium aparine* 19, 64, 127
garden orache 64, 97
Garden Organic 60
gardens 19
garlic
　three-cornered 64, 88
　wild 64, 92
garlic mustard 19, 64, 93
German grüne Sosse 84
*Geum urbanum* 19, 64, 127
gin, sloe 157
ginger
　rosehip and ginger syrup 165

*Ginkgo biloba* 64, 130
good King Henry 64, 116
gooseberries 162
goosegrass 19, 64, 127
grapefruit
　my mother's elderflower and grapefruit cordial 171
ground elder 19, 64, 86
grüne Sosse 84

H
*Hablitzia tamnoides* 35
hairy bittercress 106
hastate orache 64, 97
haws 23, 64, 114
hawthorn 19, 64, 114
hazelnuts 19, 64, 116
heartsease 184
hedge mustard 65, 172
hedgerows 18
*Hemerocallis* 19, 64, 130
henbane 115
henbit 136
Herb Bennet 19, 64, 127
herb fennel 64, 122
　Birgit's stone soup 82
　salsa verde 84
　*see also* individual herbs
Hessian grüne Sosse 84
Himalayan balsam 64, 132
holly barberry 65, 139
hollygrape, Oregon 19, 65, 139
Homecheck website 21
horseradish 64, 86
*Hosta* 30
　*H. montana* 30
　*H. sieboldiana* 30
　*H.* 'Sagae' 30
huckleberries 65, 182
*Hyoscyamus niger* 115
hyssop, anise 32

I
identifying plants 16

*Impatiens glandulifera* 64, 132
Incredible Edible Todmorden (IET) 50–5
insurance, community orchards 58

J
Jack-by-the-hedge 64, 93
jams 77–8
　damson, cardamom and vanilla jam 156
　Fallen Fruit, Los Angeles 46
Japan rose 163
Japanese knotweed 58
Japanese quince 64, 110
japonica 110
jellies 79
　quince jelly 113
　rowan jelly 173
　spicy Siberian crab apple jelly 140
Johnny jump-ups 184
*Juglans regia* 19, 64, 134
juices 78
juneberries 19, 64, 94

K
kidney stones 16
knotweed, Japanese 58
Kolker, Katy 48

L
lady's smock 64, 106
lamb's quarters 64, 115
*Lamium* 65, 136
　*L. album* 136
　*L. amplexicaule* 136
　*L. galeobdolon* 136
　*L. purpureum* 136
Land Registry 57
land use, cities 21
laws 21–2
leathers, fruit 80–1
leaves

arrangements 70–1, 75
chocolate rose leaves 164
margins 68–9, 75
pairings 74, 75
shapes 66–7, 75
tips 72–3, 75
leeks
  alpine 36
  roundheaded 92
  wild 64, 88
legal advice, community orchards 58
legislation 21–2
lemon balm 65, 142
*Leontodon hispidus* 65
*Leucanthemum vulgare* 65, 137
licenses, community orchards 58
lily, Martagon 29
lily leek 38
lime 19
  large-leaf 65, 176
  small-leaf 65, 176
linden 65, 176
local authorities 22, 57
Los Angeles 44–6

## M
*Mahonia* 139
  *M. aquifolium* 19, 65, 139
  *M. nervosa* 19
maidenhair tree 64, 130
maintenance, community orchards 61
mallow 19
  curled 35
*Malus* 65, 140
  *M. domestica* 19
  *M. sylvestris* 19, 65, 140
*Malva moschata* 35
  *M. neglecta* 19
  *M. sylvestris* 19
  *M. verticillata* 'Crispa' 35
margins, leaves 68–9, 75
marguerites 65, 137

marjoram, pot 65, 148
marsh mallow 35
Martagon lily 29
*Matricaria recutita* 19
medlars 65, 144
*Melissa officinalis* 65, 142
membrillo 113
*Mentha* 142
  *M. aquatica* 65, 142
*Mespilus germanica* 65, 144
milk sowthistle 174
Ministry of Agriculture, Fisheries and Food (MAFF) 11
mint, water 65, 142
*Monarda didyma* 32
  *M. fistulosa* 32
*Morus alba* 146
  *M. nigra* 19, 65, 146
  *M. rubra* 146
mountain ash 172
mulberries 19
  black 65, 146
  red 146
  white 146
mustard
  garlic 19, 64, 93
  hedge 65, 172
my mother's elderflower and grapefruit cordial 171
myrobalan 154
*Myrrhis odorata* 65, 148

## N
National Trust 22
Natural England 21
Nature Reserves 21
nettle-leaved bellflower 64, 103
nettles 11, 19, 65, 180–1
  nettle potato cake 181
  nettle risotto 181
  safety 16
nodding onion 36
Norway 28–39

## O
Omega-3 fatty acids 12
onions
  Egyptian walking 38
  nodding 36
  victory 36
  yellow 38
orache
  common 64
  garden 64, 97
  hastate 64, 97
  safety 16
oranges 44–6
orchards, community 57–61
oregano 65, 148
Oregon grape 19
Oregon hollygrape 19, 65, 139
*Origanum vulgare* 65, 148
Oswego tea 32
ox-eye daisy 65, 137
oxalic acid 16
*Oxalis acetosella* 65, 150
  *O. corniculata* 150
  *O. depressa* 150
  *O. lobata* 150
  *O. oregano* 150

## P
pansy 184
*Papaver rhoeas* 19, 65, 152
parks 18, 19, 21
pathways 18, 19
pears 11, 19, 65, 159
pectin 77
Perrine Puyberthier's plum tarte 155
perry pears 159
phenolic compounds 12
photosynthesis 12
pine nuts
  castagnaccio 108
plant breeding 25
planting, community orchards 60
plums 65

cherry 19, 154
  Perrine Puyberthier's plum tarte 155
pollination 60
pollution 11, 18
poppy, field 19, 65, 152
Portland Fruit Tree project 48
pot marjoram 65, 148
potatoes
  Birgit's stone soup 82
  nettle potato cake 181
pregnancy 16
preserving fruit 77–81
prickly sowthistle 174
procumbent yellow sorrel 150
*Prunus* 65, 153–7
  *P. avium* 19, 65, 153
  *P. cerasifera* 19, 65, 154
  *P. domestica* subsp. *insititia* 65, 156
  *P. padus* 153
  *P. spinosa* 65, 157
purslane 12
Puyberthier, Perrine 155
*Pyrus* 19
  *P. communis* 65, 159

## Q
quince, flowering 19, 64, 110
quince, true 64, 113
  membrillo 113
  quince jelly 113

## R
raisins
  castagnaccio 108
rampion 64
ransoms 64, 92
raspberries 11, 19, 65, 167
  Arctic raspberry 39
  raspberry vodka 167
red clover 65, 179
red whortleberries 65, 182
redcurrants 162

*Rhus typhina* 65, 161
   *R. verniciflua* 161
*Ribes nigrum* 162
   *R. odoratum* 65, 162
   *R. rubrum* 162
   *R. uva-crispa* 162
risotto, nettle 181
rivers 18
roads, pollution 18
rocket, wild 64, 118
*Rosa* 19, 65, 163–5
   *R. arvensis* 163
   *R. canina* 163
   *R. pimpinellifolia* 163
   *R. rugosa* 163
rose petals 163
   crystallised 164
   rose petal vinegar 164
rosehips 19, 163
   rosehip and ginger syrup 165
roses 19, 65, 163–5
   chocolate rose leaves 164
roundheaded leek 92
rowan 19, 65, 172
   rowan jelly 173
Royal Horticultural Society 60
*Rubus arcticus* 39
   *R. fruticosus* 19, 65, 166
   *R. idaeus* 19, 65, 167
   *R. nepalensis* 168
   *R. tricolor* 19, 65, 168
*Rumex acetosa* 19, 168
*Rumex acetosella* 19, 168

S
safety 11, 16
salsa verde 84
*Sambucus nigra* 65, 170–1
scratch tongue 64, 127
seedbeds 25
seeds 25
service berries 64, 94
service tree 172
sheep's sorrel 19, 168

shepherd's purse 64, 104
*Silene inflata* 176
   *S. vulgaris* 65, 176
Silver Lake, Los Angeles 44
Simopoulos, Artemis 12
*Sisymbrium officinale* 65, 172
Sites of Special Scientific Interest 21
sloes 23, 65, 157
   sloe gin 157
slugs 30
*Sonchus* 65, 174
   *S. arvensis* 174
   *S. asper* 174
   *S. oleraceus* 19, 174
*Sorbus aucuparia* 19, 65, 172–3
   *S. devoniensis* 172
   *S. domestica* 172
   *S. torminalis* 172
sorrel 16, 19
   common 168
   procumbent yellow 150
   safety 16
   sheep's 19, 168
   wood 65, 150
soup, Birgit's stone 82
sowing seeds 25
sowthistles 19, 65, 174
   milk 174
   perennial 174
   prickly 174
spicy Siberian crab apple jelly 140
spinach 12
   Caucasian 35
stag's horn sumach 65, 161
*Stellaria media* 19, 65, 175
sticky willie 64, 127
stinging nettles *see* nettles
stone soup, Birgit's 82
strawberries, Alpine 64, 124
sumach
   stag's horn 65, 161
   velvet 65, 161
syrup, rosehip and ginger 165

T
*Taraxacum officinale* 19, 65, 178
tarte, Perrine Puyberthier's plum 155
thistles 19, 58
   *see also* sowthistles
Thoreau, Henry David 8
three-cornered garlic 64, 88
*Tilia cordata* 19, 65, 176
   *T.* x *europaea* 176
   *T. platyphyllos* 65, 176
tips, leaves 72–3, 75
Todmorden 50–5
Tollund Man 115
toxic chemicals 11, 21
trees
   community orchards 57–61
   seeds 25
   *see also* apples, pears *etc*
*Trifolium pratense* 65, 179

U
United States of America
   Fallen Fruit, Los Angeles 44–6
   Portland Fruit Tree project 48
urban foraging
   abandoned ground 18, 19
   Fallen Fruit, Los Angeles 44–6
   land use 21
   Portland Fruit Tree project 48
   wasteland 18, 19
*Urtica dioica* 19, 65, 180–1
   *U. d.* subsp. *galeopsifolia* 180
   *U. d.* subsp. *gracilis* 180

V
*Vaccinium myrtillus* 65, 182
   *V. vitis-idaea* 65, 182
vanilla
   damson, cardamom and vanilla jam 156
varnish tree 161
velvet sumach 65, 161
Venice Beach 46

victory onion 36
Viegener, Matthias 44–6
vinegar
   elderflower 171
   rose petal 164
*Viola* 65, 184
   *V. alba* 184
   *V. canadensis* 184
   *V. odorata* 184
   *V. persicifolia* 184
   *V. tricolor* 184
   *V.* x *wittrockiana* 184
violets 65, 184
*Vitis coignetiae* 65, 184
vodka, raspberry 167

W
wallrocket, perennial 64, 118
walnuts 19, 64, 134
water mint 65, 142
wavy bittercress 104
whinberries 65, 182
whortleberries 65, 182
   red 65, 182
wild service tree 172
Wildlife Trusts 22
willow-herb, broad-leaved 19, 64, 118
Wolfert, Paula 181
wood avens 64, 127
wood sorrel 65, 150
woodlands 18

Y
yellow onion 38
Young, Austin 44–6

To Birgit for coming foraging and then turning our finds into something delicious (if you want a caterer with a difference try www.changekitchen.co.uk), to Stephen, his gardens and waterfalls, to Fallen Fruit for such a funny ride across town and herbals teas with Katy in Portland. To the Clarkes (and all at Incredible Edible) for letting us invade their kitchen and for such good funny times last summer. To those that picked: Emily, Clare, Leila (and for the nutritional advice), Debs, Grace, Saima, Becca, Emily and David, the Juliets, Dave, Nick, Joe H, Sue, Jeremy, Ingrid, Virginia, Mum and Dad. Thanks to Caroline for her dandelion recipes.

To Borra, Sophie, Charlie, Lawrence and Kyle for not blinking when I said I want to write about eating wayside weeds and making this book look so lovely.

To Simon Wheeler for coming on this odd adventure and for only mildly complaining about each mouthful. Without you, it's not a book.

But as always the biggest thanks goes to H for eating my 'spinach.'